ESSENTIAL SUBJECT KNOWLEDGE
FOR PRIMARY TEACHING

ESSENTIAL SUBJECT KNOWLEDGE
FOR PRIMARY TEACHING

NASREEN MAJID

LM Learning Matters

Learning Matters
A SAGE Publishing Company
1 Oliver's Yard
55 City Road
London EC1Y 1SP

SAGE Publications Inc.
2455 Teller Road
Thousand Oaks, California 91320

SAGE Publications India Pvt Ltd
B 1/I 1 Mohan Cooperative Industrial Area
Mathura Road
New Delhi 110 044

SAGE Publications Asia-Pacific Pte Ltd
3 Church Street
#10-04 Samsung Hub
Singapore 049483

Editor: Amy Thornton
Senior project editor: Chris Marke
Cover design: Wendy Scott
Typeset by: C&M Digitals (P) Ltd, Chennai, India
Printed in the UK

Editorial arrangement Nasreen Majid, 2023.
Chapter 1 Susan Ogier; Chapter 2 Neil Rickus,
Chapter 3 Howard Foster; Chapter 4 Caroline Whiting
and Paul Richardson; Chapter 5 Martin Sutton and
Julia Mackintosh; Chapter 6 Judy Clarke; Chapter 7
Nick Davies; Chapter 8 Jon Audain, Sarah Lloyd and
Helen Mead; Chapter 9 Cathy Burch; Chapter 10
Angela Whitehouse and Victoria Randall;
Chapter 11 Victoria-Marie Pugh; Chapter 12
James D. Holt; Chapter 13 Deborah Wilkinson;
Chapter 14 Nasreen Majid.

Library of Congress Control Number: 2023930603

British Library Cataloguing in Publication Data

A catalogue record for this book is available from the
British Library.

ISBN 978-1-5296-1194-6
ISBN 978-1-5296-1193-9 (pbk)

At SAGE we take sustainability seriously. Most of our products are printed in the UK using responsibly sourced
papers and boards. When we print overseas we ensure sustainable papers are used as measured by the
PREPS grading system. We undertake an annual audit to monitor our sustainability.

CONTENTS

ACKNOWLEDGEMENTS

Thank you to all the authors who have contributed innovative chapters, showcasing up-to-date subject knowledge in their fields. Their hard work and attention to detail has been very much appreciated throughout the development of this book.

DEDICATIONS

For my colleagues and friends, Gina Menon, Marva Rollins and Stania Baird.

Thank you for your guidance and inspiration.

For my parents – my greatest cheerleaders.

ABOUT THE EDITOR

Nasreen Majid is Associate Professor of Education at the University of Reading. Previously, she was a primary teacher, predominantly working in urban settings across London and the South East. She has two years of international teaching experience at the British School in Jakarta, Indonesia. Nasreen was an Advanced Skills Teacher for Mathematics and Science (AST). She is currently leading on a portfolio of work on climate education and sustainability at the Institute of Education, University of Reading. She has developed a framework for climate education and sustainability for trainee teachers. Nasreen has conducted research in teacher and pupil perceptions on climate change. This research will be drawn upon to frame the current thinking in the field.

ABOUT THE CONTRIBUTORS

Angela Whitehouse is a Senior Lecturer in primary Physical Education at Birmingham City University. Previously, she was a primary teacher working across different school settings within Birmingham, and a subject leader for PE throughout this time. Angela has worked within local and national networks authoring and delivering continuous professional development within school and ITE settings. She is co-founder of PE at Home, which supported schools and families with home learning PE resources during the Covid-19 pandemic and ProActive PE, which provides web-based PE resources for primary practitioners.

Caroline Whiting is co-leader of the English strand in the primary PGCE programme at Bath Spa University. Caroline has taught in primary, middle and secondary schools, has been a primary school headteacher and a local authority school improvement adviser. Currently, she is working on two English-related research projects: one on trainee teachers' perceptions of teaching English – specifically writing – and one on trainee teachers' anxiety about writing.

Cathy Burch is senior lecturer in primary languages, with responsibility for B.Ed. and PGCE students, at the University of Gloucestershire. Cathy's previous experience includes time as a primary languages teacher and co-ordinator, and as an EFL teacher in the UK and abroad.

Dr Deborah Wilkinson has worked in primary education for over twenty years and spent five years as a science co-ordinator. After teaching in primary schools for eleven years, she joined the University of Chichester where she is now a Senior Lecturer and Programme Coordinator for the Primary PGCE course. She has written a number of science books, including *Mastery in Primary Science* and *Nurturing Science*, as well as writing and editing a number of journal articles and chapters in teaching and learning books.

Helen Mead is a freelance music educator, supporting music in schools and communities. She leads sessions in SEND settings and for ITT students. She has worked as a specialist primary music teacher in schools and hubs in the South East for over 20 years. She facilitates teacher training for AYM (Awards for Young Musicians) and is a learning resources producer for Aurora Orchestra.

Howard Foster, PGCE, MBA, B.Sc. (Engineering), is a Senior Lecturer at the University of Cumbria and an experienced primary teacher. Prior to working in Education, he gained experience in heavy engineering as an assembler and designer of cranes and large structural projects before moving into the design and production management of leading-edge, high-volume safety products within the automotive safety industry, where he obtained several global patents that were subsequently put into production in motor vehicles worldwide. He has also had a product design feature on the BBC design awards TV programme.

James D. Holt is Associate Professor of Religious Education at the University of Chester. James teaches on the primary and secondary teacher education courses. He taught and supported RE in primary and secondary schools prior to his role at Chester. He is the author of *Religious Education and the Secondary School: An Introduction to Teaching, Learning and the World Religions* (Routledge, 2022) and *Understanding Sikhism: A Guide for Teachers* (Bloomsbury, 2023).

Jon Audain is a Senior Lecturer in Education at the Institute of Education, University of Winchester. Jon is the author and collaborator of over 20 books, chapters, peer-reviewed journal articles and papers, is an Apple Distinguished Educator (ADE) and Chair of the Technology, Pedagogy in Education Association (TPEA), a national subject association for evidence-informed research and education technology.

Judy Clarke has worked in primary education for over twenty years. A former headteacher, SENDCO, English and humanities coordinator, she is now a university teacher in Teacher Education and L7 PGCE Tutor at Leeds Trinity University. In 2019, she reviewed her school's subject planning, introducing a local focus, to address the revised Education Inspection Framework. Judy has a particular interest in inclusive teaching strategies and the formative links between English, history and geography. A CPD provider, she has contributed to regional history resources on the Historical Association website and delivered a workshop on the importance of visual resources and classroom talk at the association's 2022 conference.

Julia Mackintosh is a Senior Lecturer at the University of Hertfordshire, teaching primary geography on undergraduate and postgraduate teacher training courses. She also works for the National Association for School-Based Teacher Trainers (NASBTT) as their Associate Consultant for primary geography. Previously, she was a primary teacher for 13 years, working in schools in East Anglia.

Martin Sutton has taught geography in schools since 2000. He has previously been awarded Chartered Geographer status by the Royal Geographical Society, has been a Specialist Leader in Education, Head of a Secondary Geography Department and a Humanities Faculty. Martin currently teaches the primary and secondary trainee teachers at the University of Reading.

Neil Rickus is a Senior Lecturer in Computing Education at the University of Hertfordshire. In addition, he is a Computing tutor on the primary PGCE courses at University College London (UCL) and Brunel University, London, and an external examiner for Edge Hill University. Neil also undertakes work independently, including running Computing workshops, as a primary education specialist for the BCS, and as a resource developer for Cambridge University Press, the BBC and the National Centre for Computing Education (NCCE). He is a STEM Learning Senior Facilitator, a HEA Fellow, a Raspberry Pi, Microsoft and Google Certified Educator, and a CEOP Ambassador.

Nick Davies is a lecturer in education at the University of Reading. Previously, he was a primary teacher, and was mathematics subject lead in three schools in the South East of England. He was also a mathematics subject specialist teacher (MaST) and focused his MA around teachers' mathematical mindsets. Currently, Nick is studying for his Doctorate in Education, investigating a possible intervention to reduce mathematics anxiety in trainee teachers, as well as the extent that mathematics anxiety interacts with self-concept, self-efficacy, mindset and motivation in the subject.

Paul Richardson is co-leader of the English strand in the primary PGCE programme at Bath Spa University. Paul has taught in primary schools and taught English as a second language abroad to schools and universities in Thailand, Vietnam and the Czech Republic. Currently, he is working on two English-related research projects: one on trainee teachers' perceptions of teaching English – specifically writing – and one on trainee teachers' anxiety about writing.

Sarah Lloyd is a primary music Specialist Leader in Education (SLE) with significant experience supporting non-specialist teachers to deliver musical learning with their classes. She leads sessions for ITT trainees, supports leaders and teachers in schools, and is a learning resources producer for Aurora Orchestra.

Susan Ogier is a Senior Lecturer in Primary Education, specialising in Art and Design at the University of Roehampton, London. She is author of *Teaching Primary Art and Design* (2017), *Teaching Arts in the Primary Curriculum* (2021) published by Sage, as well as a series of books for children, professional and peer-reviewed journal articles, and book chapters. She holds a variety of consultancy roles, including Associate Consultant for Primary Art and Design for NASBTT, and works closely with the learned society, NSEAD. Susan's most recent book in the Learning Matters series is the revised, second publication of *A Broad and Balanced Curriculum: Educating the Whole Child* (2022).

Victoria Randall is a Senior Fellow for Education and teacher educator in primary Physical Education at the University of Winchester. Her research focuses on Physical Education curriculum knowledge, teacher education and policy. Vicky has worked across many national and European professional networks to promote and develop initial teacher education, including the European Primary

Physical Education Network and the Primary Physical Education Teacher Education Network. She is co-founder of the Primary Physical Education Assembly.

Victoria-Marie Pugh is a Senior Lecturer in Primary PSHE and RSE and Inclusion, Diversity and Global Citizenship lead across the Primary ITE courses. She is the course leader for the University Diploma in PSHE course and a member of the British Education Research Association (BERA) British Curriculum Forum steering committee. Prior to joining the university, she spent 15 years working in primary schools both in the UK and abroad, and has had experience teaching year groups ranging from Nursery to Year 10. She worked as a Specialist Leader of Education (SLE) and led PSHE networks across the UK. Victoria is currently studying for an Ed.D. with a focus on equality, diversity and inclusion and lived experiences of policy in primary schools.

INTRODUCTION

Subject knowledge plays an integral role in developing expertise. As a trainee teacher, you have a huge amount to grapple with when it comes to developing expertise in the suite of subjects within the primary national curriculum. Subject knowledge cannot be developed in isolation; it must relate to the curriculum knowledge and pedagogical knowledge, enabling ways to teach the subject with confidence. The curriculum for trainee teachers is now refined further to incorporate the ITT Core Content Framework (CCF), supporting the development of expertise during your training years and into your early career years.

This book will take you through a journey of the national curriculum, supporting you to think about each subject's positioning within the national curriculum. Details of the subject knowledge you need to know and understand are considered in detail, alongside clear examples of pedagogical knowledge in the 'how to' teach each subject in a creative way. Each chapter has several pause points with reflective questions, enabling you to stop and reflect on the content and think about how you can interpret the details for your own practice.

The CCF is explicitly drawn upon at the start of each chapter to support you to think about how your knowledge and understanding of the subject aligns with the strands of the CCF. This will support you in understanding the progress of your learning not just in your training year/s, but into your early career years, too.

The education landscape is constantly evolving and reconfiguring, while reflecting on the pressing issues of our time. Authors have therefore shared their reflections on contemporary issues in education. Each chapter reflects on aspects of diversity and decolonising the curriculum. Once again, supporting the current debate and helping you as a trainee to start these conversations with your pupils.

The book also showcases a chapter on sustainability and climate change education. By adding this chapter, we are making a clear statement on the vital need to develop practices of sustainability and climate change education for trainee teachers. Therefore, the chapter notes and understands the importance of developing sustainability and climate change education for trainee teachers to build their confidence and support them in building capacity in this vital, emerging area of study for all educators.

We hope you will view *Essential Subject Knowledge for Primary Teaching* as a constant companion for you throughout your training and beyond. When you need to look, in depth, into the structures of a subject and 'how to' teach it, this book will provide the answers. Furthermore, you will also find a section on 'developing your knowledge further', hence enabling a progression and extension of the ideas explored in each chapter.

Each chapter is written by experts in their field who have significant shared experiences of teaching in schools and the training of teachers. With this book, you are in very good hands to support all aspects of your knowledge development. We hope you enjoy reading through the chapters and 'dip' into the book chapters as and when you need to support the development of your expertise in the teaching and learning of the primary national curriculum. All the best for a successful year or more of training.

1

ART, CRAFT AND DESIGN

SUSAN OGIER

KEYWORDS: SUPERDIVERSE; CREATIVITY; HOLISTIC; INDIVIDUAL; SPIRAL CURRICULUM; TACIT KNOWLEDGE.

LINKS TO THE CORE CONTENT FRAMEWORK

High Expectations (Standard 1): 1.4

How Pupils Learn (Standard 2): 2.1

Subject and Curriculum (Standard 3): 3.2

Classroom Practice (Standard 4): 4.3

Adaptive Teaching (Standard 5): 5.2

Assessment (Standard 6): 6.5

PART 1: EXPLORING ART, CRAFT AND DESIGN

WHAT IS ART, CRAFT AND DESIGN?

Art and Design, as a subject in the English national curriculum, is a statutory area of learning for children of primary age which contributes to providing a broad and balanced curriculum for all (Education Act, 2002). Art, Craft and Design, to use the full title of this subject (hereon referred to as Art and Design), is unique in its fundamental qualities, and as such has many attributes that cannot be learned or accessed through other curriculum areas. We all know that Art and Design is an important area for children to be engaged in. It's fabulous, creative and expressive, but it is also difficult to define in terms of *what* exactly it is, as many of those innate qualities are wide-ranging, individualistic and often – dare I say it – intangible. These intriguing properties can cause tensions in a curriculum that exalts the acquisition of 'knowledge' as its primary aim. But before we fall into a lengthy philosophical debate about the nature of the beast, we should perhaps focus on the elements that particularly pertain to the teaching of Art and Design to young children. Building the range of skills and depth of understanding required by primary teachers to teach all subjects is no mean feat, and sometimes the prospect of teaching in subject areas where we are not 100 per cent confident in what learning is occurring, or where we do not feel our skills are refined enough, can be off-putting. In this chapter, we are going to explore what is meant by 'subject knowledge' in Art and Design. Hopefully, there will be a few surprises along the way.

WHY IS ART, CRAFT AND DESIGN IN THE NATIONAL CURRICULUM?

The Education Act (2002) enshrines this in law by stating that children must receive a 'balanced and broadly based curriculum', which is noted and reinforced in Part 2:1 of the 2013 version of the national curriculum (DfE, 2013a).

The concept of breadth and balance is found in a curriculum that:

(a) *promotes the spiritual, moral, cultural, mental and physical development of pupils at the school and of society, and*

(b) *prepares pupils at the school for the opportunities, responsibilities, and experiences of later life. (Part 6:78, p. 53).*

This important part of the Act ensures that wider subjects beyond the usual core areas of reading, writing and arithmetic are given some sense of status and space on the timetable, and therefore are included within national curriculum subjects.

The English national curriculum for Art and Design for Key Stage 1 and 2 contains an ambitious purpose of study, reminding us that *Art, craft and design embody some of the highest forms of human creativity*. It goes on to acknowledge that *A high-quality art and design education should engage, inspire and challenge pupils, equipping them with the knowledge and skills to experiment, invent and create their own works of art, craft and design* (2013b: 1).

These are high expectations, which is positive, but the remainder of the document itself can be viewed as rather scant in terms of guidance for teachers. While it could be perceived as freeing, due to the minimal direction given, this can be problematic for teachers who have not had much training in the subject. Later in this chapter, we shall examine the national curriculum further.

HOW HAVE PERCEPTIONS OF ART, CRAFT AND DESIGN EDUCATION DEVELOPED OVER TIME?

Art education has not always been part of the school curriculum in the UK and remains to this day a contested area of learning for a range of (often political) reasons. Attitudes towards art are engulfed in culture (Balling and Juncker, 2016; Crossick and Kaszynska, 2016), and have changed throughout recorded time. Throughout history, art has had a cyclical relationship with public perception. The Arts were once accepted as a domain for the elite, and education in art was reserved for the genius (for example, in the Renaissance period). At other times, artists have been seen as outsiders, and perhaps of low status in society. Even today, some of these attitudes likely affect how the subject is perceived despite how much our world, our attitudes, our expectations and our understandings have changed. Efland's 1990 book, *A History of Art Education*, explains the social, moral and economic constructs over time that affect the way we think about teaching and learning in this subject, including the origins of the familiar Western canon. He explains that *the ways the visual arts are taught today were conditioned by the beliefs and values regarding art, helped by those who advocated its teaching in the past* (1990: 1). Efland goes on to say that these advocates were 'socially powerful individuals' who had an agenda to influence how society evolved. An example of this influence is the introduction of art education in 'common schools' in the mid-nineteenth century, particularly through the process of *drawing*. This approach was not intended as we might now understand it – to allow children to discover their own creativity and to be able to manifest ideas from their own imagination in a visual form – but rather was meant to fill a gap in the workforce during the Industrial Revolution: teaching poor people technical drawing skills and geometry was, first and foremost, about functionality.

REFLECTION

How you perceive the status of the subject will affect the way that you come across as a teacher of art to the children in your class: your personal attitudes will affect the children's own perception of the subject.

How does this concept influence your thinking when contemplating the value of Art and Design education?

What is your perception of Art education?

How have your personal attitudes been shaped during your own education?

Do you believe that Art education should be about function and skill?

In the contemporary primary art classroom, we as practitioners are further influenced by figures from the world of art education, and particularly by those who pushed the boundaries of what art education might look like in periods of social change. One such influential pedagogue was Marion Richardson (1892–1946), an art teacher who revolutionised the concept of learning in art and design by refocusing away from the formal technical skill and drill of drawing education, which was based on copying correctly, towards more imaginative responses that were essentially child initiated and valued as such (Holdsworth, 1988). This thinking was much more in tune with other contemporaries of hers, such as the Austrian art educator Franz Cižek, and philosopher and educational reformer, John Dewey. The quality of work produced by children using Richardson's methods of 'shut-eye' painting, where children were encouraged to close their eyes and imagine their artwork without the formal tuition of learning how to draw, directly impacted upon the community of school art teachers through the public exhibition of children's artwork. This led to her being invited to lecture widely, thus spreading the word of a new approach that seemed to work well for children.

Other key progressive influencers continue to affect how art is taught and perceived. Herbert Read, Edmund Feldman and Viktor Lowenfeld need to be mentioned here as proponents for a more developmental and naturally attuned approach. These names are the big guns in relation to a more human approach to art education. Feldman's book, *Becoming Human Through Art* (1976), is the epitome of a social constructivist approach towards a subject that many policy makers might struggle to grapple with nowadays. Nevertheless, we are human beings – and it is this aspect that makes the practical experience of Art and Design a visually exciting, social and indeed humanising element of the primary curriculum, which is vitally important for a child's holistic development and well-being.

DECOLONISATION OF THE ART CURRICULUM

As we now understand the social, moral and the economic reasonings behind how Art and Design has evolved in the primary curriculum, today's audience for the subject is vastly different from that at the time of the origins of the Western canon of art education from 100 years, or 50 – or even from 20 years ago. The children who fill our schools are from as diverse a heritage as they could possibly be – *super-diverse* in fact, as coined by Koster et al. (2020), and often it feels as though the curriculum itself has struggled to keep up with the pace of change. Thompson et al. (2020) state that the English national curriculum reinforces the tenet of elitism by claiming that pupils are introduced to *the best that has been thought and said and helps engender an appreciation of human creativity and achievement* (DfE, 2013b: 3.1).

This is problematic when 'the best' and 'creativity' remain undefined and open to perhaps narrow interpretation. For example, in Art and Design it is not unusual to find the same old artists being trotted out for study in KS1 and KS2 time and again: Van Gogh, Andy Warhol, Kandinsky, and possibly a bit of David Hockney or Roy Lichtenstein.

REFLECTION

What do you notice about these choices?

Where are the women?

Where are the Black/Asian artists?

Where is the range of design and crafts from at home and around the world, created by ethnically and culturally diverse groups?

The Western canon certainly seems pervasive in this context, but particularly since the emergence of the Black Lives Matter movement in 2020, it has become urgent that schools re-evaluate the diet of examples from the world of Art and Design that children are introduced to. The notion of the Western, white, dead, male artist as the main context for learning about art is not only out of date, but is now inappropriate and narrow. The Runnymede Trust commissioned a report, to be published in 2023, the goal of which is to understand racial inequalities that exist within art education and the visual arts generally. The Trust's initial research found that DfE figures in 2017 showed that although 31 per cent of school children were from ethnic minorities, they were introduced to art by 94 per cent of teachers who were white (Freelands Foundation and Runnymede Trust, n.d.). Thus, the likelihood of teachers choosing artists who represent themselves, rather than representing the children, is high. This is why we must face our own unconscious bias when choosing artists to introduce to children, and consider making sure our choices are relevant to the audience in question.

It will be useful here to return to the DfE (2013b) national curriculum and continue to examine the Purpose of Study. This states that:

> As pupils progress, they should be able to think critically and develop a more rigorous understanding of art and design. They should also know how art and design both reflect and shape our history, and contribute to the culture, creativity, and wealth of our nation.

Given the understanding that the demographic in our schools and in wider society are 'superdiverse', DfE (2013b) explicitly gives permission to offer knowledge and understanding that is culturally rich, as well as providing wide experiences for children in our schools. We must ensure that children's learning encompasses the many influences that affect artistic outputs in order that they can critically engage with the complexities of the world in which they exist.

ART, CRAFT AND DESIGN NOW

Art and Design is a dynamic subject to teach. One of the joys of this area of learning is that, although its roots are embedded within the history of every culture on earth, it is constantly evolving in terms of themes and processes, and ways and means of working, by introducing provocations and questions – always inventing and reinventing. Art and Design involves building on the past and developing new ideas that are all about the future.

With so much going for this subject, it seems extraordinary, even senseless, that it is constantly under threat of extinction from the primary curriculum – but it is. With emphasis placed on subjects that children are tested upon, despite a supposed refocus by Ofsted to include foundation subjects (Spielman, 2017), budgetary and time pressures on the curriculum see the area of Art and Design consistently being squeezed.

Current government policy is to focus the curriculum on subjects that lead to highly paid work opportunities within a short period of leaving college. Effectively, this policy means that arts courses are now in freefall at the points of both university and higher education (Weale, 2021), with the effect that whatever happens at one end of the education system has a trickle-down effect on the others. If young people are discouraged from pursuing art, music, literature, drama, etc., with the profoundly mistaken promise that they will 'never get a job' doing that (Robinson, 2006), then they are discouraged from taking state exams in the subjects at age 16+, with the further effect of the subject having a low status at KS3, then KS2 and then KS1. The National Society of Education in Art and Design (NSEAD) has documented this decline in a survey for the year 2015–16, which found that across all phases of education professional development, the value of the subject and curriculum provision had significantly declined during the preceding five years (NSEAD, 2017). There is no sign that the situation has since improved. Before we know it, there will be a generation of children growing up missing out in this hugely important area of learning, and missing out on the possibilities it might have afforded them. Those of us with a background of further and higher education in arts subjects will know that a meaningful and fulfilling arts career does not happen overnight and sometimes takes years to establish. Yet in no way does this effort mean that the study of Art and Design is worthless – neither on a personal level nor on a societal level.

While the role of art education is seemingly losing ground in the English school system, and in many Western school systems, this is not necessarily the case in all parts of the world. Interestingly, the reverse is happening in places such as Asia, where there is an understanding of the need for creativity and critical thinking in education policy. For example, the OECD (2016) reports that the basic educational curriculum reform in China aims to promote the holistic development of students, citing the importance of developing well-rounded individuals. While in the UK, especially in England, the focus is away from the individual and a move towards a 'one-size-fits-all' system, the OECD states:

> China's focus on the all-around development of all individual learners has been supported further by the country's shift away from basic skill development towards a holistic approach to human development.

(2016: 23)

The nature of Art and Design as a discipline, and, as a school subject, means that we can hang on to some of that independence, creativity and critical thinking, because in Art and Design we are not looking for one size to fit all.

Art and Design often deals with the unknown, uncertainty and ambiguity – factors that we, as teachers, must address through difficult pedagogical challenges (Leshnoff, 1995). As so much of the curriculum is fixed on the opposite of these factors, Art and Design education can present an alternative way of thinking, doing and being, which can work well for children who thrive by learning in less formal ways. Dealing with feelings and emotions also sets Art and Design education apart from many other subject areas, where specific knowledge is taught in a linear fashion: this subject area works more along the lines of a rhizomatic paradigm (Irwin et al., 2006). This means that art practice can take the artist in any of many potential directions, and the final artwork or outcome comes about through exploratory and open-ended research. As primary teachers, we can, perhaps, look to the world of contemporary Art and Design practice to inspire approaches to use in the classroom.

WHAT MIGHT KNOWLEDGE IN ART AND DESIGN LOOK LIKE IN THE FUTURE?

Let us reflect for a moment here. What do we mean by 'knowledge' when we are thinking about Art and Design? Do we tend to automatically consider this as meaning how many facts and how much information we might be able to recall at any time? This is known as 'declarative' knowledge and is not the only kind of knowledge that we need when teaching Art and Design. The Merriam Webster definition of 'knowledge' gives a wider context for the meaning of the word, giving us another kind of knowledge that is 'procedural' or 'tacit'. This knowledge, it states, is the *condition of knowing something with familiarity gained through experience or association* (Merriam Webster, n.d.), which is more useful to us as primary teachers of Art and Design. There is a danger right now that the notion of 'knowledge' in this area of learning becomes a reductive exercise in fact finding. In the following section, we shall therefore explore the many ways we can open our minds to the full extent of the meaning of subject knowledge in this context.

PART 2: FOUNDATION KNOWLEDGE IN ART AND DESIGN

In this section, we shall explore the meaning of *subject knowledge* in Art and Design in more depth. We shall use the definition of 'knowledge' that, as we have already established, is *the condition of knowing something with familiarity gained through experience or association*, so that we are clear about how *knowledge* might be interpreted in this subject. Art and Design is first and foremost a practical subject and children will only be able to learn in this area if they are physically involved in making. As a teacher of primary Art and Design, it is of the utmost importance that you equip yourself with the understanding and skill set necessary to be able to teach it well. This means being open-minded and flexible in the way you approach planning, as well as in what happens both during and as a result of your lessons. We shall focus on two commonly used processes, so that we cover both 2D and 3D work: Drawing and Sculpture. The skills and knowledge listed in these areas can be applied to other processes that should be included during a child's primary school experience in Art and Design in order to ensure progression over time. These processes include printmaking, painting, craft-work, photography/film, installation, textiles, collage, ceramics, digital media, architecture and graphic arts.

PART 3: UNDERSTANDING THE DEVELOPMENT OF CHILDREN'S KNOWLEDGE IN ART AND DESIGN

Let's have a look at what *progression* in Art and Design might look like by taking the ideas from the last section: that progression happens by giving children high-quality experiences across a range of mediums, and by introducing them to new artists, materials, techniques and processes. The following example shows how children will develop skills, knowledge and understanding across three age phases, with a focus on *colour*.

Table 1.1 *Key process: 2D – Drawing*

Key process: 2D – Drawing	
What is this process?	**What materials are involved?**
According to the Tate website, the definition of Drawing is *essentially a technique in which images are depicted on a surface by making lines, though drawings can also contain tonal areas, washes and other non-linear marks*. This does not sound too scary when put like this, yet many people, teachers included, are worried that they 'can't draw', and teachers are afraid, therefore, that they cannot teach this process. This is often because there is a perception that a drawing must look a certain way, preferably be in pencil, and be an almost photographic representation of the object being drawn. Observation drawing can cause a good deal of anxiety for teachers, which is then reflected on to the children. Misconceptions around drawing can be easily dismissed by revisiting the definition above. It can be useful to think about Drawing as a tool with which children can explore visual representation – a form of enquiry or discovery – and, as such, a 'drawing' can take many forms. This process is fundamental to gain confidence in, as it underpins all the other art processes in some way, either explicitly (such as in printmaking, where an image is drawn onto the plate), or implicitly (such as in textiles, where perhaps images are created in planning the piece, or skills such as composition are learned through drawing and then applied when composing a photograph).	Introduce a wide range of materials for drawing, which will open up possibilities for children to visually express their ideas through mark-making. Ensure that children experience different surfaces and scale: paper, of course, but do consider offering different textures and colours, and perhaps recycled and repurposed materials, such as wallpaper samples or rolls. Do not limit children to paper as a surface when teaching drawing. Draw with chalk on the playground floor; use felt pens or oil pastels to draw on natural materials, such as autumn leaves; draw with string or tape by gluing it into a design or shape. If you are lucky enough to live near a beach, draw on a large scale with sticks in the sand or by placing pebbles into a design. Forget pencils for a while and introduce children to drawing with willow charcoal. This highly malleable and expressive material will loosen up and release the most nervous artist.

(Continued)

Table 1.1 (Continued)

Key process: 2D – Drawing

Which artists can I look at?

These are famous Western artists well known for their drawings, many of whom you will know. You might, however, notice that they are all dead, white, Western males, so you will need to expand this range of examples if you use them:

www.artst.org/famous-drawing-artists/

Do look at contemporary drawings as well as more traditional ones, and observe the different ways that artists use drawing. This will help you to develop children's understanding of this important process and to reduce anxiety.

For inspiration, look at the blog www.drawingsandnotes.com, where you will find a range of approaches by different contemporary artists by clicking on the artist's name. For example, look at the way that Tacita Dean uses a vintage index card and collage to make a drawing, check in with André Butzer's wonderfully scribbly line drawings, or

watch the video by Kara Walker talking about her process and the themes that interest her:

www.drawingsandnotes.com/kara-walker-drawings/

What are key techniques for drawing?

Sketch vs. drawing – what is the difference? It's important that you know, so have a look at this blog which explains this well: www.artst.org/sketch-vs-drawing/

You can use the same techniques as you would use in sketching to begin a drawing. You might make quick, skeletal, gestural marks, with which to map your drawing. Encourage children to keep the sketchy marks rather than erase them, as this will add depth and interest to the final piece. Show them examples such as Rodin's Cambodian dancers where many lines are used to depict gesture and movement, or even Leonardo da Vinci's drawings where lines are redrawn over and again until the artist is happy with the result.

Shading, using tone and adding dark and light areas to a drawing can be best taught through using material such as charcoal, which can used to create very black areas by pressing hard and adding compressed charcoal, or very light areas, by using light pressure and smudging, and every shade in between – maybe adding white chalk to emphasise highlights.

Mark-making can be taught through an experimental approach using any drawing material: ask children to use drawing material to represent different textures, for example. Children might use the materials to make dots, dashes sweeping marks, smears, etc.

How do I introduce this process?

Just as in PE we would expect to have some warmup activities to prepare our bodies for exercise, in Art and Design we do the same. You will need to think about the focus of your lesson: what skills are you focusing on? Then devise a short, enjoyable activity that links to that focus to warm children up for learning. For example, if you are focusing on observational drawing, you might start the session with 'no drawing – drawing'! This is by asking the children to trace an object or shape by just pointing their finger and tracing the shapes they notice in the air. It is an easy next step to do the same thing but record the shapes onto paper with some drawing materials.

What key vocabulary do I need to know?

You have already met some of the vocabulary that you can introduce in this section. It is useful if you use the correct terms for materials and techniques with children so that they hear and use these terms too. Develop their language skills by encouraging them to use descriptive words when discussing their mark-making efforts:

line	blend
tone	shape
mark	shading
light	texture
dark	gesture
smudge	value

Key process: 2D – Drawing

What skills do I need?	How do I assess this process?
Essentially you need to be open-minded and want to have a go at building your own skills and confidence in the process of drawing. This includes understanding what drawing has to offer as a way for children to communicate with you, and with a wider audience.	It is important to value children's drawings for what they are – children's drawings! How we draw is as personal, and each individual will have to find their own way with this. So, this might imply that it is impossible to assess – wrong! We can assess children's progress in Drawing over *time*. Familiarise yourself with some of the theory around children's development in drawing, such as Lowenfeld's developmental stages of drawing, which can be found in a useful context here: https://uploads.theartofeducation.edu/2021/05/73.1StagesofDrawingDevelopmentReferenceGuide.pdf
The way that an individual draws is as personal as their own fingerprint. Therefore, there is not a 'norm' – a grid that you can measure your children against in relation to their age or stage. You must leave all your preconceptions of what children should achieve, and by when, aside – which is both challenging and affirming.	
Have faith in children's innate desire to express themselves through the medium of the drawn image and enjoy and celebrate their efforts by encouraging them in every way possible.	The key takeaway is that children develop visually literacy at different rates and are dependent on their experience of physically engaging in the processes of artistic exploration. As Lowenfeld says, *For children art is a way of learning – not something to be learned.*
Build your own confidence and skills by engaging in some personal PD! Try this gently encouraging drawing programme: https://cravepainting.com/sketching-project/#outline	
Don't forget that this programme is for adults. You need to keep things fun, fluid and frequent when working with children.	

Table 1.2 Key process: 3D – Sculptures

Key process: 3D – Sculpture	
What is this process?	**What materials are involved?**
The *Merriam Webster Dictionary* (2022) describes sculpture as:	Traditionally, materials such as wood, stone, metal and other hard materials are used to create sculpture, and many of these are inappropriate to use with young children for health and safety, as well as practical and budget limitations. We can and should simplify the materials that we use for sculpture with children by using as much reclaimed material as possible. By using materials that are freely available, with little or no cost, means that we are not imposing unnecessary anxiety on children, or ourselves as teachers, for being 'wasteful' when things go awry. Using reclaimed and recycled material and objects means that we can accommodate some sense of freedom to explore and experiment without restraint, and we can allow true creativity to bloom.
The action or art of processing (as by carving, modelling, or welding) plastic or hard materials into works of art: a three-dimensional work of art (such as a statue); to form an image or representation of from solid material (such as wood or stone); to form into a three-dimensional work of art.	
We can see from this that sculpture is essentially about the creation of an artwork that will occupy a physical space in our world – it might be viewed from all sides and could be measured in terms of its volume and weight. The three dimensions that we are talking about here are height, width and depth. By reflecting on the language that we have used to describe Sculpture, we can already start to see how this process links directly to mathematical and scientific concepts: indeed, many skills are developed while making sculpture. This means that children utilise important critical skills, such as an ability to question and seek alternative solutions, as well gain sensory and tactile understanding to comprehend principles of how things work, such as gravity and properties of materials. They will gain further skills in resilience and perseverance.	Cheap and free materials you can construct sculpture with are items such as: paper, cardboard, plastic sheeting, plastic bottles, foam, wood, matchsticks, lolly sticks, foil, bamboo sticks, wire, pipe cleaners – basically, anything!
	You will also need to provide joining and cutting materials, such as tape, zip-ties, coloured electrical tape (adds colour), string, scissors, wire cutters, PVA glue, cellulose paste (for papier-mâché).
	With KS2, you might want to use craft knives with a cutting board if this can be supervised.
Sculpture as a process is often last choice for teachers, as it can be messy, chaotic and noisy. However, for some children, this will be their preferred way of making art, so it is important that all children are given the opportunity to make, build and learn to use materials in the only way afforded by creating works in three dimensions.	If carving with children, you will need soft wood, such as lime, and specialist wood-carving tools, which is better with KS2. With younger children, carve into bars of soap to change the shape just by using everyday cutlery knives from the kitchen.
	Modelling techniques involve a range a different materials and different processes. For this, you would need to buy in bags of clay. Try to go for natural, rather than air-drying clay, which is harmful for the environment due to the fact that it is full of plastic fibres.

Key process: 3D – Sculpture

Which artists can I look at?	What are key techniques for sculpture?
Because of the presence in real space and time and the physicality of sculpture as a textural object, it can be engaging as a process for young children. Expanding children's understanding of the diversity and range of contemporary sculpture can both inspire and motivate children to want to find out more.	*Construction* is an additive process that involves using joining techniques to build and create structures.
Choose artists who exemplify your teaching point: if you are planning a project that focuses on space, look at an artist whose work represents that in an explicit way, such as the mobiles of Alexander Calder, who had a career as an engineer before becoming an artist: www.tate.org.uk/art/artists/alexander-calder-848	You might encourage children to explore shape and space by constructing with a range, or a limited range, of recycled materials to see what they do with the materials. How can they change the shape/nature of the material? How can they join materials together to make a new shape that will stand up?
If your project centres on structure, shape and geometry, show them an artist such as Anthony Caro: www.anthonycaro.org/	Construction techniques will form the structure for papier-mâché or plaster bandage sculptures, which can be finished off by adding layers of tissue paper to the wet surface or painting when dry.
or Phyllida Barlow:	*Modelling* is concerned with manipulating soft material that can be moulded by hand – for example, clay work or other malleable material, such as salt dough, damp sand, etc.
www.royalacademy.org.uk/art-artists/name/phyllida-barlow-ra	*Carving* involves cutting through a defined design onto a predefined surface, such as wood/soap/clay.
If your project is concept based, look at Rachel Whiteread. This is a super artist to study if you are planning a project that involves casting techniques: https://gagosian.com/artists/rachel-whiteread/	*Casting*: place a layer of clay into a container and impress natural objects into the clay, or leave in their entirety on a bed of clay. Pour Plaster of Paris over and let it set. Peel away the clay and remove the objects to reveal the cast.
or Martin Creed, who uses art to question our preconceptions of commercial value:	
www.contemporary-art.org/Sculpture/	
Here is a website where you will find a range of interesting contemporary artists with a focus on Sculpture:	
www.contemporary-art.org/Sculpture/	
If you are looking for a more traditional focus for your sculpture project, you can find some examples of important artists on this e-resource:	
https://mymodernmet.com/famous-sculptures-art-history/	

(Continued)

Table 1.2 (Continued)

Key process: 3D – Sculpture	
How do I introduce this process?	**What key vocabulary do I need to know?**
Discuss the concept of three-dimensionality by highlighting the physicality of the world we live in: we exist in a 3-D environment, so why wouldn't we represent our ideas, thoughts and concerns about the world in 3-D too?	There is much scope to extend and develop children's language skills through sculpture projects. You will need to acquaint yourself with terms related to the process you are teaching. These might include the following, but this list is not exhaustive:
A trip to a gallery, sculpture park or walk around the locality to look at public art sculptures/statues is a great kick-off for a sculpture project.	form, shape, space, mould, smooth, build, construct, join, bend, strong, rigid, attach, bind, spatial, structure, solid, tear, volume, relief, balance, movement, maquette, geometric, mobile, assemblage, sculpt, carve, statue, cut, design, engrave, whittle, tone, shadow, curve, adjacent, straight, size, scale, etc.
You can also use the process of collage as a way into starting a sculpture project, focusing on shape and form through layering: children will have a lot of practice of cutting and sticking in a variety of contexts, and it is an inclusive art form, as children who might be developing an anxiety about not being 'good' at drawing can achieve satisfying results. Developing their understanding of collage as an art form will automatically build on children's previous learning in using and applying visual language.	
Show children how we can transform materials into three dimensions: take a sheet of paper and a pair of scissors; make a variety of cuts into the paper (zig-zags, curves, fringes, etc.), taking care to keep the paper as one piece. Hold the paper up and twist it around and look at the shapes that have been created by the cutting process. Tape/hang it up to emphasise the shapes. Shine a spotlight to emphasise the shadows that are created by the 3-D shapes and make drawings of these using at least A3 or preferably A4 size paper, with charcoal and chalk. This is a great way to get children to consider three-dimensionality before launching your main focus for the sculpture project.	

Key process: 3D – Sculpture

What skills do I need?

As a teacher, you will need to acquaint yourself with the techniques that you want to teach by having a go yourself. It is important to know how the process might work, how long it might take and what might not work so well. There is nothing wrong with learning alongside the children in art lessons, but you will need to stay one step ahead of them and be able to support anyone who is struggling or finding some challenges. You will need to refine your observation skills so that you are aware of individual children's needs and be open to children surprising you with their ideas and with what they are able to achieve.

How do I assess this process?

Assessment in the process of Sculpture, as in all processes that come into the subject area of Art and Design, must be addressed with sensitivity and encouragement at the heart. Children's confidence in creative work can be fragile, and a dismissive remark can go a long way to destroy it. Learning and progression in this area will happen, but it needs consistent and varied experiences throughout a child's primary years, offering a range of materials and techniques. It is not possible to keep a tick list of how, what and when children 'achieve' in this subject in the same way as many other areas of learning. Learning takes place more along the lines of Bruner's 'spiral curriculum' rather than in a linear way, so only by giving children positive and joyful experiences in art will they grow and develop as artists. By placing the sculptures on display and asking children to photograph them and to reflect on their learning – either verbally or by writing journal entries in their sketchbooks – you can document both the process and children's individual progress.

Table 1.3 Colour with year group

Year group 1/2	Learning objectives	Activities to develop the skills and understanding	Next steps
Process: Painting **Prior experiences:** Children will almost definitely have had the experience of painting in their Early Years setting. They should, for example, have had free access to a painting easel for independent experimentation with colour and representation. They should have had experience of mixing colours, and have tried out a variety of media commonly used in painting to achieve a variety of effects, such as dropping dry powder paint onto wet paper; using block watercolour with wax resist; using a range of tools for painting, including hands, fingers and feet.	**Aims:** At KS1, we want to build on the children's enjoyment and enthusiasm for Art and Design that they will bring with them from their Early Years learning. So, here our intention is to keep those feelings going by designing projects that will keep children interested and that are low stakes in terms of pressure for children to produce something that should conform to a prescribed model. A painting project can be taught across several lessons and should cover a range of knowledge for learning to use paint. Imaginative responses should be encouraged. **Intentions:** The focus will be on COLOUR so that children begin understanding that there is a vast range of colours: bright; dull; fluorescent; natural; pastel; skin tones; clashing colours, etc. to choose from when creating artwork. They will learn to mix colours: primary; secondary; tertiary in a fun but structured way, and learn to choose colours – sometimes intuitively, sometimes for a particular purpose. They will be introduced to a range of artists who use paint in different ways to communicate with their audience.	1. Take a colour walk in the school/ local environment/gallery trip. 2. What are primary colours? How do we make secondary colours? Set up colour-mixing stations. How many shades of green/purple/orange can they make? Can they give their colours names? 3. What are tertiary colours? Who can mix the muddiest colour? Who can create grey tones? 4. What can we add to paint to give it texture? What materials can we use as painting tools to create patterns and add texture? 5. Can we make our own paintbrushes and paint from natural materials? What happens when we apply one colour on top of another? What happens when we place one colour next to another? What are cold colours? What are hot colours?	Ensure children are introduced to a range of artists who use paint in different ways –Frank Bowling is a good example. Continue to plan to expand their understanding of how adaptable the medium is – for example, by pouring paint or by creating effects, such as adding salt to wet colour.

Table 1.4 Colour with year group 3/4

Year group 3/4	Learning outcomes	Activities to develop the skills and understanding	Next steps
Process: Printmaking **Prior experience:** Children will have had a good deal of practice printing with objects, such as toys, shapes, natural materials, fruit/vegetables, household items, etc. in the Early Years and KS1. They should have been introduced to processes using both additive – for example, collagraph – creating a block for printing using textured surfaces, and subtractive (drawing into polystyrene tiles for press-printing) techniques and methods.	**Aims** Printmaking is an inclusive art process, as it is easy for everyone to achieve a successful outcome, no matter how they might feel about their own ability as an artist. In lower KS2, we want to move children's understanding of printmaking up a notch or two, and start focusing on more complex ideas and techniques that are appropriate within their developmental stages. What is a print? Why do artists make prints? What can be achieved through this process that can't be achieved through painting or drawing? **Intention** A print occurs when media is transferred from one surface to another, and by making changes to the surface we want to print from we can explore lines, textures, colour and tone through personal themes. Children will engage in drawing without the pressure of being judged and learn about colour contrasts and layering. They will learn to work with 'happy mistakes' and to rework ideas through a sequence of procedures.	1. What is a print? Make a block by rubbing oil pastels on paper. Place two pieces of paper over the block and draw by pressing hard onto the back of the paper. Lift and admire the transfer. 2. Research some images: look at source material to develop your topic or theme. Sketch and make colour notes. Look at contrasting/ harmonious/ complementary colours. Children can choose their own colour palette. 3. Children should mix their own colours from primaries. Use rollers to print background colour (use poster paint on large-scale work or printing ink if on a small scale). 4. Draw into polystyrene block. Print choosing colours that will lay on top of background to provide a contrast. 5. Draw more detail into the polystyrene block and cut areas of the block away. Print again, using a third colour. Use a dark colour to add drama and to allow lighter colours to shine through.	Take the concept of using colour contrasts further by planning colour experiments, such as making a pastel painting or print with clashing colours. Print or paint a range of papers with different colours and use these to create collages to explore the idea of shape and colour. Look at abstract artists such as Patrick Heron or Elizabeth Murray for inspiration.

Table 1.5 Colour with year group 5/6

Year group 5/6	Learning outcomes	Activities to develop the skills and understanding	Next steps
Process: Textiles – Batik **Prior experience:** By Upper KS2, children should be confident with paint and with using colour in many different media. They should know the difference between poster paint, powder paint and watercolour, and how to achieve different effects by adding substances, such as flour or earth to make it thick, or by watering it down to create pale hues. They should have experienced working in colour on a variety of surfaces, such as cardboard, cloth, paper, etc. They should have good fine motor control, hand eye co-ordination and be confident in drawing. Children might well have had a chance to have a go at wax resist using wax crayons or candle and watercolour at some point in their journey through primary school, but as Batik is a resist method, this will need to be refreshed in their memory.	**Aims** It is always good to keep an exciting art process for children who are coming to the end of their primary year, perhaps one that they have not tried before. This shows them that we trust them to use resources sensibly and respectfully. Batik is a great way for children to build on their knowledge of using colour, their understanding of layering and working through a sequence of processes to produce satisfying outcomes. The aim is that children are working independently and with autonomy to develop their piece of work. **Intentions** Children will learn to apply knowledge and skills of drawing to design an image or pattern. Batik is both an art and a craft, and the historical and cultural background will also be interesting for children. They will learn to use specialist equipment safely and to discover alternative ways to achieve similar effects using low-cost/low-impact materials.	1. Negotiate a theme or topic with your class or ask children to develop their own as individuals. Ask children to research and collect reference information and images. Use sketchbooks to explore ideas. 2. Children can make a series of sketches using wax resist drawings to help them decide on the final design and colour scheme for their batik. 3. Introduce and demonstrate how to use batik hot wax kettles and 'tjanting' bowls, including safety advice. Children make line drawings on white cotton fabric pieces using the tjanting. 4. They add colour to the dried wax drawings by using either fabric paint or watered-down acrylics to complete the design. 5. Sandwich the dried fabric between sheets of newsprint and iron the wax out. Alternatives: use glue or flour paste instead of hot wax, which will wash out easily.	The batik pieces can be embellished with embroidery and by sewing on beads and sequins. The pieces can be sewn into cushion-covers or made into wall-hangings or flags. It is important to display the work to give children a sense of audience for their work, so involve them in organising as art exhibition, so that parents and the school community can enjoy their artwork. Children in Years 5 and 6 can build and organise their own portfolio of art experiences to take with them to share with their secondary school art teacher.

PART 4: DEVELOPING YOUR KNOWLEDGE OF ART AND DESIGN FURTHER

The 2020 Covid-19 global pandemic reignited fresh emphasis on art education as part of a recovery mechanism to help children re-engage with being in school after, in some cases, months of absence. Teachers employed practical activities that helped children settle socially and emotionally, using materials, techniques and processes. The art classroom became a safe space for discussion, reaffirming friendships and re-establishing routines. This highlights the often-hidden benefits of good art education: that, when well organised, a calm and purposeful art classroom becomes a social space and an important release from an otherwise relentless curriculum. In this chapter, we have examined some of the key learning and processes that it is important for you to understand to teach the subject well, and with pedagogy that is appropriate for teaching Art and Design to primary-aged children. This material is, however, not exhaustive and you will need to find ways to develop and expand your knowledge in this subject area by considering the following suggestions.

- Keep an eye out for professional development opportunities, either locally by joining a teacher subject network group or nationally by joining a subject association, such as the National Society for Education in Art and Design (www.nsead.org/).

- Keep a critical eye on some of the resources you might find online, as some commercial products for teachers are not always pedagogically sound. If you are tempted by some of these products, ask yourself the following questions:

  o Is this challenging (in a good way) for children? Or is it too easy?

  o Are a diverse range of artists, craftspeople and designers being introduced? Or are familiar famous artists being advocated as examples?

  o Are children's ideas and creative efforts valued? Or are they expected to copy/reproduce a prescribed outcome and made to feel unsuccessful if it is not exact?

  o Are children able to take ownership and make their own decisions in their work? Or are they working to a predetermined brief?

  o Will the resulting outcomes be individual and diverse? Or will the pieces look identical?

- Try to make this as enjoyable for yourself as possible by visiting art galleries and exhibitions to get ideas for art projects that suit your class. What is going to grab their attention and maintain it? We are so lucky that we are free to do this in Art and Design – there are no exams or tests in this subject, so we are free to develop children's (and our own) creativity as individuals.

- NSEAD has many resources for primary teachers, including advice on how to interpret the national curriculum and on assessment and progression. These high-quality resources are designed by primary art and design experts and are free to all. www.nsead.org/resources/curriculum/

- Find out more about the research project, *Visualise: Race and Inclusion in Art Education*, at: https://freelandsfoundation.co.uk/research-and-publications/runnymede-trust

- Tate has some great resources for teachers including a glossary of art terms. See: www.tate.org.uk/art/art-terms

- Best of all is Tate Kids, which will inspire you to use a range of modern and contemporary artists with children. See: www.tate.org.uk/kids

REFERENCES

Balling, G and Juncker, B (2016) The value of art and culture in everyday life: towards an expressive cultural democracy. *The Journal of Arts Management Law and Society*, 46: 231–42. DOI: 10.1080/10632921.2016.1225618

Crossick, G and Kaszynska, P (2016) *Understanding the Value of Arts & Culture*. The AHRC cultural value project. Swindon: Arts and Humanities Research Council. Available at: www.artshealthresources.org.uk/docs/understanding-the-value-of-arts-culture-the-ahrc-cultural-value-project/

DfE (2013a) Education Act (2002) An Act to make provision about education, training and childcare, Part 6, Chapter 32, p78. Available at: www.legislation.gov.uk/ukpga/2002/32/part/6/data.pdf

DfE (2013b) *National Curriculum for Art and Design KS1-3*. Available at: www.gov.uk/government/publications/national-curriculum-in-england-art-and-design-programmes-of-study

Efland, A (1990) *A History of Art Education: Intellectual and Social Currents in Teaching the Visual Arts*, Columbia University, New York and London: Teachers College Press.

Feldman, E.B. (1976) *Becoming Human Through Art: Aesthetic Experience in the School*. Upper Saddle River, NJ: Prentice-Hall.

Freelands Foundation and Runnymede Trust (n.d.) *Visualise: Race and Inclusion in Art Education*. Available at: https://freelandsfoundation.co.uk/research-and-publications/runnymede-trust

Holdsworth, B (1988) Marion Richardson (1892–1946). *International Journal of Art and Design Education*, 7 (2): 137–54.

Irwin, RL, Beer, R, Springgay, S, Grauer, K, Xiong, G and Bickel, B (2006) The rhizomatic relations of a/r/tography'. *Studies in Art Education*, 48 (1). Available at: https://opensiuc.lib.siu.edu/cgi/viewcontent.cgi?httpsredir=1&article=1004&context=ad_pubs

Koster, I, Verschraegan, G and Clycq , N (2020) Repertoires on diversity among primary schools children. *Childhood Journal*, 28 (1). Available at: https://doi.org/10.1177/0907568220909430

Leshnoff, SK (1995) Art, ambiguity and critical thinking. *Art Education*, 48 (5): 51–6.

NSEAD (2017) 2015–16 *Survey Report: How has Government Policy Impacted on Art, Craft and Design Education?* Available at: www.nsead.org/download/file/650/

OECD (2016) *Education in China: A Snapshot.* Available at: www.oecd.org/china/Education-in-China-a-snapshot.pdf

Robinson, K (2006) Do schools kill creativity? *TED*. Available at: www.ted.com/talks/sir_ken_robinson_do_schools_kill_creativity

Speilman, A (2017) Enriching the fabric of education. *Festival of Education, speechtranscript.* Available at: www.gov.uk/government/speeches/amanda-spielmans-speech-at-the-festival-of-education

Thompson, P and Maloy, L (2020) *The Benefits of Art, Craft and Design Education in Schools: A Rapid Evidence Review*. Centre for Research in Arts, Creativity and Literacies, University of Nottingham. Available at: www.researchgate.net/publication/358662186_A_Rapid_Evidence_Review_of_Arts_Craft_and_Design_Education_in_Schools

Weale, S (2021) Funding cuts go ahead for university arts courses in England. *The Guardian.* Available at: www.theguardian.com/education/2021/jul/20/funding-cuts-to-go-ahead-for-university-arts-courses-in-england-despite-opposition

2

COMPUTING

NEIL RICKUS

KEYWORDS: ALGORITHM; PROGRAMMING; COMPUTATIONAL THINKING; COMPUTER SCIENCE; INFORMATION TECHNOLOGY; DIGITAL LITERACY; ONLINE SAFETY.

LINKS TO THE CORE CONTENT FRAMEWORK

How Pupils Learn (Standard 2): 2.2

Subject and Curriculum (Standard 3): 3.1, 3.2, 3.3, 3.5, 3.7

Classroom Practice (Standard 4): 4.2, 4.3, 4.4, 4.8, 4.9

PART 1: EXPLORING COMPUTING WHAT IS COMPUTING?

The national curriculum subject of Computing (DfE, 2013a) enables children to understand our digital world. Computing is a practical subject, focusing on using computational thinking (CT) and creativity, and consists of three interrelated strands:

- Computer Science (CS) – applying fundamental Computing principles to solve problems, including the development of algorithms and programs.

- Information Technology (IT) – using information technology to solve problems and develop digital content.

- Digital Literacy (DL) – using technology creatively and purposefully, while interacting with it safely and responsibly.

Computing differs from the previous Information and Communications Technology (ICT) through its emphasis on solving problems through applying CT skills and the need to create purposeful projects. There is also a greater focus on how computers function.

While the programme of study contains statements related to digital literacy and the safe usage of technology, online safety requires a whole-school approach (DfE, 2019), including links to safeguarding and the guidance on Relationships and sex education (RSE) and health education (DfE, 2021).

The subject should not be confused with the general usage of technology in education. The teaching of Computing will regularly require the use of technology and may enable children to develop their digital literacy skills, although simply using technology, such as to reinforce the learning of multiplication tables, does not constitute coverage of this distinct curriculum subject.

REFLECTION

What was your experience of Computing-related subjects when you were at school? For example, did you enjoy lessons and do you still use skills taught when working or studying?

What is your view on Computing being taught in primary schools? For example, should the subject be taught to young children or is it more suitable for secondary-aged pupils?

Is the content of the Computing national curriculum appropriate for preparing children for their future education and careers? For example, should there be more focus on using applications or is it important that pupils understand how computers work and how to develop programs?

WHY IS COMPUTING IN THE NATIONAL CURRICULUM?

The national curriculum programme of study for Computing states: *A high-quality Computing education equips pupils to use computational thinking and creativity to understand and change the world* (DfE, 2013a). The need for a comprehensive Computing education is recognised as essential for a young person's future education and career prospects, along with a key contributor to the UK's economy (Royal Society, 2017).

Having Computing as a statutory subject helps provide all learners with an understanding of digital technologies and the ability to use them effectively. In particular, it is important that people from a range of backgrounds can access Computing-related subjects as part of their future careers (Childs, 2021). As the use of digital technologies continues to become more widespread, young people have access to a range of platforms, including social media, so there is an increased need to understand how services function and how to use them safely (NSPCC, 2022).

HOW HAS 'KNOWLEDGE' IN COMPUTING DEVELOPED OVER TIME?

Since computers started to appear in UK schools in the early 1980s, children have experienced using digital devices in the classroom. While early devices, such as the BBC Micro, which was introduced to schools across the UK in 1981 and went on to sell over a million units (Arthur, 2012) may now be regarded as primitive, they paved the way for many future careers and are regarded as having a positive impact on the UK's technology sector (Nesta, 2013).

Information Technology (IT) formed part of the newly introduced national curriculum in 1988 (Ofsted, 2011), with pupils examining how they could communicate, handle data, produce computer models, and control and monitor devices. Through having such broad statements, schools were not constrained to using software packages or solving specific problems and, in theory, could tailor curriculum content to the needs and interests of their learners. However, by the mid-1990s, which saw the change from IT to Information and Communications Technology (ICT) and the publication of the Stevenson report (Stevenson, 1996), there was recognition that *the state of ICT in our schools is primitive and not improving* (Stevenson, 1996, p6) and that significant investment was needed in both training for teachers and technology infrastructure.

As technology continued to develop and internet access became more prevalent, there was a growing recognition that the ICT curriculum was not fit for purpose. Lessons within school often focused on using productivity applications, such as formatting word-processed documents or animating presentation slides, rather than solving problems through programming, or having opportunities to develop creative digital artefacts. In addition, the distinction between teaching about technology and using technology to support teaching and learning was often unclear within schools' ICT provision (Weston, 2012). The Royal Society's *Shutdown or Restart? The Way Forward for Computing in UK schools* (Royal Society, 2012) outlined how *The current delivery of Computing education in many UK schools is highly unsatisfactory* (Royal Society, 2012, p5) and it was becoming increasingly evident that the ICT curriculum needed a significant overhaul.

Following a public consultation and the subsequent removal of ICT from the National Curriculum (DfE, 2013b), Computing as a discrete subject was introduced in September 2014, with schools beginning to deliver the new statutory curriculum content. The increased emphasis on computer science was welcomed by many (Berry, 2013), along with the benefits to students' future education and job prospects (Wakefield, 2014). Along with the reforms to the national curriculum, the qualification landscape altered for secondary-aged pupils, with the ICT GCSE now no longer available for students in English schools. While Computer Science GCSE or vocational qualifications can be studied, the number of students undertaking a

Computing-related qualification at age 16 has fallen significantly in recent years (Kemp and Berry, 2019). The number of students taking Computer Science GCSE is steadily increasing, however, yet there remains a significant gender disparity in the subject and a recognition that the subject is not accessible to a wide range of learners (McDonald, 2021).

Even before the Computing curriculum became statutory, there were concerns around teachers' ability to deliver content they were often unfamiliar with (Dredge, 2014) and, despite the support available from a range of organisations, such Computing at School (CAS) (CAS, 2022), the Royal Society's 2018 *After the Reboot: Computing Education in UK Schools* (Royal Society, 2018) highlighted how significant investment was needed to develop the subject. In response, £84 million was provided by the Department of Education (DfE) to set up the National Centre for Computing Education (NCCE) in England, which continues to provide curriculum content, CPD and Computing research outputs, as discussed in more detail below.

REFLECTION

Should Computing be a subject that prepares pupils for the world of work or is it a subject area everyone should study as part of their education?

Should there be a Computing GCSE, rather than Computer Science, or perhaps separate ICT and CS-related qualifications?

Should Computing be an overarching subject, which is taught through other subject areas, rather than a discrete subject?

COMPUTING NOW

There is a growing recognition of the need for the Computing curriculum to be culturally relevant, which enables students to relate to the examples used to teach Computing concepts and to engage with the pedagogical approaches used (Sentance, 2021a). Such an approach can encourage students to identify the relevance of Computing to themselves and its importance in society. In particular, the need to decolonise the curriculum is seen as essential to making the curriculum accessible and promoting the subject as welcoming to all (Dimitriadi, 2021). Case studies used and projects selected therefore need to be carefully chosen to ensure that they relate to appropriate content. For example, when introducing the computational concept of repetition, students could examine and produce patters found in Islamic art, with further links made to relevant cross-curricular content.

Within the classroom, the pedagogy employed by teachers continues to develop, with approaches suitable for novice learners, such as PRIMM, which follow the steps of Predict, Run, Investigate, Modify, Make (NCCE, 2020a) and Parson's Problems (NCCE, 2021), where pupils rearrange pre-written sections of code, making programming activities more accessible. The importance of practical programming tasks is increasingly recognised as an important part of Computing education and should not be substituted with activities solely focusing on theoretical aspects of the subject, which is often the focus of external examinations (Berry et al., 2022). Despite this, the need to teach programming continues to be an area of concern for teachers, particularly in primary schools (Sentance and Waite, 2018), although the first two years of the NCCE have increased the support available to schools, with over 29,500 teachers engaged with the program, including 7,600 teachers benefitting from the CPD offering and the teaching resources produced being used in classrooms nationwide (NCCE, 2020b). Support is also available to schools through the loan of physical Computing kits, such as the micro:bit (2022), which have been shown to be engaging to pupils and increasingly form part of Computing schemes of work (e.g., NCCE, 2022).

As Computing is a young subject, many aspects related to teaching and learning are less well developed than more established areas of the school curriculum. The gender imbalance in the subject has long been recognised as needing to be addressed (Margolis and Fisher, 2003), with effective approaches required to attract and maintain female interest. In particular, research outlines how young women feel they don't belong in the subject, have few role models and there is a lack of encouragement (Childs, 2021). Thus, research to address these areas, such as interventions related to specific teaching approaches and subject choices, is currently being undertaken.

Significant research is also being undertaken to better understand progression within the subject, particularly when examining content related to Computational Thinking (CT). For example, learning trajectories have been produced for many concepts, such as variables (Rich et al., 2022), outlining in detail the learning required to effectively develop understanding of these complex areas. A range of research projects are also focusing on assessment within the subject, with assessing children's CT skills recognised as requiring further study (Allsop, 2019) and continuing to be a challenge for teachers (Sentance and Csizmadia, 2017).

The recent Covid-19 pandemic has seen additional support available to schools to implement learning platforms and use online learning tools, although the lack of access to technology, often referred to as the 'digital divide', continues to be an issue within the UK and across the globe (Holmes and Burgess, 2020), and is therefore a significant barrier to pupils developing their knowledge and understanding in the subject. The pandemic has also highlighted the importance of pupils needing well-developed digital skills to prepare them for future education and the workplace (Ogu, 2022), with some teachers concerned about the emphasis given to the CS aspects of the Computing curriculum, rather than focusing on IT and DL (Colnbrook, 2022).

Within other countries, changes related to the CS aspects of the subject have recently been made to curriculum content. Within Wales, computer science-related content forms part of the *Science and Technology Area of Learning and Experience* (Education Wales, 2022a) within the country's new curriculum, with the *Digital Competence Framework* (Education Wales, 2022b) providing opportunities for learners to develop skills across curriculum subjects (Crick, 2022). Similar approaches are evident in Australia, where the *Digital Technologies* curriculum content (ACARA, 2022a) is complemented by the *Digital Literacy General Capability* (ACARA, 2022b) and Cambridge Assessment International Education's Primary curriculum content (Cambridge Assessment International Education, 2022), which has Computing and Digital Literacy as distinct subjects. Many other countries include CS-related content within the curriculum, including Ireland, Scotland, Malta and Italy, although in many countries there is often a disparity between the content of the curriculum and what is actually taught in the classroom (Falkner et al., 2019). Within the USA, the CSTA K-12 CS Standards (CSTA, 2020) are adopted by many areas of the country. However, CS courses are not available in many schools, with provision more limited in less affluent and rural areas (Code.org Advocacy Coalition et al., 2019).

REFLECTION

Should there be more of a focus on Computing for all and/or how our understanding of the subject has developed? For example, should children be taught that the word 'algorithm' derives from the name of a Persian mathematician?

Should the English Computing curriculum be modified to have a separate cross-curricular focus on digital literacy skills, which is an approach often taken in other countries?

WHAT MIGHT KNOWLEDGE IN COMPUTING LOOK LIKE IN THE FUTURE?

Many countries are looking to implement CS or move from optional to mandatory teaching of the subject. In the UK, there appears to be a growing recognition for students to have access to qualifications related to digital skills, which would complement more specialist CS qualifications (BCS School Curriculum and Assessment Committee, 2021).

The research related to making the curriculum culturally relevant (Sentance, 2021a) is ongoing, with related organisations, such as Girls Who Code (2022), helping to support young people. The development and awareness of pedagogical approaches for use in classroom will continue, with resources being adapted to recognise effective learning in the subject, such as the necessary steps to introduce new concepts (NCCE, 2020c).

Since the introduction of the Computing curriculum in England in 2014, many trainee teachers have now studied the content as pupils when in school. Their existing subject knowledge means that trainees can focus more on appropriate pedagogy, rather than developing their understanding of the curriculum, which currently forms a significant part of primary initial teacher training (e.g., Edge Hill University, 2022). Research has also shown how teachers report how their self-esteem in relation to CS increases once they have been teaching the subject for a period of four years or more (Sentance, 2020).

Finally, guidance is being developed to take into account advances in artificial intelligence and machine learning (AI4K12.org, 2022). Teaching of this topic not only enables pupils to better understand the digital world, but also allows them to examine the social and ethical implications of this complex subject (Brodsky, 2020). While existing curriculum statements may be broad enough to enable pupils to study the topic, learning in this area often takes place informally and further investment is needed to develop the teaching of the subject (Sentance, 2021b).

PART 2: FOUNDATION KNOWLEDGE IN COMPUTING

Within this section, we'll initially examine computational thinking, then unpick the various curriculum statements at KS1 and KS2 to examine the key vocabulary in detail and determine what each area might look like in the primary classroom. We'll then look at the importance of developing both knowledge and skills, followed by examining online safety, including how a whole-school approach is vital to ensure that pupils can use technology safely and responsibly.

COMPUTATIONAL THINKING

Computational Thinking (CT) underpins the Computing National Curriculum (DfE, 2013a). Computers cannot think, although at times they may appear to! CT therefore involves solving a problem in a way that a computer can help us (Wing, 2006). Within the primary curriculum, we can often think of CT as several concepts and approaches (Barefoot, 2022).

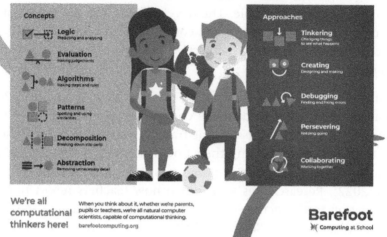

Figure 2.1 *Barefoot Computing Computational Thinking concepts and approaches*
Available at: https://www.barefootcomputing.org/resources/computational-thinking-poster. Contains public sector information
licensed under the Open Government Licence v3.0. https://www.nationalarchives.gov.uk/doc/open-government-licence/version/3/

For example, pupils could use *logic* to analyse a problem, followed by *decomposition* to break it down into smaller steps. They might use *abstraction* to focus on the key details, then produce a set of instructions, which is known as an *algorithm*, to solve the problem. Finally, they might use *evaluation* to check that the *algorithm* works as expected. For KS1 children, this could involve examining how to move a programmable toy from one part of the classroom to another, or, for UKS2 pupils, they might work on an extended project to develop a step-counter program on a physical Computing device.

CURRICULUM STRANDS

The attainment targets within the National Curriculum can be organised into Computer Science (CS), Information Technology (IT) and Digital Literacy (DL) (Berry, 2013), as outlined below.

COMPUTER SCIENCE (CS)

It is important to note that Computer Science (CS) covers two separate, yet related areas. There are the ideas and concepts that underpin how digital technology functions, and then there is the practical task of programming the computer. Pupils should be given opportunities to develop their knowledge and understanding of each aspect, which will likely include activities away from the machine, known as 'unplugged activities', plus tasks with digital devices.

KS1

Understand what algorithms are; how they are implemented as programs on digital devices; and that programs execute by following precise and unambiguous instructions.

An algorithm is a set of instructions or rules to complete a task, such as solving a problem. At KS1, an algorithm will typically be a sequence of instructions, such as the steps to make a jam sandwich or move around a maze. Algorithms produce a correct outcome, although some algorithms are more efficient than others. For example, there might be more than one set of instructions to enable someone to walk home from school, but a certain route is likely to be faster than the others.

A program enables an algorithm to be undertaken by a digital device through writing and entering instructions in a way that it can understand. These instructions, known as code, need to be precise and unambiguous, so the machine can undertake or execute them. Any electronic device that takes an input, processes it based on a program, then gives an output, can be classed as a digital device. Therefore, pupils will also need to consider other devices around them, such as smart speakers, microwave ovens and self-driving cars.

Create and debug simple programs.

Through having opportunities to create simple programs, pupils can develop their understanding of algorithms and how instructions can be undertaken by computers. For KS1 pupils, this will often involve using picture-based blocks to move objects around a screen or entering directional instructions for a programmable floor robot.

When writing a program, it is unusual for it to work first time, so pupils will need to debug, or fix errors. Through fixing these mistakes, or bugs, pupils develop soft skills, such as resilience and perseverance.

Use logical reasoning to predict the behaviour of simple programs.

It is not sufficient for pupils to simply write programs; they also need to be able to use their logical reasoning to explain and justify what they predict a program will do. For example, a pupil might explain where they believe a floor robot will end up through acting out the instructions with one of their peers.

KS2

Design, write and debug programs that accomplish specific goals, including controlling or simulating physical systems; solve problems by decomposing them into smaller parts.

As pupils move into KS2, they now need to design programs, in addition to having opportunities to write and debug. Pupils will need to break problems down through decomposing them into smaller parts. For example, if producing a program in Scratch, pupils will need to consider the graphics and sounds alongside the required algorithms and program code. There is an opportunity here for controlling or simulating physical systems to gain a better understanding of the digital devices outlined above. This will increasingly involve the use of physical Computing devices, such as the micro:bit or Crumble microcontroller.

Use sequence, selection, and repetition in programs; work with variables and various forms of input and output.

The programs produced at KS2 will involve more advanced concepts as they move beyond a simple step-by-step sequence of instructions. Repetition enables specific instructions within a program to be repeated. At KS2, this might typically involve instructions taking place a certain number of times, such as when writing a program to draw a regular hexagon, or indefinitely, often referred to as *forever*, which will continue until the program ends and might involve continually moving an object in a certain direction.

Selection involves the computer carrying out different instructions depending on whether certain conditions are met, such as whether the answer to a question is correct or not. Within many programming languages, we use *if, then, else* decisions to program the computer and determine the next instructions that should be carried out. For example, within a mathematics quiz, *if* the correct answer is entered, *then* the text 'Well done!' could be displayed, otherwise the text 'Unlucky' could be displayed.

Finally, variables enable programs to store data while it is being executed. Variables can be used to store a range of data, such as numbers, letters or text, with the data stored within the variable altered by the program if required. Within a quiz programmed by a pupil, they might use a variable to store a score. The score variable might be set to zero when the program begins, then increased by one every time the user gets a question correct.

The inputs used by pupils at KS2 will often involve the keyboard and mouse, although they might also use microphones, webcams or buttons and sensors on physical Computing devices. Outputs could be a digital device's screen or speakers, although they could also involve motors and LEDs.

Use logical reasoning to explain how some simple algorithms work and to detect and correct errors in algorithms and programs.

The problems pupils will examine and solve when using their logical reasoning will become more complex at KS2 as they explain the thinking and choices they have made when creating algorithms. As the complexity of programs also increases, a more systematic approach is needed to detect and correct errors, which will also enable pupils to develop their logical reasoning.

Understand computer networks including the internet; how they can provide multiple services, such as the World Wide Web.

Computer networks consist of many computers connected together to share information. These computers are typically connected either wirelessly, using radio or satellite signals, or through copper or fibre-optic cables.

The internet is a global network of computer networks. It provides multiple services for its users, such as webpages on the World Wide Web, social media platforms and collaborative tools. Other services include email, instant messaging, video conferencing and streaming audio/video.

Computers on a network may connect to servers, which are dedicated machines handling these services to provide content, such as emails, webpages or videos. To send data across a network, it is split into small chunks, known as *packets*, and passes through other machines, such as *routers* and *switches*, to reach its destination. These packets then get put back together by the recipient and the machine undertakes the requested action. For example, a computer might send some data to a server to start a video on YouTube, which it then starts sending back, or a computer might send an email, which is then passed on from the server to the recipient's inbox.

Within the classroom, pupils can mimic the behaviour of a network and pass packets around the classroom. They might also examine network infrastructure around the school, such as the location of wireless access points.

Appreciate how [search] results are selected and ranked.

To catalogue webpages, search engines use web crawlers to visit pages and make copies of their content, along with examining links between pages. This content is then indexed, with a record made of keywords and phrases. When a search is made, results are selected from the index. When deciding on the order results should be displayed, each page is ranked based on an algorithm to determine the relevance and quality based on the keywords searched for.

INFORMATION TECHNOLOGY (IT)

KS1

Use technology purposefully to create, organise, store, manipulate and retrieve digital content.

The opportunities for pupils to create digital content are significant, ranging from using typical office-based applications, such as producing word-processed documents and presentations, to engaging multimedia content, such as digital art or video. Pupils may also create programs, as outlined above.

As pupils create digital content, it is important they organise it. This could involve ensuring that the frames of animation are in the correct order or organising data within a pictogram. Pupils will also need to store their digital content, such as in an appropriately named file, which they can later retrieve.

Pupils might also manipulate digital content. This could involve editing an image, or even combining digital content, such as through overlaying text on a montage of photographs. When working with digital content, it is important that technology is used purposefully, including considering the intended audience.

KS2

Select, use and combine a variety of software (including internet services) on a range of digital devices to design and create a range of programs, systems and content that accomplish given goals, including collecting, analysing, evaluating and presenting data and information.

This builds on KS1 by placing an emphasis on pupils having to both select and combine software, rather than solely having to use it. In addition, as with the KS2 statements related to programming, pupils now have to design, instead of just having to create.

Alongside software installed on digital devices, pupils might use internet services, such as collaborative tools or web-based applications, to accomplish given goals for a particular purpose and audience. Data and information might take many forms at KS2, such as audio, video, text and images, which children can work with to produce their own programs, systems and content.

Pupils might also work with data through collecting and analysing it, then going on to critically evaluate it, such as through examining trends and patterns, or discussing the reliability. Pupils should also have opportunities for presenting their work through increasingly complex digital artefacts, such as webpages, edited video and 3D models.

Use search technologies effectively.

While an understanding of how search results are selected and ranked will develop pupils' understanding of how search engines work, it is important they can also use search technologies effectively. Pupils therefore need to be able to choose appropriate keywords and interpret the results presented.

DIGITAL LITERACY (DL)

KS1

Recognise common uses of information technology beyond school.

Pupils can view and interact with information technology within the classroom and beyond school. They should be able to recognise common uses, whether it is a digital alarm clock or a self-service checkout at the supermarket. Pupils should also recognise information technology used by others, such as within the workplace or for entertainment purposes.

Use technology safely and respectfully, keeping personal information private; identify where to go for help and support when they have concerns about content or contact on the internet or other online technologies (please also view the related 'Online safety' section below).

When using technology, pupils need to be guided to use it safely and respectfully, such as through ensuring that they access age-appropriate content and communicating with people they know in a considerate manner. Personal information should not typically be shared online by young people, and children require guidance as to what they can and cannot share.

Pupils will often have concerns about content or people they contact on the internet or other online technologies. They therefore need to know where to go for help and support, which would typically involve speaking to a parent/carer or teacher, although other services, such as Childline, could also be accessed.

KS2

Be discerning in evaluating digital content.

When examining search results and viewing digital content, such as webpages or images online, pupils need to be discerning in evaluating it. Pupils could consider whether the material presented is factually correct, relevant to their work and from a trustworthy source. Pupils might also be given opportunities to consider the reasoning behind initially creating the content, such as to influence a certain group of people, along with whether it is has been purposefully made to spread disinformation, such as 'fake news'.

Understand the opportunities [computer networks] offer for communication and collaboration.

Closely linked to both CS and IT, along with online safety content, pupils can further develop their understanding of how tools enabling communication and collaboration can be used and the opportunities they provide. For example, pupils might consider how electronic communication methods enable real-time video calls or how collaborative tools enable digital content to be edited.

Use technology safely, respectfully and responsibly; recognise acceptable/unacceptable behaviour; identify a range of ways to report concerns about content and contact (please also view the related 'Online safety' section below).

As pupils move into KS2, there is now an emphasis on using technology responsibly and the need to recognise acceptable or unacceptable behaviour. Along with considering the impact of their behaviour online, pupils will also begin to consider the legal and ethical implications of using technology, such as through examining copyright, plagiarism and security.

Pupils at KS2 also need to be able to identify a range of ways to report concerns about content and contact as they begin to use technology more independently. For example, pupils could be made aware of the tools available in the applications they use, along with how to report concerns to others, including CEOP and the police.

KNOWLEDGE AND SKILLS

There is often a significant cross-over between the three strands when delivering Computing lessons and sufficient coverage should be given to each area of the curriculum. In addition, children need opportunities to develop both knowledge and skills within the subject, often referred to as 'declarative knowledge' or 'knowing that' (Ofsted, 2022), and 'procedural knowledge' or 'knowing how' (Ofsted, 2022), respectively. Within the primary Computing curriculum, examples of declarative and procedural knowledge are as shown in the table below.

Table 2.1 Declarative and procedural knowledge

Knowledge	Computer Science (CS)	Information Technology (IT)	Digital Literacy (DL)
Declarative	Function of movement blocks available within a programming environment	Different spreadsheet formulae available to calculate totals	Different features of untrustworthy online content
Procedural	Implement a selection statement to check the value of a variable within a programming environment	Create a stop-frame animation using a tablet-based application	Enter appropriate keywords into a search engine

ONLINE SAFETY

While the Digital Literacy aspects of the curriculum cover aspects of online safety, *Keeping Children Safe in Education* (DfE, 2022a) recognises the importance of online safety being addressed across the school by all members of staff. It is vital that schools see online safety as a potential safeguarding issue, with their approach 'reflected in the child protection policy' (DfE, 2022a, p36), rather than simply a technology-related problem. Content should therefore not solely be delivered with Computing sessions and schools should have a well-sequenced online safety curriculum in place, along with staff having opportunities to develop their knowledge and keep up to date with the latest developments in the subject (Ofsted, 2022).

The teaching of online safety needs to ensure that pupils develop underpinning knowledge and behaviour, with DfE guidance (DfE, 2019, pp6–8) suggesting six focus areas for pupils. To address these areas, pupils need a range of age-appropriate digital skills, which are outlined in detail within *Education for a Connected World* (DfE, 2020). For example, within the *Online relationships* aspect at Y4, pupils can *describe strategies for safe and fun experiences in a range of online social environments (e.g., livestreaming, gaming platforms)* (DfE, 2020, p12).

Teachers should therefore develop their knowledge and understanding of the various digital skills and knowledge outlined in the guidance above. Teachers should also ensure that they are aware of the technologies used by pupils both inside and outside school, including their benefits and risks, along with their wider safeguarding and child protection responsibilities related to online safety.

PART 3: UNDERSTANDING THE DEVELOPMENT OF CHILDREN'S KNOWLEDGE IN COMPUTING

Due to the broad statements evident within some areas of the national curriculum, it can be challenging for teachers to determine progression. Many schemes of work suggest the order content should be taught in, such as Learning Graphs within the Teach Computing curriculum (NCCE, 2022).

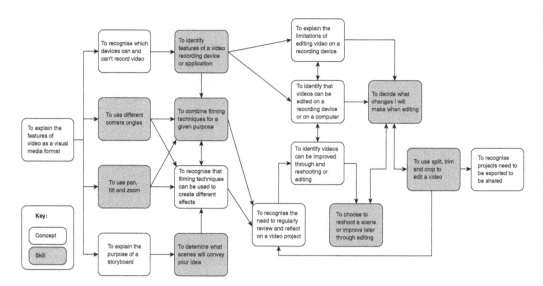

Figure 2.2 A section of a learning graph showing the progression in concepts and skills for the Y5 – Creating Media – video production unit of the Teach Computing curriculum
Available at: https://teachcomputing.org/curriculum/key-stage-2/creating-media-video-editing. This document is licensed under the Open Government Licence v3.0. https://www.nationalarchives.gov.uk/doc/open-government-licence/version/3/

Table 2.2 below outlines how pupils' knowledge and understanding of programming and computational thinking can be developed between Years 1 and 6. Two learning outcomes from the Teach Computing Curriculum (NCCE, 2022) are included per year group, with possible activities and next steps described for each outcome.

Table 2.2 Development of knowledge and understanding of programming and computational thinking – Years 1–6
Two learning outcomes from the Teach Computing Curriculum (NCCE, 2022) are included per year group. This NCCE document is licensed under the Open Government Licence v3.0. https://www.nationalarchives.gov.uk/doc/open-government-licence/version/3/

Year group	Learning outcomes	Activities to develop the skills and understanding	Next steps
Year 1	Writing short algorithms and programs for floor robots and predicting program outcomes.	Investigating buttons and their function on a floor robot (Bee-Bot). Moving a robot between different locations, then planning out a route for the robot.	Designing and producing outfits for the Bee-Bot.
	Designing and programming the movement of a character on-screen to tell stories.	Investigating and combining instructions within a block-based programming environment (ScratchJr). Adding sprites, then designing and programming an animation.	Recording sounds for characters within the animation to say.
Year 2	Creating and debugging programs and using logical reasoning to make predictions.	Giving instructions to others, along with predicting the outcomes of algorithms. Design and create a mat for a floor robot, then write a program to move between different locations.	Write a story about Bee-Bot's day when exploring different locations on the mat.
	Designing algorithms and programs that use events to trigger sequences of code to make an interactive quiz.	Investigating different instructions within ScratchJr to trigger events. Design and program a quiz, including evaluating it with their peers.	Ask questions related to a different curriculum to reinforce pupils' knowledge and understanding.
Year 3	Creating sequences in a block-based programming language to make music.	Investigating a block-based programming environment (Scratch) and getting sprites to move. Sequencing commands, including those to produce different musical notes.	Combine music producing programs to create a class orchestra.
	Writing algorithms and programs that use a range of events to trigger sequences of actions.	Experimenting with various events, including keyboard control, in Scratch. Using drawing tools to make different lines, then move a sprite around a maze.	Investigate maze-related stories and include relevant sections within programs.

(Continued)

Table 2.2 (Continued)

Year group	Learning outcomes	Activities to develop the skills and understanding	Next steps
Year 4	Using a text-based* programming language to explore count-controlled loops when drawing shapes.	Entering basic commands in Logo to draw different letters. Examining different patterns and how they can be created using loops. Designing and creating wrapping paper.	Examine different properties of shapes to investigate, altering the number of sides and angles.
	Using a block-based programming language to explore count-controlled and infinite loops when creating a game.	Investigating different types of repetition within games using Scratch. Animating letter sprites using loops. Modifying existing games, then designing and creating a game.	Set up a Scratch arcade for younger pupils to play each game.
Year 5	Exploring conditions and selection using a programmable microcontroller.	Connecting different outputs to the Crumble physical computing device. Controlling programs with different inputs using selection. Designing, programming and evaluating a fairground ride.	Designing and producing fairground marketing materials to promote the various rides.
	Exploring selection in programming to design and code an interactive quiz.	Investigating selection within Scratch. Using if, then, else statements to ask questions and give different responses. Designing and developing a quiz.	Modifying the quiz to ask random multiplication questions for Y4 pupils.
Year 6	Exploring variables when designing and coding a game.	Examining how variables are used within Scratch. Investigating how variables are used within existing games, then designing a game. Programming the game and improving it based on feedback.	Enhance the game through including further variables, such as by recording a user name and high score.
	Designing and coding a project that captures inputs from a physical device.	Using inputs and outputs when programming the micro:bit. Implementing selection statements to use sensors and record data using variables. Designing and making a step counter.	Undertake a science investigation examining someone's height and the number of steps needed to cover a certain distance.

*While there is no requirement for pupils at KS2 to use a text-based programming environment, which has the user typing in instructions instead of dragging blocks together, many pupils are able to enter commands successfully.

Other sequences of lessons could focus on the broad topics outlined below, although there is often a cross-over between different aspects of the curriculum.

- Digital content (typically two sequences of lesson per year group), such as digital painting and writing for KS1, and video production and web design for KS2.

- Computer systems and networks, including examining technologies around us for KS1 and looking at how the internet and search functions for KS2.

- Information and data, which could involve grouping data and creating pictograms for KS1, followed by data logging and spreadsheet modelling for KS2.

BUILDING ON EXISTING KNOWLEDGE

Within Computing, there will often be extended periods of time between examining different areas of the national curriculum, along with pupils using hardware and software. Therefore, planning should consider the need for pupils to re-examine concepts and technologies before addressing new content, such as through using explorative and unplugged activities. Schools may also look for opportunities for retrieval practice and cross-curricular links to support learners to develop their knowledge and understanding.

The sequence of lessons outlined above develop both knowledge and skills related to the topic. However, consideration should also be given to pupils' ability to use the specified digital device. For example, if entering data into a spreadsheet, pupils might first need explicit teaching around mouse usage, such as when to left and right click, and how to enter text effectively, such as using the shift key to produce a capital letter.

PEDAGOGICAL APPROACHES

When teaching Computing, a broad range of strategies (Waite, 2021) can be used to effectively deliver curriculum content and engage learners. It is particularly important to avoid pupils simply copying instructions or having overly structured tasks, which can be demotivating and of limited benefits to pupils. For example, project-based learning activities can provide opportunities for pupils to apply and develop their knowledge and understanding, along with being creative in the design and production of their digital artefacts. Projects also enable pupils to have an audience for their work, the theory of constructionism outlining how this is likely to lead to improved outcomes (Berry, 2014).

To support pupils in developing their knowledge and understanding, concepts and key vocabulary should be examined, rather than focusing on the hardware or software being used. For example, rather than stating 'We're doing Scratch today', teachers might explain how they are 'sequencing instructions'. New ideas and concepts will often be introduced away from the machines as *unplugged* activities. While these activities are beneficial in the classroom, it is necessary to link them back to related activities on the machines, which helps children secure their understanding of these complex concepts. We often refer to this approach as a *semantic wave* (NCCE, 2020c).

Supportive structures can form parts of lessons, such as PRIMM (Predict, Run, Investigate, Modify, Make) and Use–Modify–Create (NCCE, 2020a), as outlined above, which enable pupils to gradually develop their understanding, rather than being asked to quickly undertake a cognitively demanding task. Modelling is also useful for novices, through using approaches such as worked examples and live coding to demonstrate processes.

ONLINE SAFETY

Extensive resources are available to support the delivery of online safety-related content, including lesson plans and resources from *Project Evolve* (SWGFL, 2022) to deliver each of the statements from *Education for a Connected World* (DfE, 2020). These resources need to form part of carefully planned content within the whole school's curriculum, alongside a school's safeguarding responsibilities and relationships education, relationships and sex education (RSE) and personal, social, health and economic (PSHE) education (DfE, 2021).

REFLECTION

- What projects might pupils work on to develop their knowledge and understanding of Computing, while enabling them to be creative and have an audience for their work? For example, could links to other curriculum areas be utilised, or could there be a focus on a pupil's interests, such as video games?

- How much emphasis should schools place on developing digital skills, such as the ability to use a keyboard and mouse? For example, will children develop skills as part of their Computing lessons, or do further opportunities need to be provided elsewhere?

- How could you deliver the curriculum if pupils only have access to a few devices, only a certain type of devices (i.e., only laptops or tablets), or limited access to the internet? For example, might unplugged activities be useful, or collaborative approaches, such as pair programming? (NCCE, 2019)

PART 4: DEVELOPING YOUR KNOWLEDGE OF COMPUTING FURTHER

SPECIALIST ORGANISATIONS TO SUPPORT YOUR DEVELOPMENT

Computing at School (CAS) – www.computingatschool.org.uk/ – provides a range of support for Computing teachers, including regular CAS Community meetings, which are held nationwide – www.computingatschool.org.uk/cas-communities

CAS also has also produced a number of resources, including:

- *Computing in the national curriculum – a guide for primary teachers*, available at: www.computingatschool.org.uk/resource-library/2014/september/computing-in-the-national-curriculum-a-guide-for-primary-teachers

- *Quickstart Computing – A CPD toolkit for primary teachers*, available at: www.computingatschool.org.uk/media/pk1jtzrr/quickstartcomputing-primary-handbook.pdf

- *Leading primary computing: reflections from the subject leader community*, available at: www.computingatschool.org.uk/leading-computing/primary-leaders-toolkit

The National Centre for Computing Education (NCCE) – https://teachcomputing.org/ – also provides significant support for teachers, including:

- Training/CPD – https://teachcomputing.org/courses – can lead to an externally recognised certificate in computing teaching: https://teachcomputing.org/primary-certificate

- *Pedagogy quick reads* – https://blog.teachcomputing.org/tag/quickread/

- Full, progression mapped, scheme of work – https://teachcomputing.org/curriculum

READING TO SUPPORT YOUR DEVELOPMENT

In addition to the guidance from CAS and the NCCE above, the following texts enable you to further develop your subject knowledge.

Allsop, Y and Sedman, B (2015) *Primary Computing in Action*. Melton, Woodbridge: John Catt Educational.

Beauchamp, G (ed.) (2016) *Computing and ICT in the Primary School: From Pedagogy to Practice*. London: Taylor & Francis.

Bird, J, Caldwell, H and Mayne, P (eds) (2017) *Lessons in Teaching Computing in Primary Schools*. London: SAGE.

Burrett, M (2016) *Bloomsbury Curriculum Basics: Teaching Primary Computing*. London: Bloomsbury.

Caldwell, H and Smith, N (eds) (2017) *Teaching Computing Unplugged in Primary Schools: Exploring Primary Computing Through Practical Activities Away from the Computer*. London: SAGE.

Cross, A, Borthwick, A, Beswick, K, Board, J and Chippindall, J (2016) *Curious Learners in Primary Maths, Science, Computing and DT*. London: SAGE.

Liukas, L (2015) *Hello Ruby: Adventures in Coding.* New York: Feiwel & Friends.

Livingstone, I and Saeed, S (2017) *Hacking the Curriculum: Creative Computing and the Power of Play.* Melton, Woodbridge: John Catt Educational.

Parton, G and Kemp-Hall, C (2022) *Mastering Primary Computing.* Melton, Woodbridge: John Catt Educational.

Turvey, K, Potter, J, Burton, J, Allen, J and Sharp, J (2016) *Primary Computing and Digital Technologies: Knowledge, Understanding and Practice.* London: SAGE.

Hello World magazine, which is published three times a year and is available in print for free for UK educators, contains guidance, lesson plans and the latest computing news – https://helloworld.raspberrypi.org/

RESOURCES TO SUPPORT THE DELIVERY OF COMPUTING CONTENT

Other providers have resources available, such as schemes of work, lesson plans and CPD content.

- Barefoot: www.barefootcomputing.org/

- BBC Bitesize – KS1: www.bbc.co.uk/bitesize/subjects/zyhbwmn KS2 – www.bbc.co.uk/bitesize/subjects/zvnrq6f

- Code-it: http://code-it.co.uk/

- iLearn2: www.ilearn2.co.uk/

- Kapow: www.kapowprimary.com/subjects/computing/

- Purple Mash: www.2simple.com/purple-mash/

- Rising Stars (Switched on Computing): www.risingstars-uk.com/series/switched-on-computing

FILM, TV AND RADIO PROGRAMMES TO FURTHER YOUR UNDERSTANDING OF THE SUBJECT

- *Imitation Game* (2014): www.imdb.com/title/tt2084970/

- *The Secret Rules of Modern Living* (2015): www.imdb.com/title/tt5818010/

- *Hidden Figures* (2016): www.imdb.com/title/tt4846340/

- Radio 4: *Controlling the Unaccountable Algorithm*: www.bbc.co.uk/programmes/b085wj18

- Radio 4: *Analysis – Algorithm Overlords*: www.bbc.co.uk/programmes/b0b4zxcn

REFERENCES

ACARA (Australian Curriculum, Assessment and Reporting Authority) (2022a) *Digital Technologies*. Available at: https://v9.australiancurriculum.edu.au/f-10-curriculum/learning-areas/digital-technologies/foundation-year_year-1_year-2_year-3_year-4_year-5_year-6_year-7_year-8_year-9_year-10?view=quick&detailed-content-descriptions=0&hide-ccp=0&hide-gc=0&side-by-side=1&strands-start-index=0&subjects-start-index=0 (accessed 3 October 2022).

ACARA (Australian Curriculum, Assessment and Reporting Authority) (2022b) *Digital Literacy*. Available at: https://v9.australiancurriculum.edu.au/f-10-curriculum/general-capabilities/digital-literacy?element=0&sub-element=0 (accessed 3 October 2022).

AI4K12.org (2022) Available at: https://ai4k12.org/ (accessed 3 October 2022).

Allsop, Y (2019) Assessing computational thinking process using a multiple evaluation approach. *International Journal of Child–Computer Interaction*, 19: 30–55.

Arthur, J (2012) How the BBC Micro started a computing revolution. Available at: www.theguardian.com/education/2012/jan/10/bbc-micro-school-computer-revolution *The Guardian*. (accessed 3 October 2022).

Barefoot (2022) Computational Thinking Poster. Available at: www.barefootcomputing.org/resources/computational-thinking-poster (accessed 3 October 2022).

BCS School Curriculum and Assessment Committee (2021) *BCS Landscape Review: Computing Qualifications in the UK*. Available at: www.bcs.org/media/8665/landscape-review-computing-report.pdf (accessed 3 October 2022).

Berry, MG (2013) The new computing curriculum – some thoughts. Available at: http://milesberry.net/2013/02/the-new-computing-curriculum-some-thoughts/ (accessed 3 October 2022).

Berry, MG (2014) *Computing in the National Curriculum: A Guide for Primary Teachers*. Available at: www.computingatschool.org.uk/resource-library/2014/september/computing-in-the-national-curriculum-a-guide-for-primary-teachers (accessed 3 October 2022).

Berry, MG, Curzon, P, Cutts, Q, Hoyles, C, Peyton Jones, S and Saeed, S (2022) Practical programming in computing education. Available at: https://static.teachcomputing.org/Practical+Work+in+Computing+Apr+22.pdf (accessed 3 October 2022).

Brodsky, J (2020) Why children need to learn about artificial intelligence. Available at: www.forbes.com/sites/juliabrodsky/2020/11/12/why-children-need-to-learn-about-artificial-intelligence/ (accessed 3 October 2022).

Cambridge Assessment International Education (2022) Curriculum. Available at: www.cambridgeinternational.org/programmes-and-qualifications/cambridge-primary/curriculum/ (accessed 3 October 2022).

CAS (Computing at School) (2022) The community for computing teachers. Available at: www.computingatschool.org.uk/ (accessed 3 October 2022).

Childs, K (2021) What makes an impact on gender balance in computing education? Answers from experts. Available at: www.raspberrypi.org/blog/formal-non-formal-learning-opportunities-computing-education-impact-on-gender-balance/ (accessed 3 October 2022).

Code.org Advocacy Coalition, Computer Science Teachers Association, and the Expanding Computing Education Pathways Alliance (2019) *2019 State of Computer Science Education*. Available at: https://advocacy.code.org/2019_state_of_cs.pdf (accessed 3 October 2022).

Colnbrook, G (2022) It's vital we teach ICT basics – not just coding. Available at: www.teach-wire.net/news/its-vital-we-teach-ict-basics-not-just-coding/ (accessed 3 October 2022).

Crick, T (2022) An introduction to computer science in the new curriculum for Wales. *Proceedings of the 53rd ACM Technical Symposium on Computer Science Education*, 2: 1142 (SIGCSE 2022). Available at: https://doi.org/10.1145/3478432.3499134

CSTA (Computer Science Teachers Association) (2020) *CS Standards*. Available at: https://csteachers.org/page/standards (accessed 3 October 2022).

DfE (Department for Education) (2013a) *National Curriculum in England: Computing Programmes of Study*. Available at: www.gov.uk/government/publications/national-curriculum-in-england-computing-programmes-of-study (accessed 3 October 2022).

DfE (Department for Education) (2013b) *Consultation Report: Changing ICT to Computing in the National Curriculum*. Available at: https://assets.publishing.service.gov.uk/government/uploads/system/uploads/attachment_data/file/193838/CONSULTATION_REPORT_CHANGING_ICT_TO_COMPUTING_IN_THE_NATIONAL_CURRICULUM.pdf (accessed 3 October 2022).

DfE (Department for Education) (2019) *Teaching Online Safety in Schools*. Available at: www.gov.uk/government/publications/teaching-online-safety-in-schools (accessed 3 October 2022).

DfE (Department for Education) (2020) *Education for a Connected World*. Available at: www.gov.uk/government/publications/education-for-a-connected-world (accessed 3 October 2022).

DfE (Department for Education) (2021) *Relationships and Sex education (RSE) and Health Education*. Available at: www.gov.uk/government/publications/relationships-education-relationships-and-sex-education-rse-and-health-education (accessed 3 October 2022).

DfE (Department for Education) (2022a) *Keeping Children Safe in Education*. Available at: www.gov.uk/government/publications/keeping-children-safe-in-education--2 (accessed 3 October 2022).

DfE (Department for Education) (2022b) *UKCIS Online Safety Audit Tool*. Available at: www.gov.uk/government/publications/ukcis-online-safety-audit-tool (accessed 3 October 2022).

Dimitriadi, Y (2021) Reflections on decolonising the computing curriculum. Available at: https://helloworld.raspberrypi.org/articles/hw16-reflections-on-decolonising-the-computing-curriculum (accessed 3 October 2022).

Dredge, S (2014) Kids coding at school: 'When you learn computing, you're thinking about thinking'. *The Guardian*. Available at: www.theguardian.com/technology/2014/sep/22/computing-bcs-uk-computing-curriculum (accessed 3 October 2022).

Edge Hill University (2022) Primary initial teacher education: curriculum plan. Available at: www.edgehill.ac.uk/wp-content/uploads/2022/04/Computing-Curriculum-Plan-PG.pdf (accessed 3 October 2022).

Education Wales (2022a) *Science and Technology*. Available at: https://hwb.gov.wales/curriculum-for-wales/science-and-technology/ (accessed 3 October 2022).

Education Wales (2022b) *Digital Competence Framework*. Available at: https://hwb.gov.wales/curriculum-for-wales/cross-curricular-skills-frameworks/digital-competence-framework (accessed 3 October 2022).

Falkner, K, Sentance, S, Vivian, R, Barksdale, S, Busuttil, L, Cole, E, Liebe, C, Maiorana, F, McGill, MM and Quille, K (2019) An International Comparison of K-12 Computer Science Education Intended and Enacted Curricula. In *Proceedings of the 19th Koli Calling International Conference on Computing Education Research (Koli Calling'19)*, 4: 1–10. New York: Association for Computing Machinery, New York. Available at: https://doi.org/10.1145/3364510.3364517

Girls Who Code (GWC) (2022) Available at: https://girlswhocode.com/en-uk (accessed 3 October 2022).

Holmes, H and Burgess, G (2020) 'Pay the wi-fi or feed the children': Coronavirus has intensified the UK's digital divide. Available at: www.cam.ac.uk/stories/digitaldivide (accessed 3 October 2022).

Kemp, PEJ and Berry, MG (2019) *The Roehampton Annual Computing Education Report: Pre-release Snapshot from 2018*. London: University of Roehampton. Available at: www.bcs.org/media/2520/tracer-2018.pdf (accessed 3 October 2022).

Margolis, J and Fisher, A (2003) *Unlocking the Clubhouse: Women in Computing*. Cambridge, MA: The MIT Press.

McDonald, C (2021) Number of girls taking GCSE computing drops in 2021. Available at: www.computerweekly.com/news/252505254/Number-of-girls-taking-GCSE-computing-drops-in-2021 (accessed 3 October 2022).

micro:bit (Micro:bit Educational Foundation) (2022) Available at: https://microbit.org/ (accessed 3 October 2022).

NCCE (National Centre for Computing Education) (2019) *Quick Read: Using Pair Programming to Support Learners*. Available at: https://blog.teachcomputing.org/quick-read-pair-programming-supports-learners/ (accessed 3 October 2022).

NCCE (National Centre for Computing Education) (2020a) *Quick Read: Using PRIMM to Structure Programming Lessons*. Available at: https://blog.teachcomputing.org/using-primm-to-structure-programming-lessons/ (accessed 3 October 2022).

NCCE (National Centre for Computing Education) (2020b) *Impact Report* Available: https://static.teachcomputing.org/NCCE_Impact_Report_Final.pdf (accessed 3 October 2022).

NCCE (National Centre for Computing Education) (2020c) *Quick Read: Using Semantic Waves to Improve Explanations and Learning Activities in Computing*. Available at: https://blog.teach-computing.org/quick-read-6-semantic-waves/ (accessed 3 October 2022).

NCCE (National Centre for Computing Education) (2021) *Quick Read: Improving Program Comprehension through Parson's Problems*. Available at: https://blog.teachcomputing.org/quick-read-improving-program-comprehension-throughparsons-problems/ (accessed 3 October 2022).

NCCE (National Centre for Computing Education) (2022) *Teach Computing Curriculum*. Available at: https://teachcomputing.org/curriculum (accessed 3 October 2022).

Nesta (2013) The legacy of BBC Micro. Available at: www.nesta.org.uk/report/the-legacy-of-bbc-micro/ (accessed 3 October 2022).

NSPCC (2022) *Keeping Children Safe Online*. Available at: www.nspcc.org.uk/keeping-children-safe/online-safety/ (accessed 3 October 2022).

Ofsted (2011) *ICT in schools 2008-11*. Available at: https://assets.publishing.service.gov.uk/government/uploads/system/uploads/attachment_data/file/181223/110134.pdf (accessed 3 October 2022).

Ofsted (2022) *Research Review Series: Computing*. Available at: www.gov.uk/government/publications/research-review-series-computing (accessed 3 October 2022).

Ogu, EC (2022) Meeting digital skills demand today – and tomorrow. Available at: www.itu.int/hub/2022/07/meeting-digital-skills-demand/ (accessed 3 October 2022).

Rich, KM, Franklin, D, Strickland, C, Isaacs, A and Eatinger D (2022) A learning trajectory for variables based in computational thinking literature: using levels of thinking to develop instruction. *Computer Science Education*, 32 (2): 213–34. DOI: 10.1080/08993408.2020.1866938

Royal Society (2012) *Shut Down or Restart? The Way Forward for Computing in UK Schools*. Available at: https://royalsociety.org/-/media/education/computing-in-schools/2012-01-12-computing-in-schools.pdf (accessed 3 October 2022).

Royal Society (2017) *After the Reboot: Computing Education in UK Schools*. Available at: https://royalsociety.org/~/media/events/2018/11/computing-education-1-year-on/after-the-reboot-report.pdf (accessed 3 October 2022).

Sentance, S (2020) How is computing taught in schools around the world? Available at: www.raspberrypi.org/blog/international-computing-curriculum-metrecc-research-seminar/ (accessed 3 October 2022).

Sentance, S (2021a) Delivering a culturally relevant computing curriculum: new guide for teachers. Available at: www.raspberrypi.org/blog/culturally-relevant-computing-curriculum-guidelines-for-teachers/ (accessed 3 October 2022).

Sentance, S (2021b) How do we develop AI education in schools? A panel discussion. Available at: www.raspberrypi.org/blog/ai-education-schools-panel-uk-policy/ (accessed 3 October 2022).

Sentance, S and Csizmadia, A (2017) Computing in the curriculum: challenges and strategies from a teacher's perspective. *Education and Information Technologies*, 22: 469–95. Available at: DOI: https://doi.org/10.1007/s10639-016-9482-0

Sentance, S and Waite, J (2018) Computing in the classroom: tales from the chalkface. *it – Information Technology*, 60: 103–12.

Stevenson, D (1996) *Information and Communications Technology in UK Schools: An Independent Inquiry*. Available at: https://rubble.heppell.net/stevenson/ICT.pdf (accessed 3 October 2022).

SWFGL (Southwest Grid for Learning) (2022) *Project Evolve*. Available at: https://projectevolve.co.uk/ (accessed 3 October 2022).

Waite, J (2021) The computer science student-centred instructional continuum. Available at: https://blog.teachcomputing.org/the-computer-science-student-centred-instructional-continuum/ (accessed 3 October 2022).

Wakefield, J (2014) Does a five-year-old need to learn to code? Available at: www.bbc.co.uk/news/technology-29145904 (accessed 3 October 2022).

Weston, C (2012) Scrapping 'ICT'. Available at: https://edtechnow.net/2012/01/18/scrapping-ict/ (accessed 3 October 2022).

Wing, J (2006) Computational thinking. *Communications of the ACM*, 49: 33–5.

3

DESIGN AND TECHNOLOGY

HOWARD FOSTER

KEYWORDS: DESIGN; TECHNOLOGY; MANUFACTURE; QUALITY; VALUE; METACOGNITION; COGNITIVE DEVELOPMENT; NEEDS ANALYSIS; SPECIFICATION; EVALUATE; OPTIMISE; PATENT; AESTHETIC; FUNCTION.

LINKS TO THE CORE CONTENT FRAMEWORK

High Expectations (Standard 1): 1.1, 1.4, 1.6

How Pupils Learn (Standard 2): 2.1, 2.2, 2.6, 2.7, 2.8, 2.9

Subject and Curriculum (Standard 3): 3.1, 3.2, 3.4, 3.7

Classroom Practice (Standard 4): 4.2, 4.5, 4.6, 4.7, 4.10

Adaptive Teaching (Standard 5): 5.3, 5.5, 5.7

Assessment (Standard 6): 6.1, 6.4, 6.6

Managing Behaviour (Standard 7): 7.1, 7.4, 7.5

PART 1: WHAT IS DESIGN AND TECHNOLOGY?

Classroom Design and Technology is *learning being put into action*. Pedagogically, *Design* is a process that can give a context to learning across the curriculum, While *Technology* is the result of accumulated knowledge and the application of skills, methods and processes.

All manufactured items from beds to bridges to buildings, cars to cartons to canoes, slippers to submarines to smart phone – literally everything man-made is the result of this synergy between Design and Technology.

The products that impact our lives every day are also a window into times past. The advancement of technology changes the world, and it is now progressing at a faster and faster pace. For example, after 5,000 years using the horse and cart as transport, we have moved through the combustion engine to electric vehicles like the Tesla in a mere 160 years. From the first powered flight by Wilbur and Orville Wright in 1903 to Neil Armstrong's moon landing in 1969, a period of only 66 years – one lifetime!

Communications technology such as iPhones, tablets and computers were in the realms of science fiction only 40 years ago; good design changes lives for the better. Educators must prepare children with knowledge and competences that will impact them for the rest of their lives. This chapter frames subject and pedagogical knowledge for trainee teachers, and aspires to provide both an historical and contemporary sociological context that will be relevant in an authentic way that intersects all aspects of the English national curriculum.

Products well designed and manufactured have value, from the pen you write with to the seat you comfortably sit on. Good D&T teaching should enable the student to understand and answer for themselves questions such as:

- How does this work?

- How was it made?

- What makes it good?

- Could I improve this?

- What does the world need now?

Understanding Design and Technology prepares learners to participate and make positive contributions to our society. The drive towards human, social, economic and environmental sustainability through a green revolution will see the UK undergo tremendous changes in how we live our lives. Sustainable design will necessitate that there is a move away from disposable products towards those that are durable and recyclable. The move away from carbon fuels towards energy efficient methods of generating electricity from wind, wave and solar power is accelerating. Water conservation and air quality will also become much more to the forefront than earlier generations. Increasing food production and the elimination of food waste will also grow in necessity (Bauermeister and Diefenbacher, 2015).

Developing an interest in design at a primary age will help give context and make sense of many elements of the maths, science and art curriculums, which can be even more significantly built on through secondary schooling. Children may not be aware, but careers that use DT skills include fashion designer, product designer, architect, software engineer, engineer, carpenter, chef, and many more. Educators need to explain why DT is important for the future welfare of us all.

This chapter will provide a clear support framework that outlines the knowledge required by teachers to develop their own capability and reflect on how DT is potentially a powerful tool to develop student metacognition by resolving relevant and authentic problems in order to meet a defined need.

REFLECTION

How would you start a conversation about the importance of D&T with your pupils?

WHY IS DESIGN AND TECHNOLOGY IN THE NATIONAL CURRICULUM?

The national curriculum requires that primary children engage in three important development activities while developing knowledge in four areas of technology: Designing, Making and Evaluating. Importantly, the generality of these areas gives the teacher a great opportunity to be creative and explore areas of interest in planning a context or a specific product to design.

Table 3.1 National curriculum Design and Technology areas of study

Technology areas to study	Example
Textiles and fashion	Working with fabrics, for example, to make cushions, bags, puppets
Static structures	Bridges, towers, buildings, statues
Dynamic mechanisms	Moving vehicles, toys
Electrical systems	Application of motors, bulbs and buzzers to make simple models and toys
Principles of nutrition	Baking skills and healthy snacks

Combining intellectual thought with stimulating and creative practical actions is arguably at the centre of constructivist learning and is more effective in terms of cognitive development than the passive acquisition of knowledge alone. Therefore, it ought to be part of every child's educational entitlement from an early age. It gives the child a toolbox of skills to facilitate their own learning. It is what enables *learning to learn by thinking explicitly about their learning.*

The educational theorist Abraham Maslow said, if the only tool you have is a hammer, then *you tend to see every problem as nail* (Maslow, 1966).

By using D&T as a means of developing metacognition in a child, we are preparing them for a world that we do not yet know. Good D&T teachers should reflect on whether their lessons are broadening and deepening knowledge of the curriculum, while concurrently developing skills with an awareness of what constitutes good quality. As teachers, it is a key goal to promote child self-belief. Pupils are given the opportunity to succeed in a safe, healthy and enjoyable environment that encourages them to be discerning, while recognising quality – valuable skills for adulthood and their future economic well-being.

In primary planning, we look towards setting 'I can' objectives and goals that relate to skills and attributes that are useful for lifelong learning and holistic development, and will help to develop self-awareness and metacognition in children. To be discerning and recognising quality is a desirable life skill that is developed through a student's growing belief that they can succeed in accomplishing tasks.

Table 3.2 'I can' development

Enabling	I can work independently and as part of a team
Capability and skill	I can draw, model and communicate thoughts and ideas to others
Confidence	I can articulate opinions on what I like and dislike, and articulate why
Recognition	I can pick the appropriate tools, techniques and processes
Safety awareness	I can work safely, using a range of tools
Understanding	I can explain how the world around me works and predict change in the future

REFLECTION

How do you think the 'I can' approach can facilitate the development of potential with your pupils?

HOW HAS 'KNOWLEDGE' IN DESIGN AND TECHNOLOGY EDUCATION DEVELOPED OVER TIME?

Mankind's growing knowledge and technology has had the effect of making the world change more and more quickly. Look at structures: for 3,000 years the height of the tallest structure was the Great Pyramid, then followed the Norman structures such as Lincoln Cathedral in the eleventh century. In this early period, natural building materials were used such as stone, straw, clay and rammed earth. Being heavier and weaker structurally limited their use in terms of building taller buildings. However, these traditional materials have many sustainability advantages and tend to have a much lower carbon footprint than the modern steel, aluminium, concrete and glass buildings of today. It was not until the 1880s, after the Industrial Revolution which started in the late eighteenth century, that these new materials and techniques led to buildings suddenly getting taller and taller. It took over 4,000 years for mankind to build a structure 169 metres high – the Washington monument – but the development of materials and the engineering knowledge of how to utilise their properties has resulted in an exponential growth in the height and quantity of tall of buildings that has changed what our cities look like. This is a fascinating way to introduce the different styles of architecture from around the world, past and present. Increasingly, today's designers, contractors and manufacturers are realising that the environmental benefits of traditional materials can be combined with modern materials using today's technology to optimise material performance. By exploring the use of traditional materials and knowledge of the properties of materials, along with advanced manufacturing methods, enables students to appreciate the different architectures around the world.

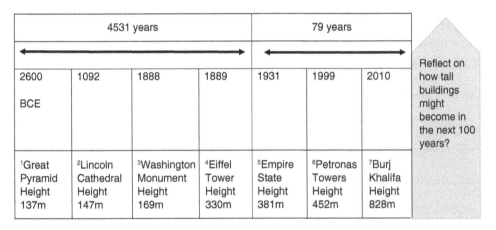

Figure 3.1 *Impact on structures of advancement in Design and Technology*

1. (2022, pyramid-of-giza.com)

2. (2021, lincolncathedral.com)

3. (2015, National Geodetic Survey)

4. (2022, www.toureiffel.paris/en/the-monument/key-figures)

5. (2022, www.esbnyc.com)

6. (2022, *Encyclopædia Britannica*)

7. (2022, www.burjkhalifa.ae)

REFLECTION

How is the speed of technical innovation impacting the classroom?

DESIGN AND TECHNOLOGY NOW
CROSS-CURRICULAR OPPORTUNITIES WHEN TEACHING D&T APPROPRIATELY

In the Early Years Foundation Stage, Design and Technology forms part of the learning that children acquire under the section 'Knowledge and Understanding of the World' of the Foundation Stage curriculum. This also covers geography, history, ICT and science. For example, one topic area – bridges – will involve the teacher researching and sharing different bridges from around the world and from different time periods, thus providing opportunities to examine geographic locations and, by comparing old bridges with new bridges, discussing how they were built and the materials used. The aim is to arouse curiosity, which can be further developed through play, as children learn to build with paper and card using tape and glue, and learn how to knock them down by discovering areas of weakness. It is particularly important to develop language and speaking skills into the early years. For example, staying with the bridge context, the class can research and discuss different designs and use evaluative language such as:

- oldest/newest;
- strongest/weakest;
- longest/shortest;
- metal/non-metallic;
- closest/furthest away.

Encourage opportunities to develop speaking and listening by expressing their favourite bridge design and articulating why they like it, what it was made from and how it was built.

Further encourage the use of the language of designing and making – for example, words such as join, connect, quality, material, assemble.

Progression into KS1 and 2 sees projects become more open-ended, with greater challenges and needs to be met, such as targets for the span and load capability – for example, can a toy remote-controlled car be driven over the bridge? This introduces aspects of numeracy and science into the challenge.

D&T both relies upon and contributes to other areas of the national curriculum, as discussed below.

Mathematics: Driven by the need to complete a task, concepts such as estimating, measuring spatial awareness symmetry and numerical operations can be given a context that promotes the development of skills earlier than usual.

Science: Investigating and exploring the properties of materials, energy and forces will all become important considerations in solving design problems. Professional designers acquire knowledge from almost any area of human activity to resolve a vast range of design problems.

Art: A care and appreciation of what they make and understanding that good design involves both form and function. Design aesthetics can be developed through drawing and sketching. The ability to visualise in terms of concept sketches in a 3D format like isometric or oblique along with 2D visualisations using orthographic projections are useful visualisation skills (Figure 3.2).

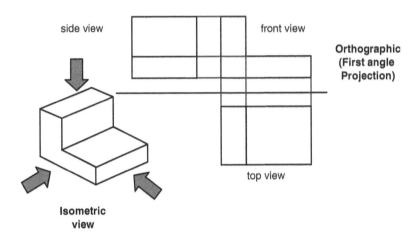

Figure 3.2 Illustrating visualising a design

Humanities: The humanities can provide starting points for design and technology activities. History gives opportunities to study technology from past times alongside the pace of change going on all around us now, while geography can explore developments from other parts of the world and consider how it is affecting the planet. The world's religions have been a source of many iconic designs in terms of iconography and places of worship. The impact of global warming and the importance of green technologies is also relevant and certainly current.

Personal Social and Health Education: Design and Technology can provide situations in which social and communication skills can be nurtured. Specifically, oral and graphical capabilities, along with personal qualities such as the ability to listen to others' ideas and to negotiate and compromise, when necessary, to persevere in the face of setbacks in order to make progress. By considering where products come from, the teacher can create class empathy with those workers involved in the production process – for example, exploring Third World sweatshops.

Generally, develop the natural curiosity that children have by noticing and discussing everyday materials around them – for example, household furniture and kitchen utensils, clothing, etc. – and reflect on how and where they were made, and the importance of using the right tool for the job. Encourage and support the correct use of a range of tools, such as scissors, hole punch, stapler, glue spreader, rolling pin, cutter. By KS2, these should include small hacksaws, set squares, hand-powered drills, needles and threads. For older children in KS3, begin to introduce ideas of casting and machining using YouTube films of the workplace.

WHAT MIGHT KNOWLEDGE IN DESIGN AND TECHNOLOGY EDUCATION LOOK LIKE IN THE FUTURE?

It is in the new technologies that progress has driven society forward even faster than structures. Look at the world of electronic devices – particularly, mobile phones, smart TVs, computer technology and, most dramatically, the internet. The signs are that the digital age we live in is likely to see this advancement in technology accelerate even more quickly, necessitating a future population and workforce with strong D&T competences. Remember, today's science fiction will become tomorrow's reality. Tomorrow's technology is already on the horizon.

Design and Technology skills are integral to tackle the pressing problems of our time. The impact of climate change is happening around the world, and scientific innovation and adaptation are key areas that will support humanity to adapt to the way our plant is changing. Design and Technology skills are vital in supporting the creative, innovative and green solutions to addressing this global emergency.

REFLECTION

What do you know about the following technologies of tomorrow?

- Augmented Reality Immersion
- Driverless cars
- Nano technology

- Green energy generation

- Artificial Intelligence

- Household robotics

- Holograms

- Smart materials – i.e., smart glass

- 3D printing

- Vertical farming

- Hyperloop transportation technology

Why not make a basic knowledge organiser of each area?

PART 2: THE FOUNDATION KNOWLEDGE OF MODERN D&T METHODOLOGY

William Edwards Deming and Joseph Juran were two of the most influential industrialists of the twentieth century. They introduced the quality systems that drove the industrialisation of Japan following the Second World War, successfully turning it into a vibrant, modern leader of technology and innovation by the end of the twentieth century. Among their many pronouncements are two quotes that are at the heart of why D&T is so useful in developing children's metacognitive strategies:

Quality is pride of workmanship (Deming, 1982).

Quality can be defined as 'Fitness for Purpose' (Juran, 1998).

Children learning to be proud of producing their best work, alongside knowing when their work meets expectations, involves having critical awareness of their own thinking and understanding that it is this act of *learning how to learn* that develops metacognition. Metacognition helps students to become independent learners who can monitor their own progress and take control of their learning as they read, write and solve problems in the classroom. Strong metacognitive skills will benefit learning in all subjects, but it is the application of the D&T process that can give many opportunities to develop these skills. To make a product that is fit for purpose, the starting point is to know what the product needs to do – a needs analysis requires the student designer to reflect and critically analyse.

For example, look at slippers, football boots and ski boots. We wear these on our feet, but they all do different jobs and are made from different materials.

Table 3.3 Needs analysis for footwear

Slippers	Football boots	Ski boots
Mainly indoor use	Outdoor use	Fits tightly to foot and encloses ankle like an endoskeleton
Comfortable to lounge in	Comfortable for running	
Insulated for warmth	Waterproof	
Attractive and stylish	Lightweight	Strong and robust
Easy to put on and take off	Secure when worn	Can bind securely onto the ski
Non-slip	Good grip, non-slip on wet grass using studs	Insulated and warm
Sole to be waterproof		Waterproof
Low cost	Resilient to impact	Flexible when leaning forward but rigid side-to-side
	Flexible	
	Stylish	

As technology keeps improving, then the opportunity to create new inventive designs also increases. However, the approach to follow is a long-established process that does not change. This is particularly the case within education, which aims to build on what has gone before rather than being leading edge. The primary classroom would, for example, focus on understanding how to design and make authentic representations of what footwear technology we have today – for example, slippers, with one eye on perhaps the idea of Hover Boots in the future. The next section will look at the pedagogical process of design that needs to be consolidated into classroom learning.

REFLECTION

Consider how a consequence of cognitive development is that, when children are faced with a problem that they have never come across before, *they choose to think*.

Why is this?

REFLECTION

How do knowledge organisers help to deepen understanding?

DT KNOWLEDGE ORGANISER KS1 AND 2 FREESTANDING STRUCTURES

CONTEXT: MY FAVOURITE STATUE

Overview Research of freestanding structures.

They can stand up supporting their own weight.

They need to be strong, rigid and stable without being attached to anything other than its foundations.

Stuctures are built for a purpose they may be functional or aesthetic or both.

They can be very large like a bridge, building or tower or quite small like a piece of furniture like a chair

EXAMPLES OF STATUES THAT ARE FREESTANDING STRUCTURES

Name : Statue of Liberty

Location : New York, USA

Completed 1886

Designer: Frédéric Auguste Bartholdi and Gustav Eiffel

It was made as a symbol of the USA s commitment to freedom and democracy

ENGINEERING DESIGN FEATURES

Despite its towering height, this hollow sculpture was made from thin sheets of hammered copper, To support this the engineer Eiffel designed an ingenious skeleton of wrought iron trusses that allow the statue to be anchored to its foundation and yet sway in the wind. Look at Eiffel's other great structure the Eiffel Tower in Paris.

Name : Angel of the North

Location : Gateshead, England

Completed 1998

Designer: Antony Gormley

It was made as a symbol of hope for the future symbolising the transition from the industrial to the information age.

ENGINEERING DESIGN FEATURES

The foundations are as deep as the fabricated steel structure, 200tonnes of concrete with 32 tonnes of reinforcing steel anchor it to to the solid rock below. The structure itself is stiffened by ribs that run its length making it rigid and stable to withstand wind loads of 160mph.It is make from a special alloy of steel and copper to give it its rusty look whilst protecting it from further corrosion(rusting).

Name : Christ the Redeemer

Location : Rio de Janeiro, Brazil

Completed 1933:

Designer: sculptor Paul Landowski

It was made to celebrate Brazil's 100th year anniversary of its independance from Portugal.

ENGINEERING DESIGN FEATURES

1400tonnes Tiers of concrete blocks shaped in clay molds. gradually extended the construction upward, and once the core was finished, the statue was covered with tiles of soapstone from Sweden.

(Continued)

MAKING PLAN	MATERIALS	KEY VOCABULARY	HEALTH AND SAFETY
Refer to your design sketch and dimensions for the statue carefully.	Plastic bottle , papier mache, card, polystyrene clay	Structure	Wear an apron, roll up sleeves and tie long hair back.
Decide on which materials you will use to make your statues shape.	Chicken wire	Freestanding	Always walk carefully in the classroom and do not carry tools
	Balsa.	Foundation	
Have you a plinth or wide base design that will make the freestanding statue stable and not fall over.	PVA Glue	Rigid	Remove bags and trip hazards
	Screws	stiff	
	Tape	Stable	Follow instructions carefully
	Paints	Unstable	
What skills will you need to cut shape and join the different parts?		Centre of Gravity	Clean up after yourself
		Weight	Use safety goggles when cutting or drilling
What will the statue be mounted on for stability?		Support	
		Robust	
How will you keep the ce		plinth	
ntre of gravity as low as possible ?		Balanced	
		Mass	
How will the statue be secured ?		Anchored	
		Connected	

EVALUATE THE DESIGN	MY FAVOURITE STATUE
How well does it meet the your needs in terms of aesthetic of function or both.	

How well does it meet the your needs in terms of aesthetic of function or both.

What problems did you have to overcome and how did you resolve them?

It it fit for purpose?

How could you improve it?

How could it be made more stable and robust?

Statue of Liberty

Figure 3 continued DT knowledge organiser ks1 and 2 for freestanding structures - science and understanding context: my favourite statue

CONTEXT: MY FAVOURITE STATUE

WHAT MAKES STRUCTURES STABLE

The centre of gravity (The point where the structures mass is acting) is kept directly above its base. This is why most tall structures have a wide base.

The structure needs to be rigid and not tilt because when a structure tilts its centre of gravity moves. If it moves outside its bas it will all collapse. Keep the centre of gravity as low as possible .

KEY SCIENCE UNDERSTANDING

A sound understanding of the science is essential for successful innovation. Think of the structure as a child. The center of gravity on a person is approximately at the belly button. When the child is sitting on its bottom. The centre of gravity is low and close to its bottom (the base). The centre of gravity is acting through the base so the child is stable. When the child stands on one foot its base is much smaller if it tilts over until the centre of gravity passes outside its foot or base it becomes unsteady . As the centre of gravity moves further away from the foot/base it become completely unstable and falls over.

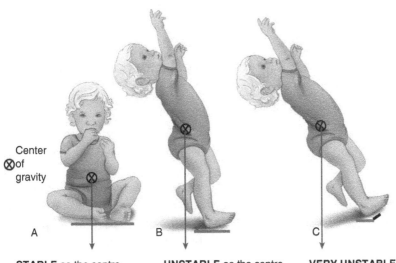

Center of gravity

A

STABLE as the centre of gravity is acting through the base

B

UNSTABLE as the centre of gravity is acting outside the base

C

VERY UNSTABLE as the centre of gravity is acting outside the base the child is now **FALLING OVER**

Figure 3.3 Exemplar knowledge organiser

SYSTEMS THINKING FOR DESIGN AND TECHNOLOGY

This methodical process approach is a core principle driving design quality. Therefore, understanding how to plan a series of lessons is vital for successful engagement and learning of principles and a resultant outcome that is fit for purpose, a source of pride giving the class a sense of achievement. Simply put, the process is a holistic approach in which the learning combines to create a synergy in learning beyond that of just making a product as if it were a mere craft exercise.

Effective D&T lessons develop self-awareness that enables individuals to monitor, reflect and analyse their own performance and that of others. Students who can do this are more likely to learn more effectively and therefore make more progress. Learning to learn (metacognitive development) enables students to deduce what they would do differently next time if they experience a setback, failure or make a mistake. A series of design lessons employs a range of learning strategies – namely:

- **Spaced practice** – students get to review and recall learning at regular intervals.

- **Elaboration** – students explain and describe concepts and processes in detail and depth, making links and comparing ideas to their own real-life experiences.

- **Use of concrete examples** – examples and models of existing products are used to facilitate understanding and knowledge growth.

- **Dual-coding** – the combination of verbal and visual representations and kinaesthetic learning complement and help make sense of learning.

- **Interleaving** – students are challenged to think about and actively recall information from across the curriculum and apply this relevant knowledge to their decision making.

- **Retrieval practice** – the D&T process requires students to regularly recall relevant information from their long-term memories.

Design and Technology not only enhances the thinking and decision-making powers of young people, it also enhances their conscious awareness of those thought processes. 'They not only learn to think and make decisions, but they also know (and can see) that that is what they are doing' (Kimbell et al., 1996, p31). The term 'metacognition' has been applied to this phenomenon.

The table below gives a general outline of typical topic areas for design activity, although remember, you need not be limited to this list – you can pick any area of interest.

Table 3.4 D&T themes for the primary teacher

Moving pictures – use as an introduction to pop-up books and cards	9–11 hours
Playgrounds – draw, then model the ideal playground using craft materials	8–10 hours
Eat more fruit and vegetables – design and make the healthy fruit kebab	6–8 hours
Homes – research architect models, then design your perfect home and make a model	8–10 hours
Vehicles – make a wheeled vehicle, research cars, trains, trucks	9–11 hours
Puppets – finger and sock puppets, shadow puppets	6–8 hours
Winding up – gravity-powered toys, windmills and gears	8–10 hours
Buzzer game – links to science: electrical circuits with buzzer, polarity, etc.	6–8 hours
Packaging – pupils will look at food packaging and see why it is and how it does its job	8–10 hours
Sandwich snacks – think about different food groups; design and make their own sandwiches	6–8 hours
Moving monsters – investigate how air can produce movement and how this can be used in simple pneumatic mechanisms	9–11 hours
Photograph frames – different styles and materials to secure a photo	8–10 hours
Money containers – different styles, materials and ways store money	8–10 hours
Storybooks – pop-up story books and binding	6–8 hours
Flight – research the story of flight and the different principles by making paper planes and water-powered rockets	9–11 hours
Musical instruments – research orchestra and design alternative percussion, string and wind instruments	6–8 hours
Baking – design, bake and decorate a themed cake	8–10 hours
Moving toys – learn about cams and sliders, axles and drives	9–11 hours
Shelters – design and make a woodland bivouac	6–8 hours
Textiles – slippers/puppets/bags/cushions/T-shirt designs	8–10 hours
City planning – design and model facilities such as parkland, shopping mall, sports stadium, fairground, etc.	9–11 hours

PEDAGOGICAL APPROACHES THAT CAN BE USED TO DEVELOP DESIGN AND TECHNOLOGY CAPABILITY

Teachers need good knowledge and modelling skills alongside an ability to plan and prepare in advance of starting the process. The breadth of potential design areas is such that on many occasions the teacher is learning along with the students. Good preparation will enable the teacher to predict potential problems and help them fulfil their role of 'more knowledgeable other' and arbiter of quality. On school visits, I have entered classrooms in which the children have made a single paper slipper. This is *not* design, as one paper slipper serves no purpose and has no value in terms of being fit for any purpose.

A classic KS2 project is to make proper, wearable 'fit-for-purpose' slippers. This develops practical skills in measuring, cutting, gluing and sewing, alongside knowledge of the properties of materials and assembly methods. It even offers the opportunity to look at the social implications of the mass production of footwear by examining sweatshops in the Third World. To do this well and make fit-for-purpose slippers as a design activity can take a half-term and six to eight lessons, as described in Table 3.5 below.

By learning how to follow this design process competently, the children are learning skills that will enable them to thrive in adulthood and be successful in the future. This entails more than just improving literacy and numeracy skills alongside general knowledge. We need a broad, flexible and motivating education that recognises the different talents of all children and delivers excellence for everyone. A role of the teacher is to recognise and promote young people's interests and creative capacities and then to provide the conditions in which they can be realised. This is essential both in itself and to promote forms of education that are inclusive and sensitive to the cultural diversity and understanding of how society might evolve in the future.

REFLECTION

D&T is an essential school subject because it can lead to economic and domestic benefits. Do you agree? Reflect on why this may be the case.

Table 3.5 Lesson plan sequence

Lesson	Learning activity
1. Define a need and context	Often the origin of a new product is a problem or something that society requires. It will have a value if done well. Decide on a product to make and why. What do the class like/want/need – i.e., slippers?
2. Research and evaluate existing product designs and start the knowledge organiser	Examine existing products by taking them apart and explore how they were made and how they might be improved in terms of performance, reliability and cost. Understand what materials were used and how it was assembled – i.e., for slippers, a waterproof non-slip sole joined to an absorbent and cushioning layer along with an insulating comfortable upper.

Lesson	Learning activity
3. Complete a design needs analysis and establish the design criteria	Remembering that 'fit-for-purpose' defines quality, brainstorm what the product must do and establish what good will look like. A great needs analysis lists the desired outcomes or goals for the designed product. The quality of the needs analysis will greatly influence the eventual outcome - i.e., the slippers should be robust and comfortable when worn, as well as attractive to look at.
4. Generate conceptual ideas and decide on the type of slipper to design	A slider type does not require a heel, which simplifies assembly with few component parts. Where possible, think KIMS - Keep Its Manufacture Simple.
5. Focused practical tasks - FPTs	*Before* starting to make any slippers, there are skills to learn: making and cutting out templates; measuring and checking; spreading glue; sewing.
6. Making the product in the required quantity	Look at how assembly lines work and, in small groups, establish production cells - for example, one group uses a template to cut out each element of the soles and uppers and another group checks the work (quality control). When component parts are made and checked, other groups/cells will glue soles together and then join soles to uppers. A round-robin approach is taken to ensure that all children have a go at each process. Discuss sweatshops in the Third World as a philosophy session.
7. Evaluate through testing and optimise	Slippers are examined and a sample checked for quality, robustness and wearability. How might they be tested?
8. Optimisation	Each child can then optimise their slippers and show individual creativity by adding improvements and embellishments that creatively personalise them.
9. Presentation of the finished design	Wear slippers in class with pride and take them home. Can the class articulate their learning?

D&T lessons offer a context for a class to develop their understanding and creativity. Context can fulfil the need for a reason why to undertake a task. Focusing on skills in isolation can kill interest in any discipline. Many people have been put off by mathematics for life by endless rote tasks that did nothing to inspire them with a context of why there is a purpose of value. The real driver of creativity is an appetite for discovery and a passion for the work itself. When students are motivated to learn, they naturally acquire the skills they need to get the work done. Their mastery grows as their creative ambitions expand. A driver of design excellence is the idea that 'better never stops' – there is always room to improve a product in a search for optimum performance. For example, the England women's national football team (the Lionesses) won the European championship in 2022 because they were motivated to improve their skills, fitness and teamwork; they also had the best equipment in comfortable strips and boots.

Thinking back to the needs analysis of the football boot, reflect on how they have improved over the last 90 years (footballboots.co.uk). Would the Lionesses still have won if they had worn boots from the 1930s?

By looking closely at a products evolution, it becomes apparent that both process and knowledge are critical. The ability to conduct research skills are promoted through the development of knowledge organisers which can direct and support what is taught in each lesson. You can shape your lesson planning around these to ensure that you cover the key learning over a sequence of lessons. In D&T, a good knowledge organiser will impact both creativity and quality of design produced, while also forming a basis for assessing outcomes based on it.

PART 3: UNDERSTANDING THE DEVELOPMENT OF CHILDREN'S KNOWLEDGE IN DESIGN AND TECHNOLOGY
A PROCESS MODEL FOR PLANNING DESIGN AND TECHNOLOGY

The government expectations are that lessons should be inspiring, rigorous and practical. Pupils design and make products that have worth by solving real and relevant problems within a variety of contexts. Pupils learn how to evaluate past and present technology and its impact on how well it meets market needs. They learn a process to harness creativity and become resourceful, innovative, enterprising and capable citizens. The analytical nature of high-quality design and technology education makes an essential contribution to the culture, wealth, and academic well-being of the nation as it develops a broad range of subject knowledge drawing on disciplines such as mathematics, science, engineering, computing and art. Successful D&T teaching involves a series of lessons that systematically takes the class through the design process of:

DESIGN – MAKE – EVALUATE – KNOWLEDGE DEVELOPMENT

A 'better by' design approach involves carefully designed experiences that help children develop the confidence that they can mould and shape the world through their ideas and actions. Innovation doesn't come from a genius mind; it comes from a mindset that 'better never stops'. Author and international educational adviser, Sir Ken Robinson, contended that *Creativity is the process of having original ideas that have value* (Robinson, 1999). The comparison with effective Design and Technology is easy to see. He contends that creativity is putting your imagination to work and innovation is putting new ideas into practice. He argues that creativity should be treated with the same status as specific subjects like literacy. Few would argue that creativity is not a highly desirable element for success in literacy and, like D&T, it also has its logical processes to scaffold activities or example story mountain planning. Children are often told how the world is, while an appreciation of D&T helps them perceive ideas about how the world could be. Where do great ideas come from? Some people appear naturally creative, but the reality is that all children have imaginations and an inclination towards creativity. D&T offers an approach that should harness and promote individual creativity. A rigorously creative approach can act as a scaffold that can gradually develop ideas into products. Creativity is not about artistry and nor is it about the 'lightbulb moment' (The Niche Marketeer, 2021). Becoming an innovator can be learned and practised by anyone with the appropriate knowledge, resources and drive. Learning to successfully harness creativity makes a more confident and proactive learner capable of innovation. A consequence of promoting creativity is that it develops confidence and thinking skills in all curriculum areas. Cultivating and refining these skills, knowledge and ideas is desirable for anyone wanting to develop an approach to mastery in the classroom. The creative D&T process cycle model below aims to provide learning outcomes shaped to support trainees in building their knowledge, attitudes, values, behaviours, competences and capabilities. These areas will underpin an understanding of how to develop lesson content to support their pupils in understanding the core process to be followed.

Elmer (2000) argues that *the language of technology is indisputably a concrete one – of images, symbols and models. Without this language it is just not possible to conceive of technological solutions.*

REFLECTION

To what extent do you agree that creativity can be described as the confluence of intrinsic ability or self-motivation, domain-relevant knowledge and abilities, and relevant skills?

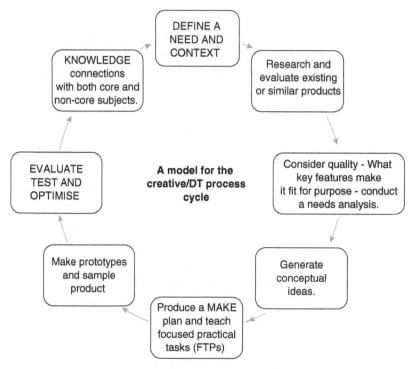

Figure 3.4 Module for the creative D&T process cycle (Foster, 2020, University of Cumbria)

Table 3.6 below shows how this model might look in terms of lesson aims over a series of lessons that will cover the process in terms of national curriculum aims and development of metacognition in students.

Table 3.6 National curriculum alignment with the D&T process and impact on metacognition

NC D&T STEPS	LESSON	CLASSROOM D&T LESSON AIMS (7 LESSONS)	METACOGNATIVE STRATEGIES DEVELOPED
Design (I&EA)	1	Define a need and define the context.	Reflection and mental scripting.
Investigating and evaluating activities	2	Research and evaluate existing products.	Research and recording skills.
	3	Consider quality. What key features make it fit for purpose? Conduct a needs analysis.	Critical reflection using prior and new learning.
	4	Generate conceptual ideas.	Working independently and with peers. Working with others.
Make	5	Produce a 'making' plan and teach focused practical tasks (FTPs).	Arranging a workspace and schedule. Planning and preparation. Guided practice.

NC D&T STEPS	LESSON	CLASSROOM D&T LESSON AIMS (7 LESSONS)	METACOGNITIVE STRATEGIES DEVELOPED
	6	Make prototypes and sample product.	Work ethic and following instructions/plans. Problem solving, monitoring and rectifying errors.
Evaluate	7	Test product. Does it do what it needs to do? Is it *fit for purpose*? How can the product be improved/optimised? Present final product design.	Evaluating task success, recognising good quality and adjusting as needed. Using structured reflection.
Subject knowledge	All	Make connections with both core and non-core subjects. Technical: maths, science. Facts: history, geography.	Activating prior knowledge. Explicit instruction.

In considering D&T by the end of KS2, students need to be aware that if an idea is novel with a clear inventive step, it can be patented. This gives the inventor protection to stop others stealing the idea. It is well worth researching products that have been patented and then commercially exploited making the inventors wealthy.

In primary schools, most ideas are not novel. The students make their own versions of existing products as described in Table 3.7 and exemplified below.

REFLECTION

How does what you have just learned relate to what you already knew?

Table 3.7 Examples from the classroom – what does good look like?

Paper-folding skills and simple mechanisms	Links to literacy and art. Take the group's creative writing and design a pop-up book. The skills learned are simple: using a paper linear slider, rotary mechanisms and pop-up features, gluing and binding skills. These skills are the same as those needed to make pop-up celebration cards for Mother's Day or Easter.
Textiles: making puppets	Cross-curricular links with literacy and art. In small groups, the class undertake some creative writing – for example, a new story or a reworking of a traditional story or tale. In art, they draw/paint the characters in the story, then research how these might be represented as a puppet, and follow the design process to research into how to make sock puppets and finger puppets. They then follow the process to make the puppets and, on completion, they can be used to retell and dramatise their story in a puppet show.

(Continued)

Table 3.7 (Continued)

Up-cycling	Use waste plastic bottles to make elegant, stylish or fun vases or outdoor bird-feeders.
Static structures	Links to maths and science. Set a challenge to build the tallest tower capable of holding a 750g weight without collapsing using a fixed amount of material - e.g., straws and sheets of A4 paper sheets, lolly-pop sticks, etc. The class will learn about stability, struts, stiffness, rigidity. Alternatively, undertake to design a bridge.
Moving vehicles	Design a car to travel in a straight line down a ramp with an egg as a passenger. Good maths links to make the axles parallel and at a right angle to the structure. Learn about friction and measure velocity and distance travelled. Research car crash safety.
Classic buzzer game	Test hand and eye co-ordination. Put the electrical understanding of circuits to a practical use. Reflect on how this approach might be used for other uses such as an alarm.
Outdoor learning	Design and build a practical functional bivouac, fully insulated with structural integrity giving protection from the elements - waterproof and windproof.
Make a working hovercraft	Using a plastic cup and a Styrofoam pizza base, put electrical circuit knowledge into practice. Learn about mass and lift alongside careful hand-assembly skills.
Make a pirate ship	Design a pirate ship from plastic milk bottles. Learn about forces, buoyancy and stability.

REFLECTION

How has your mindset towards D&T altered after reading this chapter?

PART 4: DEVELOPING YOUR KNOWLEDGE OF DESIGN AND TECHNOLOGY EDUCATION FURTHER

SOME READING TO SUPPORT YOUR DEVELOPMENT

Cole, E (2003) *A Concise History of Architectural Styles*. New York: Herbert Press.

Lo, C (2012) Old as the hills: traditional building materials in the 21st century. Accessed at: www.designbuild-network.com/analysis/featuretraditional-building-materials-21st-century/

Rutland, M and Spendlove, D (n.d.) Creativity in design & technology. Accessed at: https://dandtfordandt.files.wordpress.com/2016/09/creativity-in-design-technology.pdf

University of East Anglia (n.d.) Strategies for effective learning. Available at: www.futurelearn.com/info/courses/early-career-teachers/0/steps/164332 (accessed 9 December 2022).

Weinstein, Y and Sumeracki, M (2019) *Understanding How We Learn: A Visual Guide*. London: Routledge.

WEBSITES RECOMMENDATIONS

AQA. GCSE Design and Technology. Available at: www.aqa.org.uk/subjects/design-and-technology/gcse/design-and-technology-8552/subject-content

Design & Technology Association. Available at: data.org.uk

Main, P (n.d.) Metacognitive strategies in the classroom. Available at:

www.structural-learning.com/post/how-to-develop-metacognition

REFERENCES

Bauermeister, M and Diefenbacher, LH (2015) *Beyond Recycling: Guiding Preservice Teachers to Understand and Incorporate the Deeper Principles of Sustainability*. Taylor & Francis online.

Burj Khalifa (2022) Did you know? Facts & Figures. Available at: www.burjkhalifa.ae/en/the-tower/facts-figures/ (accessed 15 November 2022).

Lincoln Cathedral (2021) Cathedral floorplan: Explore the cathedral. Available at: https://lincolncathedral.com/floorplan/ (accessed 15 November 2022).

Deming, WE (1982) *Out of the Crisis*. Cambridge, MA: MIT Press.

Department for Education (2013) Design and Technology. Programmes of study: Key Stages 1 to 2. Available at: https://assets.publishing.service.gov.uk/government/uploads/system/uploads/attachment_data/file/239041/PRIMARY_national_curriculum_-_Design_and_technology.pdf (accessed 15 November 2022).

Eiffel Tower at a glance. Available at: www.toureiffel.paris/en/the-monument/key-figures (accessed: 15 November 2022).

Elmer, R (2000) Meta-cognition and design and technology education. *Journal of Design & Technology Education*, 17 (1).

Empire State Building Fact Sheet (2022) Available at: www.esbnyc.com/sites/default/files/esb_fact_sheet_4_9_14_4.pdf (accessed: 15 November 2022).

Encyclopædia Britannica (2022) Petronas Twin Towers. Available at: www.britannica.com/topic/Petronas-Twin-Towers (accessed 15 November 2022).

Football Boots History (2022) Available at: www.footballboots.co.uk/history.html (accessed: 15 November 2022).

Foster, H (2020) *Introduction to Primary Design*, module CURC 4202. Available at: https://mylearning.cumbria.ac.uk/

Juran, JM (1998) *Juran's Quality Handbook*. New York: McGraw-Hill.

Kimbell, R, Stables, K and Green, R (1996) *Understanding Practice in Design and Technology*. Milton Keynes: Open University.

Maslow, AH (1966) *The Psychology of Science: A Reconnaissance*. New York: Harper & Row.

National Geodetic Survey (2015) 2013–2014 survey of the Washington Monument. NOAA Repository. Available at: https://repository.library.noaa.gov/view/noaa/9319

Niche Marketer, The (2021) Creativity – that lightbulb moment is actually a process. Available at: https://thenichemarketer.com/creativity-that-lightbulb-moment-is-actually-a-process/ (accessed 15 November 2022).

Pyramids of Giza Facts: 12 interesting facts you didn't know (n.d.). Available at: https://www.pyramid-of-giza.com/pyramids-of-giza-facts/ (accessed: 15 November 2022).

Robinson, K (1999) *All our Futures: Creativity, Culture and Education*. London: Department for Education and Employment.

4

ENGLISH

CAROLINE WHITING AND PAUL RICHARDSON

KEYWORDS: LITERACY; TALK; INTERCONNECTED; TRANSCRIPTION; COMPREHENSION; DECODING; VOCABULARY; COMPOSITION; PURPOSE; AUDIENCE.

LINKS TO THE CORE CONTENT FRAMEWORK

Subject and Curriculum (Standard 3): 3.2, 3.3, 3.5, 3.6, 3.7, 3.9, 3.10

Classroom Practice (Standard 4): 4.1, 4.5

PART 1: EXPLORING ENGLISH

WHAT IS ENGLISH?

At first, it may seem obvious as to what 'English' is, but it can be difficult to define (Cambridge Assessment, 2013). Upon further research, it becomes clear that it covers so many areas between the aesthetic (literature) and functional (skills) (Laugharne, 2007). Additionally, as a primary phase subject, English is often seen as synonymous with that of 'literacy'. It is important to understand the meaning and implications of both these terms. Both are underpinned by our prime means of communication: our language. But these are also socially constituted terms that bring with them underlying assumptions and perceptions.

The term 'English' encompasses the system of our particular language code, whether it is thought, spoken, written or read. 'Literacy' carries with it the ability and skill to work with that code. However, there are many different kinds of literacy – functional, technical, creative – linked to particular communities. You will see both terms used in statutory and guidance documents, and in materials and programmes offered to support schools, often without the distinction being made clear. A key thing to remember is that to effectively carry out your job as a teacher of English, you need not only to understand and be able to use the code, but also to understand the detail and interdependence of its elements, the importance of its variety and potential in implementation, and its key role in communication in a range of contexts.

WHY IS ENGLISH IN THE NATIONAL CURRICULUM?

English as a subject has been readily regarded during the twentieth and twenty-first centuries as a fundamental component in education, which has given it a pre-eminent place in the national curriculum. Young (2014) states that constructing a curriculum helps to make a subject possible to learn in schools because it sets limits to make learning achievable. Currently, English is organised in four areas: reading; writing; vocabulary, grammar and punctuation; spoken language. This chapter will develop your understanding of these areas in greater detail, but it will also briefly explore the historical tensions behind the construction and interpretation of English within the national curriculum. If we understand that a curriculum is a selection of knowledge (Wood, 2012), this raises questions as to who has 'selected' this knowledge and decided upon what should and should not be included in the national curriculum. In addition, decisions have been made in how this knowledge should be interpreted, structured and organised. For instance, the Department for Education states that children need to learn to read fluently, and to write accurately and coherently (DfE, 2022a). This can reduce English to performing a functional, rather than an aesthetic role (Laugharne, 2007) in children's lives. There are arguments that this deficit perspective towards English can have a negative impact on children's learning, and can lead to the discrimination of particular groups. Cushing (2022) has identified this issue within the context of 'racially minoritised' children's use of vocabulary, often referred to as the 'word gap'. He explains how something that seems so common sense, and is believed to be addressing a social justice imperative, is in fact discriminatory. As he posits, 'What if poor, racially minoritised children don't have a word gap at all, but simply use language in ways that defy the measurements used to claim that a gap exists in the first place?'

HOW HAS 'KNOWLEDGE' IN ENGLISH DEVELOPED OVER TIME?

This functional role can lead to the teaching of the 'basics' to ensure there are sufficiently skilled workers for the economy (Gee, 2004), whereas an aesthetic role for English emphasises the importance of reading for pleasure; to provide children with the abilities to develop 'culturally, emotionally, intellectually, socially and spiritually' as individuals. In recognising that curricula are a selection of knowledge (Wood, 2012), it is possible to identify the historical influences previous generations had in constituting what is 'official' and 'real' knowledge, and why it should be included in the present national curriculum.

The *Newbolt Report* (1921) identified the lack of English teaching, particularly in elementary schools, and proposed that certain types of 'knowledge' were considered crucial in achieving social mobility for the working classes. This knowledge was the acquisition and demonstration of both spoken and written 'standard English' and the learning of technical skills, such as reading. In acquiring this knowledge, the working class, who were often considered illiterate, would benefit from the enhancement of their cognitive skills, which was believed to lead to an improvement of their economic prospects and ultimately make them better citizens (Street, 1984). Although initially the report seems primarily 'functional' (Laugharne, 2007) in its interpretation concerning the role of English, there is recognition in the aesthetic role that English plays, such as developing children's enjoyment of literature to help equip them with an understanding of life. Knowledge in the context of this report was to achieve social mobility for the working classes and build an appreciation of English literature, a motivation that is explored further in this chapter. Thus, this concept of knowledge is divided in two ways: propositional knowledge, which is the 'knowing of facts', and procedural knowledge, which is 'know-how' (Wood, 2012, p71). We will see later that this reductive conceptualisation of knowledge is still influential today.

The functional and aesthetic role of English would be developed in further detail in the *Hadow Report* (1931) which reiterated the importance of forming correct habits in speaking and writing, but also emphasised reading for pleasure. What was most notable was the move away from knowledge being presented as something to be mastered, and the recognition and inclusion of children's interests and sense of curiosity as well – what we would now refer to as 'child-centred education'. This was a significant shift from knowledge being a system of expertise, created and owned by specialists, and imposed top-down on children (Gee, 2004). Curriculum knowledge can often implicitly become self-validated as official knowledge, leading to other forms of knowledge being seen as of lesser importance (Wood, 2012). For instance, this perspective can overlook and downplay the legitimacy of children's own knowledge that they bring and share with the classroom community. There are examples today where writers such as Janks (2010) emphasise the need for teachers to recognise and celebrate the sophisticated forms of oral literacy practices and knowledge that children bring into the classroom from various other sociocultural and socioeconomic groups in society.

This major tension, which still besets education today, is deciding what is at the heart of the educational process: the child or the curriculum? The *Plowden Report* (1967) emphasised that the main educational role of primary schools was to build on and strengthen children's intrinsic interest in learning. A significant point that was made concerning children's progress was that teachers should *not assume that only what is measurable is valuable* – a point that is still relevant today. It also argued for more flexibility in the curriculum so that knowledge would not fall into neatly separate compartments and instead proposed a broader approach to education. This emphasised that the child at the centre of the learning experience (examples of which you can see in good early years' practice today) where the 'curriculum' is fitted around the needs of the child. A knock-on effect of this approach could have been that English as a subject could be somewhat lost among the focus on broader approaches to curriculum. Any concerns of this sort dissipated with the introduction of the national curriculum.

ENGLISH NOW

The first primary national curriculum was published in 1989. The *Cox Report* (1989) outlined the attainment targets and the programmes of study. It is set out under the headings 'speaking and listening', reading and writing'. Through a number of iterations, the national curriculum has developed to what it is today. The introduction of key stages, 'standard assessment tasks' (SATs) for core subjects, carried with them an expectation of what an 'average' child at the end of a key stage would achieve. 'Tasks' became 'tests' and the link to accountability was made through the publication of league tables, and the criteria applied to the assessment, the most testable and measurable (Whetton, 2009). With assessment outcomes, high stakes matter for individual teachers, schools and local authorities; the tendency, therefore, to focus on teaching to the tests is perhaps not surprising. Slimmed down in 1995, an even closer focus on the 'workings' of English was a feature of a further revision first taught in the autumn of 2000 (DfEE, 2000a).

> *The study of English helps pupils understand how language works by looking at its patterns, structures and origins. Using this knowledge pupils can choose and adapt what they say and write in different situations.*

(p43)

The primary English curriculum was supplemented by a non-statutory framework document, the 'Literacy Strategy' (DfES, 2006), promoted by the government through local authorities, which came to eclipse the actual national curriculum document. It was detailed and brought additional focus to the machinations of grammar (DfEE, 2000b), thus heralding the necessary development of teachers' technical knowledge in grammar, punctuation and genre. The success of the strategies was claimed in the improvement in SATs outcomes and the narrowing of differences between schools, areas and pupil groups (DfE, 2011).

The most recent change of any significance was in 2014 when the change in government resulted in a completely new curriculum and new assessment criteria. There is now an even greater focus on the teaching of reading through systematic synthetic phonics (SSP), and new tests in grammar, punctuation and spelling (GPS) were established. Thus, the scope of the national curriculum still requires sound technical knowledge for both teacher and pupil, but in some cases, the terminology and key foci may have changed. For reading and writing, the national curriculum as it stands now is less focused on accelerated progress as it had been before, but more on reaching specific standards by the end of the key stage. Most schools will take the standards agenda further and apply the suggestions for content in particular groups to set standards in other years groups, too. Thus, the national curriculum becomes more than a curriculum, but a set of expectations of performance for every year group in the primary school, and assessment of pupils against the specifics of the curriculum is the gauge for its success. To be judged as literate, then, is seen as the ability to use English in the way prescribed by the national curriculum, including standards in decoding print through SSP, and a prescriptive technical knowledge of grammar, punctuation and spelling (GPS – commonly also known as SPAG – spelling, punctuation and grammar).

WHAT MIGHT KNOWLEDGE IN ENGLISH LOOK LIKE IN THE FUTURE?

There are considerable criticisms for having a narrow and reductive interpretation of the national curriculum, and the knowledge contained with it. Focusing too much on testing and accountability places the importance of economic competitiveness over more socially driven purposes for education (Ball, 2017), which can lead to economically disadvantaged children with no more than 'the basics' (Gee, 2004, p109). This can result in too many disadvantaged children being denied access to knowledge that the privileged take for granted; therefore, we need to emphasise 'knowledge' as less of a form of control and more as a source of emancipation (Young, 2018). To achieve this, Young and Muller (2010) suggest that we interpret knowledge as being 'powerful knowledge'. This is specialised knowledge that is attained through formal education which provides learners with the capacity to extend horizons. This 'powerful knowledge' must change over time, just as specialist knowledge does, and thus places great importance on moving away from held assumptions concerning the objective and a-historic nature of knowledge, and that inherited traditions should automatically and uncritically be handed down to later generations. This is because the world of language and literacy is in a constant state of transformation and the development of new technologies and popular culture are changing the face of communication and everyday literacy practices. Therefore, it is crucial to promote equal access to powerful knowledge which can help individuals, and the societies they live in, respond to new and unpredicted problems.

REFLECTION

How has reading Part 1 of this chapter changed your perception of English 'knowledge'?

What do you think is important for children to learn? Had you previously thought about both functional and aesthetic aspects of knowledge in English?

What is your response to the notion that specific types and content of knowledge in English can be discriminatory towards particular socioeconomic or racial groups?

PART 2: FOUNDATION KNOWLEDGE IN ENGLISH

English happens to be the language in which we operate. As the curriculum is presented in the larger part as the detail of taught content within the discrete parts of the English curriculum as spoken English, reading and writing, with appendices outlining grammar, punctuation and spelling, the aspects that underpin the subject as a whole may not be at the forefront of a teacher's thinking when they come to plan for learning. However, we would argue that both trainee and experienced teachers, as well as curriculum planners, should bring a broader understanding of the subject to their planning and teaching. Building on the first sections in this chapter, we should consider the relationship of children's life experiences and their relation to the current understanding of what is important knowledge in English. We would suggest that the following three perspectives are kept in mind.

LANGUAGE AS COMMUNICATION

As social beings, we have an in-built need to communicate (Tomasello, 1992). Language is our most powerful form of communication. We communicate in many different ways, but language has uniquely developed in human beings as a sophisticated, complex, flexible and expansive communication system. It is described as combinatorial: its elements can be combined in infinite ways. Language – in this case, English – can be sent and received in sound (speech) and in marks (text). In speech, it is complemented by tone of voice, facial expression and gesture. In text, the content and form are adjusted to suit the purpose and audience. As senders (expressive language), we *speak and write*; as receivers (receptive language), we *listen and read.* This forms a structure for a curriculum, but these discrete elements are wholly connected to each other, and the communicative experiences that children encounter, both in and out of school.

FROM SPOKEN LANGUAGE TO READING AND WRITING

As children develop language through their unique social interactions, they first learn the particular sounds and patterns in speech and gradually come to realise the related significance of marks on the page as we share books and other printed or digital material with them: they recognise that the marks 'say' something. They then begin to develop their own mark-making to conform with their developing knowledge of the language code, building from what is said to letters and letter combinations, to words, and on to combinations of words that build meaning through the expansion of their vocabulary and a deepening understanding of grammar. Through spoken language and reading, they begin to learn the detail of both formal and informal codes and conventions for conveying meaning in different contexts, for different purposes and audiences.

LANGUAGE AND THINKING

This progression requires the development of something more fundamental. Vygostsky (1938) wrote about the link between thought and language. He argued that language enables us to develop complex thoughts internally through 'inner speech', and spoken language (outer speech) and writing provide ways of communicating those thoughts to others. When we receive a communication in speech or text, thought enables us to interpret it. It follows, then, that as language develops, so does the depth of what we can think, and in turn what we can understand in spoken language and in reading, and thence in our capacity to put our own thoughts in writing. This framing helps us to realise that writing is the outcome of a process that starts with thought, progresses through inner speech to outer speech, and can be formalised into a suitable structure for writing. It is a long way for that thought to travel, and we can help children by encouraging them to vocalise that transition from inner speech to what they want to write.

As we start to explore the framework documents, then, we should start to draw out the interconnectedness of the elements illustrated in Figure 4.1 below.

NATIONAL CURRICULA

Statutory and guidance documents will be at the core of how your understanding of foundational knowledge, and consequently your teaching, will be framed. The statutory curriculum for English is laid out in two curriculum documents: the primary national curriculum for English (DfE, 2013) and the communication, language and literacy (CLL) sections of the Early Years Foundation Stage (EYFS) statutory framework (DfE, 2021a). The framework for the EYFS is complemented by the non-statutory Development Matters (DfE, 2021b). These latter two documents cover birth to five years, so will be in place for Reception classes.

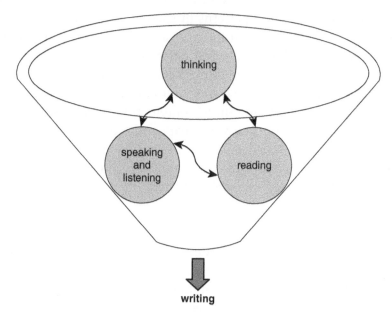

Figure 4.1 Connecting the elements

EARLY YEARS FOUNDATION STAGE

Communication and the development of oral language is emphasised, especially at the start. Reading is introduced through the sharing of books, and knowledge and understanding of the language code in text developed through the teaching of systematic synthetic phonics (SSP). Writing proceeds first through early mark-making, developing towards formal writing skills, using oral rehearsal and SSP. Development Matters gives practical suggestions on how the curriculum can be delivered. Throughout, the curriculum is delivered through direct teaching and play. Children are developing as active and motivated communicators through talk, reading and mark-making/writing. The Early Learning Goals (ELGs) outline what children should be able to do in these areas by the end of the Foundation Key Stage.

Table 4.1 Communication, language and literacy in the Early Years Foundation Stage

Prime area: communication and language EYFS Framework, pp8, 11 Development Matters, pp33-41		Specific area: literacy EYFS Framework, pp9, 13 Development Matters, pp33-41	
Aim To develop: • children's language and communication skills in order to learn across all areas of the EYFS.		**Aims** To develop: • a lifelong love of reading; • decoding and the speedy recognition of familiar printed words, transcription (spelling and handwriting); • composition.	
Key messages • *The development of children's spoken language underpins all seven areas of learning and development* (p8). • The number and quality of the conversations they have with adults and peers is crucial.		**Key messages** • Oral language is the precursor of reading and writing. • Both reading and writing involve more than one fundamental component. • Phonological awareness supports the development of reading and writing.	
Spoken English	**Reading**	**Reading**	**Writing**
• A language-rich environment; • back-and-forth interactions to aid the development of vocabulary and language structures; • covers listening and attention, understanding and speaking.	Reading frequently to children; engaging them actively in stories, non-fiction, rhymes and poems.	Reading for pleasure and to develop their knowledge of themselves and the world. It links strongly to the specific area of knowledge of the world: • reading involves word reading (decoding or 'sounding out' and word recognition) and comprehension; • decoding is taught through SSP; • children read books aloud using their phonics knowledge.	Writing involves both transcription (handwriting and spelling) and composition: • SSP supports spelling: children encode using their phonic knowledge; • handwriting is supported by good fine motor control, linking to specific area. **Physical development** • Oral rehearsal supports writing composition.

(Continued)

Table 4.1 (Continued)

Practitioners must know how to:	Practitioners must know how to:
• introduce, use and embed new words; • develop conversation, storytelling and role play; • provide opportunities to support and model language and use questions to encourage children to elaborate; • model quality talk.	• share books with children that they cannot access on their own; • make effective links across the curriculum to develop skills in all aspects of literacy; • use the school SSP programme to provide books that children can read independently and begin to write using their phonic knowledge; • provide opportunities to talk about books together; • use questions; • support home reading; • help children to orally discuss and rehearse what they want to write; • model whole sentences.

PRIMARY (YEARS 5–11)

The introduction to the English curriculum is clear in its acknowledgement of its *preeminent place in education and society* (p3).

It also emphasises the foundation that Spoken English provides not just for English, but across the whole curriculum. To underline its foundational place in the English curriculum, Spoken English is set out in a single statement for Years 1–6, but features throughout.

ASSESSMENT

Following the publication of the current national curriculum, a committee was tasked with producing a report on assessment (McIntosh, 2015). It characterised assessment in three distinct ways. The report sends a clear message that these three assessment processes are each with a different purpose and a different audience (pp18–21) and warns against using the language of the statutory assessments for purposes for which they were not intended. Uniquely for core subjects, of which English is one, the expectations of attainment at particular ages are assessed against a specific set of national criteria and benchmarks that can be easily measured, and which are set out in Table 4.3 (Roberts, 2022).

Schools have to be mindful of statutory assessments. Although they relate directly to the content of the national curriculum, they do not cover all aspects of the curriculum, but on the knowledge outlined in the programmes of study that are most easily measurable by the assessment processes presented: mark schemes for tests, baselines for successful outcomes and structured frameworks for teacher assessment. They therefore tend to focus on the functional aspects of discrete elements

Table 4.2 The primary English curriculum

	Reading	Writing
The rest of the English curriculum is set out with discrete programmes of study (PoS) for reading, writing, vocabulary, grammar and punctuation. This content is presented by year group, although the full national curriculum document makes clear that it is not statutory for particular content to be taught at a particular time, and attainment targets represent the whole of the Key Stage content.		
	Spoken Language	**Aims**
	Aims	To use their knowledge of a wide vocabulary, and understanding of grammar and writing conventions *to write clearly, accurately and coherently, adapting their language and style in and for a range of contexts, purposes and audiences* (p3).
	To support development across the curriculum, cognitively, socially and linguistically.	
	Aims	**Key messages**
	• To read easily, fluently and with good understanding.	• Writing consists of, and pupils need competence in:
	• To develop a love and appreciation of reading; to read for pleasure and information.	○ transcription (spelling and handwriting) *and*
		○ composition (articulating and structuring ideas).
	Key messages	• Pupils should plan, revise and evaluate their writing.
	• Pupils need competence in the two dimensions of word reading and comprehension.	• Grammar and punctuation are tools for writing.
	• Letters on the page represent the sounds in spoken words.	
	• A wide range of literature (fiction and non-fiction) should be both read and discussed.	
	• Develops imagination, knowledge of themselves and the world.	
	• Provides a 'treasure house of wonder and joy'.	
Spoken Language		
Aims		
To support development across the curriculum, cognitively, socially and linguistically.		
Key messages		
• Spoken language is laid out in a single statement for all year groups.		
• Speaking and listening are not included discretely.		
• Speaking and listening underpins the development of reading and writing.		
• The quality of what they hear and speak is vital.		
• Pupils must be assisted in making meaning clear.		
• Pupils must participate in discussion, role play and drama.		

(Continued)

Table 4.2 (Continued)

Speaking	Listening	Word reading	Comprehension	Transcription	Composition	Vocabulary, grammar and punctuation
Practitioners must know how to:		**Practitioners must know how to:**	**Practitioners must know how to:**	**Practitioners must know how to:**	**Practitioners must know how to:**	**Practitioners must know how to:**
• utilise their understanding that spoken language is *reflected and contextualised within the reading and writing domains, demonstrating the interconnectedness.*		• teach systematic synthetic phonics (SSP). This is statutory for decoding for beginner (unskilled) readers; • teach speedy recognition of familiar words using the school's SSP programme.	• provide opportunities for pupils to listen to, discuss and read a wide range of literature; • draw on children's linguistic knowledge, including vocabulary, grammar and knowledge of the world.	• utilise their understanding that spelling includes phonics (link between sounds and letters), morphology (word structure) and orthography (spelling structure); • use the school's SSP programme to teach encoding; • teach the words in the spelling glossary.	• develop pupils' awareness of: – audience; – purpose; – context; • develop a wide knowledge of vocabulary and grammar.	• use key terms in the vocabulary, grammar and punctuation; • use Appendix 2 of the National Curriculum to support discussion about language.

of the subject. Although the government acknowledges – for example, in the KS1 assessment guidance for 2022 (DfE, 2022b), that *pupils will have a wider range of knowledge and skills than those covered by statutory assessment* – the link to accountability carries the potential for schools to focus in their practice on these particular measurable outcomes, to the detriment of other aspects of the curriculum.

Table 4.3 *Statutory assessment in English*

Statutory summative assessment		
N.B. Assessments were paused for two years due to the pandemic and resumed for the school year 2021–22. The introduction of the reception baseline was delayed by a year. Key Stage 1 assessments will be made non-statutory in the year 2023–24.		
Reception	**Key Stage 1**	**Key Stage 2**
Baseline assessment An assessment against an assessment framework to take place within the first six weeks of school. It measures early vocabulary, phonological awareness and early comprehension. Designed *to create school-level progress measures for primary schools which show the progress that pupils make from reception until the end of Key Stage 2* (KS2). **The Early Years Foundation Stage Profile** The main purpose of the EYFSP is to support a successful transition to Key Stage 1 (KS1) by informing the professional dialogue between EYFS and Year 1 teachers. Although not intended as an accountability measure, the data of achievement against the Early Learning Goals are still published.	**Year 1 phonics screening check** This is a check of phonic knowledge, using single real and made-up words. Children are told which are the made-up words. These are designed to discourage children from using alternative strategies. Due to the introduction of the baseline assessment when children start school, these Year 2 assessments to inform reported outcomes will become non-statutory in 2023–24. **Reading test** A timed comprehension test. **Teacher assessments in writing** Assessed against a published framework. **Optional grammar, punctuation and spelling test** A timed test of knowledge in the national curriculum appendices.	**Reading test** A timed comprehension test. **Teacher assessments in writing** Assessed against a published framework. **Grammar, punctuation and spelling tests** Timed test of knowledge in the national curriculum appendices.

BEYOND FUNCTIONAL: KNOWLEDGE FOR EFFECTIVE TEACHING OF A PRIMARY ENGLISH CURRICULUM

This chapter aims to emphasise an understanding of knowledge in English beyond the scope of nationally standardised assessments. It is easy to get bogged down with assessment against limited attainment criteria and teach directly to them, but the broader aspects are key to children's progress in the subject and to remember them, and have them underpin practice. This can result in success in these assessments, but also in a richer understanding of English and make a stronger foundation for developing children's knowledge and progress, and future learning in the subject.

In terms of your own subject knowledge, we might look at it like this: you need to know the 'stuff' of English – what structural elements of the language are called and how they work. You therefore need to recognise them in speech and text, to be able to explain, use and model them, show how they work together, not just according to conventions to achieve 'correctness', but also to manipulate them for effect, to communicate intended meanings, to meet their purpose, to reach the intended audience. Although the curriculum is presented in discrete areas, it is crucial for us to recognise the interconnectedness of thought, the development of oral language (both listening and speaking), reading and writing, all the while remembering that language is a communication system driven by our social and cultural identities. This means that you also need to be an enthusiast for your subject, to know how to engage children, to value and link to what they already know, to have them motivated, to want to understand how language works so that they can use it to express themselves more fully, to enrich their lives, their knowledge, their understanding, to open up that 'treasure house of joy' – all to position themselves for future learning and options for the future, not just to get marks in an assessment.

Table 4.4 aims to summarise the key points. Be a reader and writer yourself, see yourself and all your children as readers and writers, then you can share your knowledge and enthusiasm and be able to model how language works, and the richness it brings of itself, and of and to the wider curriculum.

Table 4.4 Key things to remember

Talk is fundamental to the whole curriculum; it supports the development of thinking and all forms of communication and literacy.	Listening, attention and speaking are equally important. Talk is intrinsically linked to the development of thought, both as speaker and listener, and underpins the development of reading and writing. Opportunities for talk must be planned. It depends on a practitioner's knowledge of how to incorporate and model these.
Phonics is important for early readers and writers, but is not the only reading component to learn.	Phonological awareness (distinguishing between sounds) underpins the development of phonic knowledge and begins the journey to knowledge of the formal code-linking sound to marks on the page. Systematic synthetic phonics (SSP) is the statutory approach for schools in England, although the programme itself is the choice of the school. Decoding (sounding out of letters or combinations of letters, known as graphemes) supports reading. Encoding (blending the sounds, or phonemes, represented by individual letters or combination of letters) supports spelling and writing.

Reading opens doors to themselves and the wider world.	Reading involves word reading and comprehension; comprehension is an active process drawing on pupils' knowledge and life experiences.
	Reading for pleasure is not an afterthought – it is fundamental.
	In addition to phonics, word recognition must be taught alongside comprehension to help develop fluency and vocabulary.
	A wide range of fiction and non-fiction should be shared – read to, and with children, as well as developing their independent reading.
	Reading and discussion about quality texts are an effective starting point for writing.
Grammar and punctuation hold writing power.	Secure knowledge of terms and functions provides a shared metalanguage to discuss texts and writing with children.
	Grammar and punctuation are not transcriptional tools; when well understood, they can be chosen carefully to develop meaning and effective communication.
	Carefully selected texts demonstrating effective use of grammar and punctuation can support children's own attempts at writing.
Writing is complicated. It depends on the development of thought, spoken English and reading.	Spoken language and reading are necessary components in the development of writing, both over time and in lesson planning.
	Early writers are new to the writing code.
	Writing involves both transcription and composition.
	The transcriptional elements of spelling and handwriting/keyboard skills increase fluency and make writing easy to read.
	A secure knowledge of grammar, punctuation and vocabulary provides the widest scope to transfer thoughts and vocalised ideas on to the page.
The broader elements of English.	We are active participants in speaking, listening, reading and writing.
	Children's engagement will be facilitated by knowing children as individuals and being aware of what they bring, and by offering choice and agency.
	The components, although laid out discretely, are inextricably linked; sequencing of learning can make deliberate opportunities to secure those links.

PART 3: UNDERSTANDING THE DEVELOPMENT OF CHILDREN'S KNOWLEDGE IN ENGLISH

Our ambition for English, then, should be for children to acquire not only the skills and knowledge of the discrete elements that make up the curriculum, but also, by knowing them well, the positive attitude to the study of English that will empower them to become motivated and effective speakers and listeners, readers and writers. We have already heard how societal influences dictate what is deemed important; attention to this has the potential to both empower but also disempower and discriminate against children in their learning of English. However, through the subject of English, despite any perceived confines of the national curriculum or its associated assessments, we can celebrate and explore the complexity of language and literacy. Statutory and guidance documents provide a clear framework, but with your secure contextual and functional knowledge, these frameworks can provide the vehicle for effective English teaching for all primary pupils.

PROGRESSION IN THE NATIONAL CURRICULUM

The curriculum content is presented as a progression through the Key Stages as shown in Table 4.5.

Table 4.5 How the primary national curriculum for English is set out

	Spoken English	Reading	Writing	Vocabulary, grammar, punctuation	Spelling
Key Stage 1	Years 1–6	Year 1	Year 1	Year 1	Year 1
		Year 2	Year 2	Year 2	Year 2
Key Stage 2		Lower Key Stage 2	Lower Key Stage 2	Year 3	Year 3
				Year 4	Year 4
		Upper Key Stage 2	Upper Key Stage 2	Year 5	Year 5

It is worth noting that in the full national curriculum publication (DfE, 2013, p16) it states that it is not statutory to teach this content at this time. In practice, however, schools generally keep to the structure as it is laid out, and this will guide your planning for progression.

Linking back to all you have read in this chapter, there are a few key messages to bear in mind when planning for progression:

- Continue to develop talk; aim for progression in the expression of more complex thought and argument and remember that this is most effective through collaborative opportunities.

- Make explicit links from reading to writing.

- Identify texts that demonstrate what you want to show the children.

- Help children to recognise how authors use language for effectiveness.

- Use shared metalanguage (refer to the national curriculum appendices).

- Build opportunities for children to emulate what has been demonstrated; model examples of your own, vocalising your thinking.

- Let children try out things, play with vocabulary and sentence structures.

- Give choice and agency; allow children to find their own voice.

- Evaluate effectiveness together.

- Encourage editing to result in improved outcomes.

- Focus on effective communication as well as accuracy.

The following Table 4.6 is an example of progression: making links from reading to writing.

REFLECTION

How has the chapter helped you to see the interconnectedness of the discrete elements of the English curriculum?

PART 4: DEVELOPING YOUR KNOWLEDGE OF ENGLISH FURTHER

REFLECTION

How has reading the chapter helped you to think about national curricula and guidance for English as an entitlement for children as well as an expectation for schools? Can you see how it can provide a sound framework for children's progress in all aspects of English beyond statutory assessment?

SUBJECT ASSOCIATIONS

Belonging to a subject association is one of the best ways to develop your knowledge of research, policy, pedagogy and resources, including established and new children's literature. They will give you access to news, ideas, conferences, research, a professional community and more. We recommend the United Kingdom Literacy Association (UKLA). Some parts of the website can be accessed for free, but joining will broaden that access.

FURTHER RESOURCES

KEY TEXTS

A general text:

Bearne, E and Reedy, D (2018) *Teaching Primary English: Subject Knowledge and Classroom Practice*. London: Routledge.

Table 4.6 Progression: making links from reading to writing

Year group	Learning outcomes	Activities to develop the skills and understanding	Next steps
Reception	Listen to stories and demonstrate understanding when talking with others about what they have read. Retell stories. Write captions.	**Handa's Surprise by Eileen Browne** Read the story aloud. Repeat, encouraging the children to comment, question and discuss. Draw their attention to the pictures and what is happening. Reread the story at many points over the next few weeks, varying your focus or the way you do this to maintain the children's interest. For example, you could read one page and then pause before turning over, encouraging the children to say what comes next. Alternatively, you could read the story aloud but miss out the names of the fruits for the children to say. These kinds of strategies build familiarity with the story, help develop vocabulary and instil language skills such as sequencing.	Ask the children to sequence the story, using illustration from points in the story, or to retell the story to each other, using the book to show the cards, puppets or the book itself, using your modelling of reading stories to an audience. They could write captions on a storyboard, using their phonic knowledge to attempt plausible spellings.
Year 2	Participate in discussion about books. Use expanded noun phrases to describe and specify.	**Owl Babies by Martin Wadell** Read and reread the story aloud using story props – there are many different kinds of props you can collect or make, from plastic owls, fluffy owls of different sizes, knitted owls, magnetic story pieces, etc. Using a big book version, shared reading can enable children to join in the reading and allow you to focus their attention on aspects of the print. • Groups can read the book together with or without adult support. • Children could read or retell the story onto tape, together with sound effects. • Different language versions could be provided with support from bilingual support teachers or parents. • Children could read the story with you in groups, with multiple copies of the book. Discuss the story further in small groups, with children sharing their own responses to the owlets' predicament and their own	Collect examples of noun phrases from the story and present them to the children on large strips of paper – e.g., old bit of ivy, small branch, three baby owls. Ask them to read these and see if they recognise them from the story. Explain how a noun phrase gives us more information about a person, place or thing and can be used to make a story more exciting. Show children sentences from the story and, using shared writing, model how a noun can be expanded to include a noun phrase – e.g., "'Or a fox with big claws got her,' said Percy' could become "'Or a fox with big claws got her,' said Percy'. Allow the children to write some of their own ideas onto post-it notes and add these to sentences from the story. Create a bank of ideas on a display or large board and share them together.

Year group	Learning outcomes	Activities to develop the skills and understanding	Next steps
Lower Key Stage 2	Participate in discussions about books that are read to them and those they can read for themselves, building on their own and others' ideas. Identify how language and structure contribute to meaning.	**The Iron Man by Ted Hughes** Read Chapter 3, 'What's to be done with the Iron Man'. Talk about the scrapyard and all the things that were there. Have the section of the text that describes the scrapyard displayed for the children to see on an interactive whiteboard (IWB). What does the Iron Man think of the scrapyard? Pick out some of the phrases – e.g., 'greasy black stove'. Ask the children to turn to a partner and jot down some phrases together describing objects in the yard. Ask each pair to select one of these to read out and then put their ideas together on a flip chart or the IWB to create a class scrapyard poem.	Ask the class to help you improve the rhythm and structure of the poem. For example, phrases such as 'clink clink' could be used as a refrain. Read the poem out in different ways as a class.
Upper Key Stage 2	Identify how language, structure and presentation contribute to meaning. Writing: select appropriate grammar and vocabulary, understanding how such choices can change and enhance meaning. Proposing changes to vocabulary, grammar and punctuation to enhance effects and clarify meaning. Cohesive devices, single and multi-clause sentences.	**Skellig by David Almond** Discuss how the structure of sentences can provide cohesion, economy of writing and emphasis through the repetition of words or phrases or sentence structure. Identify examples of two often used structures in the book: 1. Paragraphs, or sections of paragraphs, where most sentences begin with the same subject pronoun, often 'I' or 'she'. See, for example, pp9, 16, 22, 23, 25. Sometimes the 'I' is omitted so it reads like a list: p30. 'I left him . . .' 2. Several short sentences of similar structure. These are often one-clause sentences or, if more than one clause, they are independent (look for co-ordinating conjunctions – and, but, or, nor, for, yet, so). Examples include on p23, *She put the book . . . ; on p26, 'I squeezed . . .; and on p30, I stood . . .* You may have been encouraging children to vary their sentences to provide interest and this is a good example of how seemingly simple structures can be used to good effect. (There are many more examples later in the book if you choose to tackle this when they have read more.) Provide an opportunity for children to find their own examples and develop discussion in pairs or groups, encouraging them to articulate the effect of the repetition and short sentences they find.	You could ask them to classify single clause and multi clause sentences, counting how many there are of each on one page to discover patterns through the book and the effects they have. You will need to revise co-ordinating and subordinating conjunctions first. You should aim to ensure they are familiar with the correct terminology and, above all, to understand the effect of these structures on the reader. They could try varying the structures, reading them out loud to each other in pairs, and articulating the difference in effect, choosing an example to share with the class. A narrative-writing task using characters and settings in the book can be used as a vehicle to try out these effects. Along with the teacher in a shared write, and then in pairs or independently, try out pairs of sentences with differences only in sentence structure. Discuss the subtle differences in meaning or emphasis.

A text to broaden your thinking about how to engage children:

Cremin, T (2015) *Teaching English Creatively*. London: Routledge.

Texts that focus on the strands of English:

Dombey, H (2010) *Teaching Reading: What the Evidence Says*. London: UKLA.

Dombey, H (2013) 'What we know about teaching writing'. *Preschool & Primary Education*, 1 (1): 22–40.

Reedy, D and Bearne, E (2021) *Talk for Teaching and Learning: The Dialogic Classroom*. London: UKLA.

A text that focuses on the use of texts to support learning in English:

McGonigle, S (2018) *Creative Planning with Whole Texts*. London: UKLA.

Further guidance for Early Years:

Early Education (2021) *Birth to 5 Matters: Non-statutory Guidance for the Early Years Foundation Stage*. St Albans, Early Education, pp66–75.

WEBSITES

Book Trust: www.booktrust.org.uk/ This is the place to go if you are looking for a book on a theme for a particular age group.

British Library: Discovering Children's Books. Available at: www.bl.uk/childrens-books. A wealth of ideas and resources.

Centre for Literacy in Primary Education (CLPE): https://clpe.org.uk/ Membership is free; this site will support you with ideas and resources.

Englicious: www.englicious.org/ This site will support you with grammar and punctuation. It is aligned closely to the national curriculum, so you can be sure you are using the correct terminology.

Reading for Pleasure: https://ourfp.org/ The site focuses on developing motivation and enjoyment in reading.

University of Exeter: Centre for Research in Writing: Writing resources for teachers: https://education.exeter.ac.uk/research/centres/writing/grammar-teacher-resources/ Debra Myhill heads up the research centre – a wealth of ideas to support the teaching of writing.

Writing for Pleasure: https://writing4pleasure.com/ Free and subscription content here.

REFERENCES

Almond, D (1998) *Skellig*. London: Hodder & Stoughton.

Ball, SJ (2017) *The Education Debate* (3rd edn). Bristol: Policy Press.

Browne, E (1994) *Handa's Surprise*. London: Walker Books.

Cambridge Assessment (2013) *What is Literacy? An Investigation into Definitions of English as a Subject and the Relationship between English, Literacy and 'Being Literate'*. Cambridge: Cambridge Assessment.

Cox, B (1989) *English for Ages 5 to 16*. London: HMSO. Crown copyright. Available at: www.educationengland.org.uk/documents/cox1989/cox89.html (accessed 19 October 2022).

Cushing, I (2022) Mind the 'word gap' – it's dangerous. *Tes magazine*. Available at: www.tes.com/magazine/analysis/general/word-gap-vocabulary-schools-racism-social-justice (accessed 3 October 2022).

DfE (2011) *The National Strategies 1997–2011*. London: DfE. Crown copyright. Available at: https://assets.publishing.service.gov.uk/government/uploads/system/uploads/attachment_data/file/175408/DFE-00032-2011.pdf (accessed 19 October 2022).

DfE (2013) *English Programmes of Study: Key Stages 1 and 2*. London: DfE. Crown copyright. Available at: https://assets.publishing.service.gov.uk/government/uploads/system/uploads/attachment_data/file/335186/PRIMARY_national_curriculum_-_English_220714.pdf (accessed 19 October 2022).

DfE (2021a) *Statutory Framework for the Early Years Foundation Stage*. London: DfE. Crown copyright. Available at https://assets.publishing.service.gov.uk/government/uploads/system/uploads/attachment_data/file/974907/EYFS_framework_-_March_2021.pdf (accessed 19 October 2022).

DfE (2021b) *Development Matters*. London: DfE. Crown copyright Available at: https://assets.publishing.service.gov.uk/government/uploads/system/uploads/attachment_data/file/1007446/6.7534_DfE_Development_Matters_Report_and_illustrations_web__2_.pdf (accessed 19 October 2022).

DfE (2022a) Our focus on literacy and numeracy – what it means in practice. Available at: https://educationhub.blog.gov.uk/2022/02/16/our-focus-on-literacy-and-numeracy-what-it-means-in-practice/ (accessed 3 October 2022).

DfE (2022b) *Key Stage 1 Teacher Assessment Guidance*. London: DfE. Available at: www.gov.uk/government/publications/key-stage-1-teacher-assessment-guidance/key-stage-1-teacher-assessment-guidance (accessed 3 October 2022).

DfEE (2000a) *National Curriculum Handbook for Primary Teachers*. London: QCA/HMSO. Available at https://dera.ioe.ac.uk/18150/7/QCA-99-457_Redacted.pdf (accessed 19 October 2022).

DfEE (2000b) *Grammar for Writing*. London, DfEE. Crown copyright. Available at: https://dera.ioe.ac.uk/4882/7/nls_gfw010702intro_Redacted.pdf (accessed 19 October 2022).

DfES (2006) *Primary Framework for Literacy and Mathematics*. London: DfES. Crown copyright. Available at: https://dera.ioe.ac.uk/14160/7/15f5c50f1b2f78d6af258a0bbdd23951_Redacted.pdf (accessed 19 October 2022).

Gee, JP (2004) *Situated Language and Learning: A Critique of Traditional Schooling*. London: Routledge.

Hadow, H (1931) *Report of The Consultative Committee on The Primary School*. London: HMSO. Available at: www.educationengland.org.uk/documents/hadow1931/hadow1931.html (accessed 19 October 2022).

Hughes, T (1968) *The Iron Man*. London: Faber & Faber.

Janks, H (2010) *Literacy and Power*. London: Routledge.

Laugharne, J (2007) The personal, the community and society: a response to Section 1. In V Ellis, C Fox and B Street (eds), *Rethinking English in Schools*. London: Continuum.

McIntosh, J (2015) *Commission on Assessment Without Levels: Final Report*. London: DfE. Crown copyright. Available at: https://assets.publishing.service.gov.uk/government/uploads/system/uploads/attachment_data/file/483058/Commission_on_Assessment_Without_Levels_-_report (accessed 19 October 2022).

Newbolt Report (1921) *The Teaching of English in England*. London: HMSO. Available at: www.educationengland.org.uk/documents/newbolt/newbolt1921.html (accessed 10 December 2022).

Office for Standards in Education (Ofsted) (2022) Research review series: English. Available at: www.gov.uk/government/publications/curriculum-research-review-series-english/curriculum-research-review-series-english (accessed 3 October 2022).

Plowden, B (1967) *Children and their Primary Schools*. London: HMSO. Available at: www.educationengland.org.uk/documents/plowden/plowden1967-1.html (accessed 19 October 2022).

Roberts (2022) *Assessment and Testing in Primary Education (England)*. London: House of Commons Library. Research Briefing, 5 December. Available at: https://commonslibrary.parliament.uk/research-briefings/cbp-7980/ (accessed 19 October 2022).

Street, B (1994) What's 'new' in New Literacy Studies? Critical approaches to literacy in theory and practice. *Current Issues in Comparative Education*, 5 (2): 77–91. Available at: www.tc.columbia.edu/cice/pdf/25734_5_2_Street.pdf (accessed 3 October 2022).

Tomasello, M (1992) The social bases of language acquisition. *Social Development*, 1: 67–7.

Vygotsky, LS (1978) *Mind in Society: The Development of Higher Psychological Processes*. Cambridge, MA: Harvard University Press.

Waddell, M (1992) *Owl Babies*. London: Walker Books.

Whetton, C (2009) A brief history of a testing time: national curriculum assessment in England 1989–2008. *Educational Research*, 51 (2): 137–59.

Wood, K (2012) *Education: The Basics*. London: Routledge.

Young, M (2014) What is a curriculum and what can it do? *The Curriculum Journal*, 25 (1): 7–13.

Young, M (2018) A knowledge-led curriculum: pitfalls and possibilities. *Impact*, 4: 1–4. Available at: https://discovery.ucl.ac.uk/10060317/1/Young_FINAL.pdf (accessed 3 October 2022).

Young, M and Muller, J (2010) Three scenarios for the future: lessons from the sociology of knowledge. *European Journal of Education*, 45 (1): 10–27.

5

GEOGRAPHY

MARTIN SUTTON AND JULIA MACKINTOSH

KEYWORDS: ENQUIRY; ENVIRONMENT; FIELDWORK; MAPPING; PLACE; SCALE; SPACE; TECHNOLOGY.

LINKS TO THE CORE CONTENT FRAMEWORK

High Expectations (Standard 1): 1.6

Subject and Curriculum (Standard 3): 3.1, 3.2, 3.4, 3.5, 3.7

Classroom Practice (Standard 4): 4.2, 4.7

Adaptive Teaching (Standard 5): 5.3

Professional Behaviours (Standard 8): 8.1, 8.2, 8.7

PART 1: EXPLORING GEOGRAPHY

WHAT IS GEOGRAPHY?

Geography has been described as the 'world discipline' (Bonnett, 2003) and is usually associated with an extremely broad array of issues, sometimes to the detriment of the subject's reputation. However, it is precisely this breadth that makes geography unique, traditionally comprising 'physical geography', which refers to the study of natural environments and processes on the earth (for example rivers, coasts, rainforests and deserts) and 'human geography', which refers to the study of topics such as cities, transport networks and population. It is a subject situated at the intersection between science and humanities. Therefore, geography is the subject that can help us to address some of the important questions in life (CCF 1.6): 'How can we tackle climate change?', 'Why has my energy bill increased?' and 'Will I need my umbrella today?' It can empower children to make good decisions in their life.

Geography is certainly not the learning of a list of inert facts about places and physical features (Geography Expert Subject Advisory Group, 2013). Geographers will tell you that the subject is 'living' (Lambert, 2009) and is happening all around us. Children themselves are excellent geographers, even before they commence formal education. By observing and asking investigative questions about the world around them, they start to make sense out of the chaotic systems and processes that they encounter every day of their lives. It is this enquiring nature that helps to define what a 'geographer' is and how they view the world around them.

WHY IS GEOGRAPHY IN THE NATIONAL CURRICULUM?

The subject of geography contributes to the primary curriculum at two levels. First, as pupils learn about places, people and the processes that form natural and human environments (DfE, 2013), they expand their mental map of the world and begin to develop the skills required to collect, interpret and communicate information from first-hand experiences and secondary sources of information. But geography has an additional and unique contribution to children's education in the primary phase. As they learn about people from other places, pupils are encouraged to value diversity, to become aware of the common needs of life and the differences in resources and opportunities that people have available to them (Catling and Willy, 2009). As they learn about the natural world, geography encourages children to engage with environmental issues, exploring how their own actions, and those of others impact on the environment at local and global levels. Geography, then, supports children to appreciate what it means to be a global citizen in the twenty-first century.

HOW HAS 'KNOWLEDGE' IN GEOGRAPHY DEVELOPED OVER TIME?

The geographical knowledge taught in primary schools reflects ideas that are considered to be geographically important by wider society, recent subject-specific developments and the ideological beliefs of those that create the curriculum (Hopkin and Martin, 2018). Studying the geography curriculum over recent years can therefore illustrate the changing focus and impact of these factors on the selection and organisation of geographical knowledge included in the primary curriculum.

In the years between 1944 and the Education Act in 1988, teachers had considerable autonomy over the geography taught in primary schools. Influenced by the *Plowden Report* (Central Advisory Council for Education, 1967), the subject was frequently taught through topics and cross-curricular approaches, and schools and individual teachers decided upon the knowledge, aims and approaches included in their lessons. Although there were some positives, national monitoring showed that there were many negatives, including an over-emphasis on human geography themes, a lack of physical geography and poor development of pupils' locational knowledge; in some cases, geography was entirely missing from the curriculum (Martin, 2013). In order to ensure parity of experience for all pupils in all subjects, a national curriculum was introduced in 1991, establishing centralised control over the knowledge taught in primary schools. To date, there have been four versions of the national curriculum (DES, 1991; DfE, 1995; DfE, 2013; DfEE/QCA, 1999). Table 5.1 compares the KS2 programme of study specified for one aspect of geography – rivers – to illustrate how the knowledge taught reflects contemporary trends and the ideological beliefs of the curriculum author.

Table 5.1 Programme of study for rivers at KS2 in the national curriculum for England

National curriculum	KS2 programme of study: rivers
1995 (DfE, 1995: 5-6)	**Rivers** In studying rivers and their effects on the landscape, pupils should be taught: • that rivers have sources, channels, tributaries and mouths, that they receive water from a wide area and that most eventually flow into a lake or a sea; • how rivers erode, transport and deposit materials producing particular landscape features - e.g., valleys, waterfalls. **Environmental change** In investigating how environments change, pupils should be taught: a. how people affect the environment; b. how and why people seek to manage to sustain their environment - e.g., by combatting river pollution.
2000 (DfEE/QCA, 1999: 114)	**Knowledge and understanding of patterns and processes** Pupils should be taught to: b. recognise some physical and human processes - e.g., river erosion, a factory closure - and explain how these can cause changes in places and environments. **Themes** c. water and its effects on landscapes and people, including the physical features of rivers (e.g., flood plain) or coasts (e.g., beach), and the processes of erosion and deposition that affect them. **Knowledge and understanding of environmental change and sustainable development** a. recognise how people can improve the environment (e.g, by reclaiming derelict land) or damage it (e.g., by polluting a river), and how decisions about places and environments affect the future quality of people's lives.
2014 (DfE, 2013: 3)	**Human and physical geography** Describe and understand key aspects of: • physical geography, including climate zones, biomes and vegetation belts, rivers, mountains, volcanoes and earthquakes, and the water cycle.

As can be seen in Table 5.1, the geography curriculum published in 1995 (DfE, 1995) reflects a traditional view of geography, albeit with a focus on answering geographical questions and requirement to study how people affect the environment. It contains a detailed specification of the geographical knowledge and understanding to be taught, with specific features and physical processes being identified. This has caused some to comment that this version of the curriculum left teachers with few opportunities for autonomy, positioning them as 'curriculum deliverers' of geographical knowledge (Hopkin and Martin, 2018).

The subsequent national curriculum (DfE/QCA, 1999) presents a different view of the type of knowledge that is considered important and worthy of study. Topographic features are no longer specified, and the topic of rivers is woven into a number of curriculum threads. Pupils learn that water has an effect on landscapes and people, and that people can improve and damage river environments, affecting the future quality of their lives. This reflects the 'creative curriculum' agenda of the early 2000s, highlighting links within and between subjects, causing many primary schools to return to the teaching of geography through topics. Overall, this curriculum emphasises skill development rather than the acquisition of facts.

The national curriculum published in 2013 (DfE) presents an interesting hybrid of previous models (CCF 3.1). Containing a core of 'essential knowledge' (DfE, 2013, p6), this curriculum is in part a return to a more traditional view of geography. Pupils are no longer required to learn about environmental issues, but they are required to learn factual knowledge about the United Kingdom, such as the names and locations of key topographical features (including hills, mountains, coasts and rivers). The specification of essential knowledge to be learned is, however, combined with less prescription in terms of topic content. For example, pupils should be taught to 'describe and understand rivers' (DfE, 2013: 3) but exactly what they should teach and how they should do this is not specified. Allied to this is the statement that *The national curriculum forms one part of the school curriculum* (DfE, 2013: 5), highlighting that schools should develop and design their curriculum beyond that specified. Reflecting the concerns of wider society, many schools provide opportunities for pupils to investigate environmental and sustainability issues, and in the 2020s are decolonising their geography curriculum in order to review how and what they teach about physical and human topics.

REFLECTION

What knowledge do you think is important for pupils to understand through their study of geography?

What other issues and topics would you add to the geography curriculum?

GEOGRAPHY NOW

The lack of diversity of pupils who study geography is an issue that is also rightly under scrutiny. The Royal Geographical Society (rgs.org, 2022) reports that *BAME students . . . are significantly underrepresented at A level and at university.* We suggest that this could be a focus of primary geography – to help recognise that geography is a subject for everyone.

REFLECTION

Why do you think that geography is underrepresented as children grow older?

How could you ensure that children see geography as a fully inclusive subject?

Movements to help to decolonise the geography curriculum are striving to eradicate terms such as 'slums' and to challenge the 'single story' (Adichie, 2009; Biddulph, 2011) – a concept where repeated negative references to a place unfairly distorts one's perception of it. Do we need to keep revisiting Bangladesh every time we need to study topics such as flooding, weather hazards, poverty or disease? The decisions that you make about which examples to use in your geography curriculum are crucial ones. Powerful learning can happen when the geography is relevant and meaningful to children's lives (Roberts, 2014; Vygotsky, 1962).

REFLECTION

Which local example of flooding could you embed in your curriculum?

To what extent do you examine differences in wealth around the UK?

The recent COVID-19 global pandemic has seen the importance of outdoor learning and engagement with the natural world included in many schools' recovery curriculums (DfE, 2021). Research has shown the well-being benefits to engaging with and learning about the natural world (Dyment et al., 2017; Harvey et al., 2020), sparking an interest in holistic Forest Schools and the exploration of local urban landscapes alike (Williams, 2019) from Early Years to Key Stage 2.

Due to a recent focus on a 'broad and balanced curriculum' (Ofsted, 2021), prompted by concerns over time allocated to core subjects at the expense of foundation subjects such as geography, the time allocated to geography and its profile in primary schools has been raised. Recent inspection frameworks suggest that at least one foundation subject will be scrutinised during each visit. This involves gathering empirical evidence on the curriculum intent, implementation and impact in an attempt to judge the quality of educational provision. Such a heightening of focus on geography has elevated its status in primary schools, but has uncovered some issues in terms of subject knowledge and confidence held by teachers. Subject associations such as the Geographical Association and the Royal Geographical Society offer excellent support through webinars, primary schemes of work, resources and TeachMeets.

It is important to appreciate that other countries in the United Kingdom have separate national curricula from that taught and learnt in England. Both the Welsh National Curriculum (Welsh Government, 2008) and the Scottish Curriculum for Excellence (Education Scotland, 2010) challenges children to conduct 'geographical enquiry' – language that does not feature in the current English version (DfE, 2013). Across the world, the geographical experiences of children vary due to differences in the curriculum that they are exposed to. New Zealanders are familiar with place-based learning, using local community volunteers and locations widen their learning (Brown, 2012), while Singaporean teachers are encouraged to use 'field-based enquiry' as their signature pedagogy (Seow et al., 2019).

It is clear that the diet varies, yet there are common ingredients that make good geographical learning. Roberts (2016) suggests that an enquiry-based approach and connecting with the pupils' own experiences are fundamental traits of learning and teaching 'good' geography.

WHAT MIGHT KNOWLEDGE IN GEOGRAPHY LOOK LIKE IN THE FUTURE?

Being regarded as a 'living' subject (Lambert, 2009), the discipline of geography is in a constant state of refresh. Every day, the news informs us of contemporary examples of flood events, droughts, journeys of migration and economic flux around the globe. It is therefore not surprising that geography will continue to change course into the future, not only in terms of new examples, but also with respect to changes in focus and completely new frontiers being pursued.

In recent times, there has been more traction towards sustainability education (Scoffham and Rawlinson, 2022) and its interrelationship with climate change education (Majid et al., 2022). Such emphasis at a school level will undoubtedly intensify, with pupils thinking about their own diet (Jones, 2019) through a sustainable, global citizen lens, prompting them to ask their teachers what they can do to make a difference (Hicks, 2019). The increasing profile of the UN's Climate Change conferences will undoubtedly help climate change and sustainability education to gain momentum in schools, with some (Dunlop and Rushton,

2022) questioning the effectiveness of current government policies in England. Subsequent iterations of the Geography national curriculum will need to include crucial omissions with regards to climate change and sustainability in order to empower pupils to make sensible decisions in the future (CCF 1.6).

PART 2: FOUNDATION KNOWLEDGE IN GEOGRAPHY

Knowledge in geography is often organised into a number of 'key' or substantive concepts. Taylor (2007) summarises the suggestions from a number of different authors, as shown in Table 5.2.

Table 5.2 Substantive concepts in geography

Space	This relates to the surface of the Earth and helps us to describe where a location is. It is used to examine the distribution (spread) of things like cities, disease, crime, deserts and where we live.
Place	When meaning is added to space, a place is 'made', such as having memories of walking through leaves in a park. Before visiting the park for the first time, it would be described as a 'space', yet after experiencing it and attaching memories, it can then be described as a 'place'.
Scale	Geographers look at how processes operate across several scales, from looking at how woodlice form part of an ecosystem in a pile of leaves, to the importing of your food from the other side of the world. Common terms used to help to describe scale include local, regional, national and global.
Connectivity	Links between places and phenomena are important to geographers. The relationships between countries who trade with each other can sometimes be a mutual one, or the reliance that a plant has on the nutrients in the soil, which itself in turn, relies on the plant for decaying leaf matter, is a good example of connectivity.
Processes	These are key to understanding how the world works. Examples include migration, evaporation, erosion, deforestation, urbanisation and precipitation.
Time	Geographers look backwards in order to look forwards. By understanding how a coastline has changed in the last 100 years, we may be able to predict how it may change in the next century. Changes in towns and cities can be seen around us on a daily basis as urban populations explode, as we move closer to having 8 or even 9 billion people on the planet.

In order to 'think like a geographer' (Jackson, 2006), we can ask particular questions that encourage this unique mindset. Storm (1989: 4) devised five key questions that we can ask in primary schools to foster this attitude:

- 'What is the place like?

- Why is this place as it is?

- How is this place connected to other places?

- How is this place changing?

- How would it feel to live in this place?'

Pro-environmental behaviours are clearly being developed with these questions, which can readily be used with photographs or pieces of texts in the classroom, or indeed when undertaking fieldwork. Storm's (1989) key questions link closely to the substantive concepts suggested in Table 5.2.

ENQUIRY APPROACH

A second way to promote good geographical thought in primary schools is to adopt an 'enquiry approach'. Roberts (2013) proposes this pedagogical attitude as a way of allowing the pupils to make sense of the geography themselves and equipping them to think critically, in a geographical way. Roberts (2013) suggests four traits that are present in geographical enquiry.

- **Question driven**, sometimes by the pupils themselves. A curiosity is ignited and the pupils 'need to know'.

- **Evidence based,** to try to answer the question(s). This can be in the form of numerical data, graphs, satellite images, photographs, maps, opinions from people, poems, newspaper articles or any other artefacts that contain deep layers of geographical meaning.

- **Geographical questions** are asked and geographical skills are used – analysing, describing and explaining patterns, mapping, analysing values, classifying and contrasting.

- **Reflection happens**. Pupils challenge evidence and think carefully about what they have learnt and how they have learnt it. Discussions about how the enquiry could be improved are key to the process.

Roberts's (2013) suggestion that geography is driven by questions, links well to Storm's (1989) ideas discussed previously. By building on these, Roberts (2013) devised a 'layers of inference' framework that challenges pupils to think more deeply about a geographical resource, as they progress through the questions, adding suggestions to each of the concentric answer boxes, with the resource placed in the centre.

- What does this tell me?

- What can I infer?

- What does it not tell me?

- What would I like to know?

It is important to acknowledge that these questions should be adjusted to suit the pupils' needs (CCF 5.3), but the principle remains the same. For example, a simplified sequence of questions may be written in response to a photograph of a flood:

- What can you see?

- What do you think has happened?

- Why has it happened?

- What don't we know?

The enquiry process lends itself to classroom talk, especially paired and group activities (CCF 4.7, 4.9), which enables the pupils to consolidate their ideas in method that is 'low stakes'. By solving a 'mystery' (Karkdijk et al., 2013), using careful crafted geographically rich clues, the children are making sense of the geography themselves, through discussion and reasoning, allowing them to make powerful connections between existing knowledge and new information (Roberts, 2013) (CCF 3.7).

MAPWORK

The use of maps is an important way that geographers acquire new knowledge and is distinctly mentioned in the Geography National Curricula for both Key Stages 1 and 2 (DfE, 2013).

Table 5.3 Key Stage 1 and 2 – Geography national curricula

Key Stage 1	Use world maps, atlases and globes to identify the United Kingdom and its countries, as well as the countries, continents and oceans studied at this Key Stage.
	Use simple compass directions (North, South, East and West) and locational and directional language – for example, near and far; left and right – to describe the location of features and routes on a map.
	Use aerial photographs and plan perspectives to recognise landmarks and basic human and physical features; devise a simple map; and use and construct basic symbols in a key.

(Continued)

Table 5.3   (Continued)

Key Stage 2	Use maps, atlases, globes and digital/computer mapping to locate countries and describe features studied.
	Use the eight points of a compass, four- and six-figure grid references, symbols and key (including the use of Ordnance Survey maps) to build pupils' knowledge of the United Kingdom and the wider world.

It is vital to expose pupils to these key mapping skills in order for them to access more learning in the future (CCF 3.5). By being able to 'read' an Ordnance Survey map by the end of their time at primary school, pupils will eventually be able to understand complicated relationships and interactions that they experience on maps in secondary school. It is important that they are shown how to do these mapping skills in primary school in order for them to build on this knowledge.

It is useful to integrate map work into lessons, rather than see it as a separate topic or module in your curriculum sequence. Regular map work, be it using an atlas, an Ordnance Survey map or a website, is important to do frequently so that the skills and understanding are maintained. The order in which the pupils encounter the skills is particularly important to think about, due to the way that they build on one another (CCF 4.2). For example, it is important to learn about 4-figure grid references before attempting 6-figures.

Table 5.4 Suggested activities for map work

Key skill	Suggested activities and topics	Misconceptions and obstacles (CCF 3.4)
Left/right/near/far	Instructing each other to turn left or right to walk round the classroom to reach a destination. Use of photos to discuss the 'foreground' or 'background'.	Confusing left and right.
Compass directions (4-point and 8-point)	Pupils can design their own mnemonic to remember 'N, E, S, W'. Explain how to work out the extra 4 points (NE, SE, SW, NW) and pupils fill in their own compass rose.	Pupils can sometimes experience literacy issues when using the words 'from' and 'to', which results in them reversing the direction of travel.
Symbols and key	Draw a sketch map of their classroom/bedroom/school. Design their own symbols to represent items and places.	Symbols must be simple and small enough to use on a map. Text is not necessary.

Key skill	Suggested activities and topics	Misconceptions and obstacles (CCF 3.4)
4-figure and 6-figure grid references	Design a treasure map with a grid over it. Integrate symbols and compass directions. Battleships games can improve understanding of grid references. Create a 'silly' story using place names from a map. Replace the names with grid references and ask pupils to complete the story and even write their own version.	The Eastings ('along the corridor') can be seen at the top of an OS map, yet in maths, the x-axis is always along the bottom of the graph. Imagining the 'tenths' on a map is difficult (Sutton, 2022).
Scale/distance	Use a ruler to measure how far places are away on a map to check the accuracy of measurement techniques. First use centimetres, then convert using simple scales - e.g. 1 cm = 1 km, building up to scales used on O.S. maps. (Remember that 1 square on these maps is a square kilometre.)	Practical issues over measuring accurately. Numeracy issues over converting measurements to real-life distances. Measurements of winding roads can be challenging. Consider using string to help.
Routes	Work towards using Ordnance Survey maps (or excerpts can be found free on Bing maps). How do the pupils walk to school? Is there another way? Can they describe their route using the map skills learnt to date? Can they be challenged by reading the relief of the land using contour heights, which are not currently on the national curriculum for KS1 or 2 (DfE, 2013).	Confusion as OS maps suddenly bring lots of information together. Colour-vision deficiency (more common in boys) may mean that differentiation and identification of some colours is more challenging. Travelling long distances on the route without describing what they are passing can lead to confusion when peers follow the route.

Sutton (2022) suggests using a template tool to help younger learners develop their understanding of six figure grid references. The moveable template allows the pupils to visualise a Northings and an Eastings grid on the grid square that they are focusing on. Without the use of the template, children can often lose their way when tracing their fingers to the edge of the map, to find the grid reference. By reducing the margin of error within the grid square itself, the pupils often gain confidence quickly.

Owens (2021) has developed an excellent free resource that will help primary teachers to 'inspire a sense of place and adventure' into OS map work. The fun activities fully engage pupils in using maps and consequently asking and answering geographical questions about the world around them in an enquiring way.

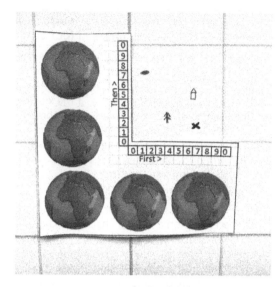

Figure 5.1 A six-figure grid reference template (after Sutton, 2022)

In order to allow primary pupils to use technology with their geography (or, more accurately, to learn geography *through* technology) the use of Geographical Information Systems (GIS) should be encouraged and is, in fact, cited on the national curriculum (DfE, 2013). This technology allows pupils to create, edit and view layers of geographical data. A simple example of this is looking at Google Maps on your phone. The digital map has layers of information that are superimposed to help you get from A to B. Information about the physical relief, buildings, roads, traffic volumes and even rainfall can be collated in one map to allow you to make sense of the world in a more measured way. This creates an excellent opportunity for pupils to explore many of the key concepts from earlier space, place, scale, change over time, connectivity, and physical and human processes.

A useful piece of software that allows primary-aged pupils to access GIS is called Digimaps for Schools. After subscribing, the user is able to access a digital version of the OS map for the whole of the Great Britain and a non-OS map for the rest of the world. This allows a number of geographical skills to be practised. Some simple suggestions are listed below, but their own website provides many more lesson ideas.

Table 5.5 Suggested digital mapping activities

Activity	Skills used
Draw a line from home to school, adding a distance.	Route mapping. Scale.
Add a photo to the map, taken on a field trip or sourced from the internet.	Adding meaning to space, creating a place. Looking for change in an area.

Activity	Skills used
Draw polygons around buildings and calculate their area.	Land-use mapping: colour code how land is being used differently – e.g., retail, forestry, residential. Suggest reasons why they are located where they are.
Use historic maps to look at how the coastline has eroded and measure its rate of retreat since 1890.	Change over time. Predict how issues may play out into the future, based on empirical evidence.
Use historic maps to draw on changes in buildings.	Look at changing use of space over time.

FIELDWORK

Geography wants to take children outside the school and into the streets and fields; it wants to take keyboard tappers out of their gloomy offices and into the rain or the sunshine (Bonnett, 2008).

Experiencing fieldwork is an essential dimension to geography (and a requirement according to DfE, 2013) at all Key Stages. By connecting the seemingly straightforward principles that they have learnt in the classroom, to the messy and chaotic real world, the pupils are given the opportunity to test out their ideas (CCF 3.5). Fieldwork links well to the enquiry process (Roberts, 2013) and allows children to experience an awe and wonder that cannot be replicated inside a building.

Fieldwork does not have to involve visiting exotic destinations such as Iceland or China, but instead should start with the 'local'. Opportunities exist within the school grounds and the local community that are rich locations for geographical learning. By adopting an approach with investigative questions, good geographical fieldwork can be very powerful indeed. Mackintosh (2022) outlines the case for fieldwork in more depth and reminds us that it is supportive of the enquiry approach (Tanner, 2021). Many of the ideas below can be coupled with the use of GIS in your classroom to help to present and analyse your findings.

Table 5.6 Suggested fieldwork ideas

Investigate	Suggested activities
Where should we locate a new school bench/pond/ vegetable garden/flower bed?	Using a digital thermometer and anemometer, measure temperature and wind speed/directions around the school. Discuss what makes an ideal site. Predict what you will find before you go. Were you right? Plot your data on a map, colour coding temperatures and using longer lines for wind strengths. Write a summary letter/presentation to the headteacher/ caretaker/grounds person.

(Continued)

Table 5.6 (Continued)

Investigate	Suggested activities
Which areas of the school grounds are most likely to flood?	Cut up a 2-litre water-bottle to make a tube. Pour a set amount of water into the tube and time it to soak into the ground (infiltration). Choose different sites - concrete, wet soil, dry soil, sand, bark, mud. What do you predict will happen? Why are we doing this? Plot your results on a map and colour code the speeds. What are the patterns? What can you suggest to help solve this issue?
What is the traffic like outside our school?	In pairs, pupils can count vehicle types (cars, buses, lorries, bikes) and direction of flow (left/right). Tally charts are useful and should be conducted safely away from the road. What do you expect to see? Why? Use bar charts and flow lines to present results on a map. Why are we doing this? (Fewer bikes, links made to climate change and sustainability.) Would we find something different on different days of the week and at different times of the day? Why?

A multitude of skills and concepts are addressed with fieldwork such as this – for example, GIS, mapping, scale, hypotheses testing, discovery, enquiry, numeracy, reasoning, justification and analysis, to name a few. Social benefits such as group work skills and the physical exercise that accompanies fieldwork is well reported (Harvey et al., 2020), in addition to the 'compelling case' for it in geography education (Lambert and Reiss, 2014, p9). The Geographical Association (n.d.) website is a rich source of fieldwork ideas that should be explored further.

PART 3: UNDERSTANDING THE DEVELOPMENT OF CHILDREN'S KNOWLEDGE IN GEOGRAPHY

In order to develop children's knowledge in geography, teachers need good subject knowledge themselves, an understanding of the elements that combine to produce a good geography lesson and how to sequence the teaching of skills and knowledge within the geography curriculum (CCF 3.2).

Recent inspections of geography teaching in primary schools (Ofsted, 2021) highlight the importance of teacher subject knowledge in the development of children's knowledge. Research by Catling and Morley (2013) identified that 'expert' primary geography teachers understand and use three types of geographical knowledge:

- **Knowledge of information about the world** – e.g., the facts that geography draws on, such as the names and locations of different countries.

- **Knowledge of concepts** – e.g., the big ideas that geography uses to understand and make sense of the world, including place, space, scale and environmental processes.

- **Knowledge as thinking geographically** – e.g., appreciating place as a significant idea and by taking an holistic approach in studies, such as exploring human and physical geography aspects and connecting local with global contexts.

These aspects of subject knowledge are also reflected in the elements of geography that should be included in a 'good geography lesson', as outlined by Roberts (2016):

- geographical data – first-hand observations or representations of the world through secondary sources;

- geographical ideas – the big ideas of geography or concepts, such as erosion or theories such as plate tectonics;

- locational contexts – the location and placing in context of the place or feature being studied.

In addition, a good geography lesson should connect with pupils' minds, building on and connecting to prior knowledge and supporting progress through the use of scaffolding (Vygotsky, 1962). It should allow pupils time to explore new information, relating it to what they already know and provide opportunities for them to make sense of this information through talking and writing (Roberts, 2016).

REFLECTION

How many of these elements did you include in the last geography lesson that you taught?

As noted by Ofsted (2021), teachers use their good subject knowledge to select and sequence curriculum content, considering how pupils build their geographical knowledge over time. A successful geography curriculum begins in the early years and builds year on year, developing pupils' expertise and knowledge so that pupils can draw on it in future learning. Table 5.7 below demonstrates how enquiry, fieldwork and mapping might be combined and sequenced to support the development of pupils' knowledge, skills and understanding across the primary phase.

Table 5.7 Development of mapping and fieldwork skills

Year group	Enquiry question	Fieldwork and mapping
EYFS	What would the Naughty Bus see in our school?	• Read the book *Naughty Bus* by Jan Oke. • Explore the outdoor area/school grounds, noting and naming features the Naughty Bus might see. • Follow a photo trail to find hidden toys. • Represent places visited using small world play.
1	How does our school change with the seasons?	• Visit one place in the school grounds four times over the year to observe weather and seasonal changes - focus on deciduous trees or plants. • Use simple weather maps and symbols. • Record seasonal changes using digital photographs and/or collections of natural objects.
2	How do we feel about the local park?	• Follow a route to and from the local park/play area, observing physical and human features. • Note how people use this place. • Express feelings about this place using happy/sad faces and plot on a map. • Discuss how we might improve the park.
3	How are rocks used in our town?	• Follow a predefined route around the local area, identify the location of buildings/natural features. • Record features using a digital mapping package and digital photographs and/or symbols, colour and a key.
4	How does our local river change from the source to the sea?	• Using OS maps, trace the route of a local river, identify the source and key features. • Make annotated drawings and field sketches to identify river features. • Collect data about river flow, shape of channel.
5	What is changing in our local area?	• Using historic OS maps, investigate how the local area has changed. • Using local news reports, investigate a current local issue - e.g., new development, traffic issues. • Collect data using questionnaires, tallies, etc. • Record findings using charts, graphs and freehand maps. • Suggest possible future changes.

Year group	Enquiry question	Fieldwork and mapping
6	How can we make the school grounds more sustainable?	• Pupils design own enquiry questions to investigate how sustainability of the school might be improved - e.g. biodiversity, use of resources, pollution. • Design and use tools to collect data - e.g., questionnaires using the Likert scale. • Use OS maps of school grounds to present findings and suggested improvements.

Starting in EYFS, pupils become familiar with their new school through first-hand sensory exploration, observation and talk, representing places using small world play. This is built upon in KS1 where pupils explore and engage with the school grounds and conduct a simple fieldwork enquiry designed to enhance their understanding of places, and human and physical geography. They identify features and record feelings on simple base maps. Finally, in KS2, pupils undertake more structured enquiries to answer geographical questions, using specific fieldwork techniques. They develop their fieldwork skills to enable them to plan and conduct their own enquiries, with guidance, by the end of the primary phase. Pupils use Ordnance Survey maps to follow the route of a river and identify changes in the local area. The varied use of maps, both current and historic, supports the progression of both map making and map interpretation skills. Table 5.7 supports the progression of pupils' competence in geographical enquiry and the development and application of skills in collecting and presenting fieldwork data (Tanner, 2021).

PART 4: DEVELOPING YOUR KNOWLEDGE OF GEOGRAPHY FURTHER

Recommended resources to develop your geographical knowledge are as follows.

PROFESSIONAL AND SUBJECT ASSOCIATIONS (CCF 8.1, 8.2, 8.7)

The Geographical Association (GA) is the leading subject association for geography teachers. It offers concessionary membership for trainee teachers and those in the early stages of their career. The GA has an excellent website that offers a wealth of resources and lesson ideas for Key Stages 1–5, across a broad range of geographical topics. Local branches, scattered around the UK, offer regular meets and the annual GA Conference is the showpiece event that attracts hundreds of primary and secondary teachers who gather to attend lectures, workshops, talks and discussion panels. www.geography.org.uk/teaching-resources

The Royal Geographical Society (RGS) attracts a broader spectrum of geographers. They too offer school resources, CPD and working groups, but the RGS also focuses on careers in the subject and study at undergraduate degree level and beyond. Their teaching resource page is well worth a visit – see: www.rgs.org/schools/teaching-resources

WEBSITES

In addition to these two associations, there are many excellent resources on the internet that will help you to plan geography into your curriculum. As geography is one of the most dynamic and fast-moving disciplines, the internet is a good way to keep up to date with access to live data, resources and ideas for lessons. The following table represents some good starting points.

Table 5.8 Useful resources for learning and teaching geography

Resource	Use	Visit
BBC Go Jetters (EYFS) Bitesize	Resources, videos and games. KS1 and KS2 video clips.	www.bbc.co.uk/cbeebies/shows/go-jetters www.bbc.co.uk/bitesize/primary www.bbc.co.uk/programmes/b006vj4c/clips
Bing maps	Free Ordnance Survey maps (change 'road view' to 'OS').	www.bing.com/maps
Check my street	Investigate local data in your area.	www.checkmystreet.co.uk
Digimaps	Web-based software for enhancing geographical thinking.	www.digimapforschools.edina.ac.uk
Field Studies Council	Plan some outdoor learning.	www.field-studies-council.org/primary-school-trips
Global dimension	A compilation of global learning resources.	https://globaldimension.org.uk/resources/
Greenpeace	Resources and games.	www.greenpeace.org.uk/all-resources/education-resources
Lizard Point	Hundreds of map and flag quizzes for all scales and places.	www.lizardpoint.com/geography
Met Office's WOW	Weather Observations Website. Investigate weather around the UK.	www.wow.metoffice.gov.uk

Resource	Use	Visit
National Geographic Kids	Resources and games.	www.natgeokids.com/uk/teacher-category/primary-resources/
Open Street Map	Crowd-sourced street map.	www.openstreetmap.org
Oxfam	Resources and games.	www.oxfam.org.uk/education/classroom-resources
Police	Crime stats in your area and beyond.	www.police.uk
Primary geography blog	Blog relating to EY and primary geography and the national curriculum.	www.primarygeography.wordpress.com
Reading International Solidarity Centre (RISC)	Resources for global learning.	www.toolkit.risc.org.uk/search
Royal Meteorological Society	Weather and climate change resources.	www.metlink.org/teaching-resources/
Ordnance Survey	Map skills and games.	www.mapzone.co.uk

PUBLICATIONS

The following publications may be particularly useful in further developing your geography knowledge and pedagogy.

Barlow, A and Whitehouse, S (2019) *Mastering Primary Geography*. London: Bloomsbury.

Catling, S and Willy, T (2018) *Understanding and Teaching Primary Geography*. London: SAGE.

Primary Geography journal, from the Geographical Association. A collection of articles written by class teachers and academics, with ideas on enhancing the learning and teaching of primary geography. Universities may well already permit you access to this publication – see: www.geography.org.uk/Journals/Primary-Geography

Scoffham, S (2013) *Teaching Geography Creatively*. Abingdon: Routledge. A wealth of lesson ideas that spans the whole of the geography national curricula for Key Stages 1 and 2 for a large range of topics.

Scoffham, S and Owens, P (2017) *Teaching Primary Geography*. London: Bloomsbury.

Willy, T (ed.) (2019) *Leading Primary Geography: The Essential Handbook for All Teachers*. Sheffield: Geographical Association.

SOCIAL MEDIA

Every resource that you use to influence your lesson design should be assessed carefully by you for bias and levels of appropriateness. The world of social media can sometimes be an excellent way to network with fellow colleagues. Geography-related Twitter users that have inspired us include the one shown in Figure 5.2. Investigate what they are discussing and also who they follow themselves.

Figure 5.2 Suggested Twitterers to follow

Geography is a subject that helps to explain the world around us, from the everyday to the exotic. Good geography asks questions about our environment and how it links to places and people. It is a relevant, contemporary, ever-changing subject that should grip the imaginations of all. Fieldwork, digital technologies and mapping can all be used to enhance its learning and teaching. An enquiry approach is a strong pedagogy to allow the pupils to make sense of the geographical evidence that they are presented with (Roberts, 2013). Geography is powerful and important, in that it can help pupils make decisions around poverty, climate change, sustainability and their own day to day lives. A carefully constructed geography curriculum can allow children to 'think like geographers' in a way that views the world through a unique lens.

REFERENCES

Adichie, CN (2009) The danger of a single story. Available at: https://sch.rcschools.net/ourp-ages/auto/2017/7/24/35784355/danger%20of%20a%20single%20story.pdf

Biddulph, M (2011) The danger of a single story. *Teaching Geography*, 36 (2): 45.

Bonnett, A (2003) Geography as the world discipline: connecting popular and academic geographical imaginations. *Area*, 35 (1): 55–63.

Bonnett, A (2008) *What is Geography?* London: SAGE.

Brown, M (2012) Developing a place-based approach to outdoor education in Aotearoa New Zealand. *Teaching and Learning Research Initiative Summary*, 1 (7).

Catling, S and Morley, E (2013) Enquiring into primary teachers' geographical knowledge. *Education, 3–13*, 41 (4): 425–42.

Catling, S and Willy, T (2009) *Teaching Primary Geography*. Exeter: Learning Matters.

Central Advisory Council for Education (1967) *The Plowden Report: Children and their Primary Schools*. London: HMSO.

DES (1991) *Geography in the National Curriculum: England*. London: HMSO.

DfE (1995) *Geography in the National Curriculum: England*. London: HMSO.

DfE (2013) *National Curriculum Programme of Study – Geography*. Available at: www.gov.uk/government/publications/national-curriculum-in-england-geography-programmes-of-study

DfE (2021) *Teaching a Broad and Balanced Curriculum for Education Recovery*. Available at: www.gov.uk/government/publications/teaching-a-broad-and-balanced-curriculum-for-education-recovery

DfEE/QCA (1999) *The National Curriculum Handbook for Primary Teachers in England, Key Stages 1 and 2*. London: DfEE/QCA.

Dunlop, L and Rushton, EA (2022) Putting climate change at the heart of education: is England's strategy a placebo for policy?, *British Educational Research Journal*.

Dyment, JE, Bell, A and Green, M (2017) Green outdoor environments: settings for promoting children's health and wellbeing. In H Little, S Elliott and S Wyver (eds) *Outdoor Learning Environments: Spaces for Exploration, Discovery and Risk-taking in the Early Years*. Crows Nest, Australia: Allen & Unwin Academic. pp. 38–58.

Education Scotland (2010) *Scottish Curriculum for Excellence*. Available at: https://education.gov.scot/education-scotland/scottish-education-system/policy-for-scottish-education/policy-drivers/cfe-building-from-the-statement-appendix-incl-btc1-5/experiences-and-outcomes/#soc

Geographical Association (n.d.) *Fieldwork Ideas and Resources*. Available at: www.geography.org.uk/Fieldwork-ideas-and-resources

Geography Expert Subject Advisory Group (2013) *Interpreting the 2014 Geography National Curriculum, Framework*. Available at: https://geognc.wordpress.com/about/support-for-key-stage-1-and-2-geography-curriculum-2014/

Harvey, DJ, Montgomery, LN, Harvey, H, Hall, F, Gange, AC and Watling, D (2020) Psychological benefits of a biodiversity-focussed outdoor learning program for primary school children. *Journal of Environmental Psychology*, 67: 101381.

Hicks, D (2019) Climate change: bringing the pieces together. *Teaching Geography*, 44 (1): 20–3.

Hopkin, J and Martin, F (2018) Geography in the national curriculum for Key Stages 1, 2 and 3. In M Jones, and D Lambert (eds) *Debates in Geography Education* (2nd edn). Abingdon: Routledge. pp. 17–32.

Jackson, P (2006) 'Thinking geographically', *Geography*, Autumn.

Jones, V (2019) Adapting our diets for global climate change: could eating bugs really be an answer? *Teaching Geography*, 44 (2): 72–4.

Karkdijk, J, Van Der Schee, J and Admiraal, W (2013) Effects of teaching with mysteries on students' geographical thinking skills. *International Research in Geographical and Environmental Education*, 22 (3): 183–90.

Lambert, D (2009) What is living geography? In D Mitchell (ed.) *Living Geography: Exciting Futures for Teachers and Students*. London: Chris Kington. pp. 1–7.

Lambert, D and Reiss, M (2014) *The Place of Fieldwork in Geography and Science Qualifications*. London: Institute of Education, University of London.

Majid, N, Reed Johnson, JA, Marston, S and Happle, A (2022) *UoR Climate Education and Sustainability ITT Framework*. CentAUR: Central Archive at the University of Reading.

Mackintosh, J (2022) *Making the Case for Fieldwork in the Primary ITT Curriculum*. Available at: www.nasbtt.org.uk/making-the-case-for-fieldwork-in-the-primary-itt-curriculum/

Martin, F (2013) The place of knowledge in the new curriculum, *Primary Geography*, 82 (3): 9–11.

Ofsted (2021) Geography in outstanding primary schools. Ofsted blog: Schools and further education & skills (FES), 21 May. Available at: https://educationinspection.blog.gov.uk/2021/05/11/geography-in-outstanding-primary-schools/ (accessed 25 October 2022).

Owens, P (2021) Teaching map work to inspire a sense of place and adventure. Ordnance Survey. Available at: www.ordnancesurvey.co.uk/documents/resources/teaching-map-skills-primary.pdf

RGS (2022) Equality, diversity and inclusion. Available at: www.rgs.org/about/equality,-diversity-and-inclusion/ (accessed 13 December 2022).

Roberts, M (2013) *Geography Through Enquiry: Approaches to Teaching and Learning in the Secondary School*. Sheffield: Geographical Association.

Roberts, M (2014) Powerful knowledge and geographical education. *The Curriculum Journal*, 25 (2): 187–209.

Roberts, M (2016) What makes a good geography lesson? Available at: www.geography.org.uk/write/MediaUploads/Teacher%20education/GA_ITE_TE_whatmakesageoglessongood.pdf

Scoffham, S and Rawlinson, S (2022) *Sustainability Education: A Classroom Guide*. London: Bloomsbury.

Seow, T, Chang, J and Neil Irvine, K (2019) Field-based inquiry as a signature pedagogy for geography in Singapore. *Journal of Geography*, 118 (6): 227–37.

Storm, M (1989) The five basic questions for primary geography. *Primary Geographer*, 2 (4).

Sutton, M (2022) Don't lose your pupils! Teaching six-figure grid references. *Primary Geography*, Summer.

Tanner, J (2021) Progression in geographical fieldwork experience. *Primary Geography*, 104: 13–17, Spring.

Taylor, L (2007) GTIP think piece – concepts in geography (Liz Taylor). Available at: www.geography.org.uk/write/mediauploads/research%20library/ga_tp_s_concepts.pdf

Vygotsky, L (1962) *Thought and Language*. Cambridge, MA: Massachusetts Institute of Technology Press.

Welsh Government (2008) *Geography National Curriculum*. Available at: https://hwb.gov.wales/curriculum-for-wales-2008/key-stages-2-to-4/geography-in-the-national-curriculum-for-wales/

Williams, C (2019) From forest school to urban school. *Primary Geography*, 100: 26–7.

6

HISTORY

JUDY CLARKE

KEYWORDS: ENQUIRY-BASED PRACTICE; SUBSTANTIVE AND SECONDARY CONCEPTS: THEMES AND SKILLS: SUBJECT-SPECIFIC VOCABULARY; FORMATIVE FEEDBACK.

LINKS TO THE CORE CONTENT FRAMEWORK

High Expectations (Standard 1): 1.3, 1.4, 1.6

How Pupils Learn (Standard 2): 2.1, 2.2, 2.5, 2.8

Subject and Curriculum (Standard 3): 3.1, 3.2, 3.5, 3.7, 3.10

Classroom Practice (Standard 4): 4.1, 4.2, 4.6, 4.7, 4.9

Adaptive Teaching (Standard 5): 5.3, 5.4, 5.6

Assessment (Standard 6): 6.1, 6.3, 6.4, 6.5, 6.6

Managing Behaviour (Standard 7): 7.1, 7.4, 7.7

Professional Behaviours (Standard 8): 8.1, 8.2, 8.5, 8.7

PART 1: EXPLORING HISTORY

WHAT IS HISTORY?

History is more than the rote learning of facts or dates. Actively enquiring into the past considers causes, continuity and change, promoting a critical understanding of how significant events shaped our world.

REFLECTION

Can you identify connections across the programme of study?

Can you identify the links between local, national and global history?

Why are enquiries that use themes to develop prior learning more valuable than memorising disconnected facts?

How confident are you about introducing diversity and decolonisation into your teaching?

WHY IS HISTORY IN THE NATIONAL CURRICULUM?

The Purpose of study across Key Stages 1–3 states that:

History helps pupils to understand the complexity of people's lives, the processes of change, the diversity of societies and relationships between different groups, as well as their own identity and the challenges of their time.

(DFE, 2013, p188)

Carefully structured primary history will identify opportunities to sequence learning encouraging pupils to interpret current local, national and global issues through a considered evaluation of the past.

HOW HAS KNOWLEDGE IN HISTORY EDUCATION DEVELOPED OVER TIME?

While dates cannot change, the way in which evidence is interpreted and presented has changed. Many historians and social commentators around the world now analyse events through a wider range of, sometimes controversial, lenses. This involves moving from the traditional, narrow, white, privileged, usually male, Western approach to evaluating the impact across a wider social, political or economic viewpoint.

This change has implications for teaching primary history. Key Stage 1 requires pupils to consider *aspects of change in national life.* Key Stage 2 pupils *should construct informed responses that involve thoughtful selection and organization of relevant historical information* (DFE, 2013, p189). Rather than repeating back facts, interrogating primary and secondary sources enables pupils to recognise the importance of historical developments, including cultural diversity. David Olusoga illustrates this; drawing on archaeology and forensic science, he shows that soldiers and traders from across the Roman Empire worked and settled in Cumbria (Olusoga, 2020).

DIVERSITY AND DECOLONISATION ACROSS THE HISTORY CURRICULUM

Schools have the freedom to interpret statutory content in ways that reflect their localities and cohorts. Introducing cultural diversity and discussing decolonisation enriches teaching. Investigating the impact of the Industrial Revolution on their local area or as a national turning point, encourages pupils to consider the wider colonial implications of the transatlantic slave trade, as well as social changes.

DIVERSITY

Diversifying the history curriculum involves focusing on events through a more inclusive, critical lens. To avoid tokenism, consider integrating the diverse stories and narratives of people who have previously been left out of traditional Western narratives across studies, rather than as an annual 'bolt-on' (Lyndon-Cohen).

Table 6.1 extends and further diversifies the non-statutory list of significant individuals in the past (KS1). Engage pupils through displays of biographical texts, including picture books.

Table 6.1 KS1: increasing diversity

Ada Lovelace	Alan Turing	Amelia Earhart
Anthea Gibson	Beatrix Potter	Emmeline Pankhurst
Floella Benjamin	Greta Thunberg	Harriet Tubman
Jane Goodall	Jesse Owens	Mahatma Gandhi
Margaret Hamilton	Martin Luther-King	Mary Anning
Mother Theresa	Nelson Mandela	Rosalind Franklin
Stephen Hawking	Valentina Tereshkova	Walter Tull

Referencing the concepts at Table 6.2 promotes diversity. Threading invasion, migration and settlement across KS2 emphasises the complexity of British society. Introducing related texts and writing tasks into English, as well as history lessons, embeds this. Take care however, to avoid anachronisms. Stone Age people did not keep diaries or read newspapers. Ask pupils to write reports that evaluate archaeological finds, and analyse similarities and differences within and across periods.

Table 6.2 S2 Developing diversity

Colony	Education	Empire
Farming	Health	Law and Justice
Power	Religion	Ritual

(Continued)

Table 6.2 (Continued)

Slavery	Society, including the role of women and childhood	Suffrage
Technology	Trade	Travel

DECOLONISATION

The English Heritage and Historic England websites identify historical links between wealth and slavery in Britain. The Historical Association's website and journal suggest ways in which primary teachers can decolonise history.

The National Trust's child-led colonial countryside project investigated the legacy of the British Empire, including colonial trade and slavery, with primary pupils. Pupils asked robust questions about artefacts, rewriting guidebooks and labels to critically deconstruct assumptions and stereotypes.

Working with Liverpool's Walker Art Gallery, the International Slavery Museum, has also developed a community-led project, asking searching questions about the significance of the trade triangle to the wealthy families who built Liverpool.

The national curriculum requires a local history study at both Key Stages. KS2 pupils must study an aspect of British history beyond 1066; the achievements of the earliest civilisations and Ancient Greece, and a non-European society that contrasts with British history. These studies should encourage pupils to ask questions, think critically and develop perspective and judgement about Britain's past and current roles and responsibilities within a local, national and global context. Table 6.3 identifies ways of extending this within the post-1066 study.

Table 6.3 Decolonising the post-1066 study

Black musicians. From the Tudors to today	City street names	Development of the British Empire
Who owns the Benin bronzes?	Who owns the Elgin Marbles?	Popularity of Georgian coffee and chocolate houses
Significant local and national buildings	Significant local and national families	Significance of the trade triangle
Statues and other commemorative artefacts: stained-glass windows and memorials, including gravestones	Sugar in your tea?	Windrush

HISTORY EDUCATION NOW

The revised national curriculum became statutory across state-funded schools in England in September 2014. Replacing the 1999 curriculum, Key Stage 1 history now identifies four focus areas. At Key Stage 2, the change removed the previous episodic units. History should now be delivered as a discrete subject, rather than as *submerged within an integrated curriculum structure* (Maddison, 2014, p5). Teaching should encourage pupils to think and talk like historians, using subject-specific vocabulary to make connections. While planned links to other subjects may be valuable, the importance of recognising history as history is vital to ensure that *pupils gain a coherent knowledge and understanding of Britain's past and that of the wider world* (DfE, 2013, p188).

Ofsted's revised Education Inspection Framework responded to concerns about *curriculum narrowing and an over-focus on data* (Ofsted, 2019, p5). The framework emphasises the importance of evidencing subject *intent* through focused, long-term planning; the *implementation* of these plans through well-informed teaching, including challenging activities, and evaluating the *impact* on pupils' learning (Fearn and Keay, 2021). This has implications for sequencing learning; securing teachers' subject knowledge through high-quality resources, including courses, and assessing formatively to check understanding. The framework confirms the importance of an ambitious curriculum across all primary schools that delivers subject-specific aims and objectives inclusively (Maddison, 2014).

WHAT MIGHT HISTORY EDUCATION LOOK LIKE IN THE FUTURE?

Planning to enrich primary history by introducing diversity and decolonisation locally, nationally and globally to reflect historians' interpretations will continue to evolve.

The significance of local and regional history is increasing nationally and internationally. The Historical Association, county and national archive offices, family history websites, social media groups and local museums provide engaging resources, including business directories, census data and historical photographs. Historic England offers free online learning resources, including an online data base, historical mapping and aerial photographs of English towns and cities. Regional Local Heritage Education managers work with schools in target areas to develop an understanding of the significance of local heritage.

Local history develops a critically important sense of place. Interrogating primary and secondary sources to evaluate the impact of history, from pre-history to the twenty-first century, on pupils' local area and the wider region establishes connections, highlighting continuity and change.

Technology is changing teaching. Animations, including 3D resources from Mozaik Education, engage pupils, bringing history to life. Interacting with visuals to compare life in Britain with, for example, life in Greece around 2000 BC/BCE is inclusive, challenging all abilities. Virtual reality headsets enhance this. Digital quizzes check prior learning and understanding formatively, as robustly as written summative tests.

Using technology to interrogate Ordnance Survey maps and record findings adds depth to historical enquiries through virtual fieldwork. Digital, including historical mapping identifies and records change locally and nationally. Table 6.4 demonstrates how making connections to physical geography, challenges pupils to investigate and explain their local area.

Table 6.4 Local invasion and migration

Roman, Saxon and Viking settlements in our area: why did they settle here?
• Search for our local area.
• Use the table of Latin, Saxon and Viking place names to identify settlements.
• Record your findings on the digital Ordnance Survey map.
• Print your map.
• Choose an example from each category.
◦ Identify the era.
◦ What does the prefix or suffix mean?
◦ Use a grid reference to locate the place.
◦ Describe the importance of physical geography.
Extension
• Can you identify other significant evidence?

Recording pupils' findings allows them to be shared on the school website or via carefully monitored social media, motivating pupils and raising the profile of history.

PART 2: FOUNDATION KNOWLEDGE IN HISTORY EDUCATION

EARLY YEARS FOUNDATION STAGE: UNDERSTANDING THE WORLD

The revised Early Years Framework requires pupils to make sense of the past. Using role play and continuous provision areas to introduce the past creates critically important opportunities to enrich vocabulary, supporting all seven areas of learning (Bradbury, 2021).

Visual resources encourage pupils to use their senses. Artefacts from, for example, Janet and Alan Ahlberg's *Peepo!*, illustrate how daily life was both similar and different in the past (Crawford, 2016).

Table 6.5 Introducing the past

Use pictures, photographs and artefacts, including toys, to highlight social and technological change. Encourage pupils to label the items.	Create mathematical opportunities to represent pupils' lives from birth. Create timelines from Lego or Multilink. Count across the years.
Develop talk, observational and motor skills by creating simple jigsaws from photographs.	Sequence familiar routine events.
Share picture books illustrating social change.	Sequence and retell stories.

Challenging pupils to use subject-specific vocabulary (Table 6.6), engages, stimulates and extends pupils' thinking, guiding, prompting understanding from the earliest stage (Alexander, 2004).

Table 6.6 Early vocabulary

After	A long time ago	Before I was born . . .	Before (named adult) was born . . .
Brother	Daughter	Different	In the past
Last week . . .	New	Old	Parent, grandparent
Picture	Photograph	Sister	Son
Story	Then	The same	Today
Tomorrow	Yesterday	What?	When?
When I was little . . .	When (adult) was little . . .	Where?	Who?

Share vocabulary with teaching assistants. Encourage them to check understanding. Pupils' spoken responses provide valuable assessment material.

The historic past is an abstract concept for Reception pupils (Jenner, 2021a). Downing and Boydell (2022) suggest that investigating the local community engages the youngest pupils, preparing them for later local history.

Discussing historic and current photographs with school staff, governors and carefully identified visitors, introduces oral history as a significant source. These early, age-appropriate, meaningful encounters embed pupils' use of the language of time and promote a sense of place, introducing *knowledge (which) will be highly generative in future* (Jenner, 2021a, p41).

KEY STAGE 1

The Purpose of study, Aims and Attainment targets for history are the same across Key Stages 1 to 3 (DfE, 2013). Key Stage 1 introduces the historic past, preparing pupils for Key Stage 2. Statutory subject content is not allocated to year groups.

The freedom to move beyond suggested examples, allows schools to plan studies which reflect their context and cohorts. Continuing to evaluate similarities and differences over time, through stories, local and family histories, engages pupils, developing their conceptual understanding (Jenner, 2021a).

Pupils move from sequencing routines to creating and interacting with timelines that construct the past, identifying intervals and durations across events and periods of time. Creating scaled timelines from Lego bricks or Multilink, organised in multiples of ten, introduces duration.

Manipulating timelines encourages pupils to actively represent the passage of time. Simple labelling, as at Figure 6.1, contextualises vocabulary, using patterns to introduce decades.

Challenge pupils to use the subject vocabulary at Table 6.7.

Table 6.7 Extending vocabulary

ancient	artefact	because	century centuries	chronology chronological order
date dates	decade decades: 1970s, etc.	evidence	generation generations	great grandparent
historians	homes houses	impact	important	memory memorial monument
modern	monarch reign	opinion	photography black-and-white photographs	painting portrait
sibling	significant	similar	source	technology

Pupils who have already sequenced events, used some historical vocabulary, and discussed similarities and differences in the past in their local area are ready to become history detectives.

CHANGES WITHIN LIVING MEMORY

Listening to stories, evaluating visual resources, including artefacts, photographs and film, and continuing to prepare questions, introduces enquiry skills. This helps pupils to understand how known adults have experienced change. Illustrating the themes suggested at Table 6.8, visually on a timeline defining – for example, Elizabeth II's 78 reign, adds depth.

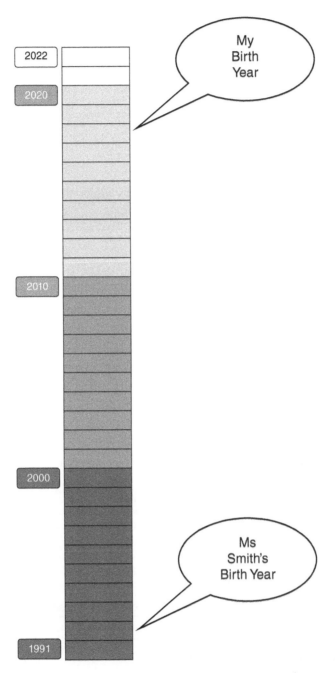

Figure 6.1 A simple timeline

Table 6.8 *Changes in living memory*

Entertainment	Fashion	Holiday destinations
Household appliances	Shopping: markets to online	Sport and leisure
Technology: telephones, televisions, computers	Toys	Travel

Table 6.9 *Investigating social change*

Investigating change: children's TV
Draw on pupils' interests and ideas to write a homework questionnaire.
Evaluate responses.
Watch the earliest programme on YouTube: • Would you enjoy watching this programme?   • Scaffold or scribe short sentences explaining why/why not.
Compile a class questionnaire for an expert witness: • Did you watch programmes on a phone?   • Can we watch your favourite programme today?   • How has TV changed since you were at school?
Interview the witness: • Record adult and pupil responses.
Display: Create a scaled timeline, with pupils from the earliest programme to today.   • Add photographs illustrating programmes and technological change.   • Add significant events – for example, the introduction of colour TV and the moon landings.   • Add pupils' questions, interview responses and pupils' observations.   • Photograph the display for pupils' books.
Reflection: • Two things I will remember ...   • One thing I would still like to know.
Scaffold sentences or scribe responses for pupils' books and the display.

NATIONAL EVENTS BEYOND LIVING MEMORY

EVIDENCING SIGNIFICANT CHANGE: THE GREAT FIRE OF LONDON

Investigating how events in the past affect pupils' lives locally and nationally today establishes connections across time. The legacy of the Great Fire of London is important. While only a few people were reported to have died, 100,000 people were rendered homeless, forcing civic and social change. Although there were some stone buildings in London by 1666, the fire prompted changes to health and safety practices nationally, including building regulations, town planning, the introduction of fire hydrants and insurance. Pupils who have located local emergency services during EYFS therefore draw on prior learning to contextualise the emergence of a national fire service. New learning, including scaffolding extracts from Samuel Pepys's diary develops skills, broadening and deepening knowledge and understanding. Mapping the spread of the fire identifies it as a significant factor in the development of modern London, creating a link to locational geography.

Table 6.10 *Impact of the Great Fire of London*

The Great Fire of London
*Photographs of The Monument, Monument Tube Station and local fire station. What is a monument? Are these photographs connected? Record responses.
Use visual resources to introduce the enquiry. Record observations.
How do we know about the fire? Extracts from Pepys's diary. Scaffold reading and discussion. Why were Pepys, King Charles I and Wren significant? Hot seat these key figures.
How did London and firefighting change? Grid/jigsaw images of artefacts, London, in 1666 and today. Compare seventeenth-century city housing and street scenes with modern cities. Compare seventeenth-century firefighting with today.
Assessment: previous photographs.* Repeat earlier questions. Reflection: The fire happened because . . . This would not happen today because . . . Two things I will remember: One thing I would still like to know: Scaffold/scribe short sentence responses.
Display: Timeline the fire and emergence of the national fire service. Add pictures and speech bubbles, recording pupils' observations.

LIVES OF SIGNIFICANT INDIVIDUALS

Identifying historic figures – for example, Elizabeth I and Elizabeth II – as lenses to compare aspects of life in different eras, encourages pupils to consider how lives have changed across longer periods (Table 6.11). Use carefully selected visuals and texts, including stories.

Table 6.11 Historic change

Buildings, pre- and post- 1666	Cooking	Education
Fashion	Holidays and travel	Homes
Leisure	Medicine	Music

LOCAL HISTORY

Continue to invite local experts into school to respond to pupils' prepared questions. Collaborate with EYFS staff to develop KS1 pupils as local experts. Responding to purposeful questioning from reception pupils will *consolidate their understanding* (Downing and Boydell, 2022, p67).

Explore the local area, using mapping to identify and record change (Table 6.12). Historical and current photographs, including your own, confirm change and similarity across time. Display photographs, mapping and pupils' observations.

Table 6.12 Local continuity and change

High streets	Housing	Parks
People	Roads	Schools
Shops	Significant buildings	Transport links

KEY STAGE 2

Key Stage 2 evaluates change, investigating cause, similarity and difference, and significance across identified British and global eras, preparing for post-1066 studies across Key Stage 3. Content is not allocated to year groups. Delivering studies chronologically may support understanding; however, there is *no statutory requirement to teach them in a* chronological sequence (Maddison, 2014, p7).

Promote deeper learning through subject vocabulary (Table 6.13), including open questions What? When? Where? Who? Recent archaeological and scientific advances add significance to revisiting how we know during enquiries. Reference local and regional history across pre- and post-1066 studies and scaffold pupils' understanding of written sources. Prepare timelines with pupils to record their developing knowledge and understanding on squared paper.

Table 6.13 KS2 vocabulary

AD/CE BC/BCE	agriculture	anachronism	ancestor	archaeology archaeologist
cause causation consequence effect	change continuity	city town village	climate climate change	colony
communication	culture	democracy	difference similarity	diversity
DNA	empires	era	excavate excavations	immigration
invader invasion	kingdoms	migration	religion	resources
settlement settler	significance significant	society hierarchy social class slavery	sources primary secondary interpret	trade trade network trade route

BRITAIN PRE-1066

THE STONE AGE TO THE IRON AGE

Recognising geographical, climate, lifestyle and technological changes across British pre-history is important. Archaeological advances trace local and national changes from palaeolithic nomadic hunter-gatherers who sheltered in caves, through mobile Mesolithic seasonal settlers, to Neolithic farming communities.

The introduction of bronze, a mixture of copper and tin which makes the metal harder than pure copper, caused further social change, including harsh child labour in mines. While the use of stone and bronze continued, the discovery of iron secured advances in farming tools and weaponry.

Table 6.14 Investigating pre-history

What was the impact of climate change during pre-history?	Hunter-gatherers, traders or farmers?
Did everyone live in a cave?	How did the Bronze Age change fashion?
How did shelters, houses and homes change across pre-history?	How did technology change lives?
What did people believe? Did this change?	Is there any evidence of pre-history in our area?

THE ROMAN EMPIRE AND ITS IMPACT ON BRITAIN

Pupils who are aware of technical advances and trade throughout pre-history will make connections, understanding that, at the time of Julius Caesar's attempted invasions in 55 and 54 BC/BCE, the Romans knew about Britain's mineral wealth. Roman expansion north in AD/CE 43 provided access to gold, silver, tin, coal and salt, in addition to copper and iron. Enslaved Britons worked the mines. Roads were built to London, securing exports across the Empire.

The change from tribal hierarchies to an increasingly Romanised society was gradual. To counter opposition, the Roman army garrisoned the country and established administrative centres, creating an efficient network of link roads from around AD/CE 80. Remains of stone walls and buildings in the north (Britannia Inferior), and the south (Britannia Superior), evidence the existence of colonial towns. Latin inscriptions on monuments and other writings develop enquiries into cultural and religious change (Table 6.15).

Table 6.15 Investigating Roman Britain

Why did the Romans trade with Iron Age Britain?	Which countries were part of the Roman Empire by AD 42?
	Map the countries and trading networks.
How did tribal leaders respond?	Would we have lived in Britannia Superior or Inferior?
	What was the impact on our region?
Did daily life change for everyone?	Why and where did Hadrian build his wall?
	Is there evidence of occupation north of the wall?
How diverse was Roman society?	What was the role of women across Roman society?
Did beliefs and religious practices change?	When and why did the occupation end?

SETTLEMENT BY THE ANGLO-SAXONS AND SCOTS

Pupils who know that not everyone in the then known world lived in the Roman Empire will understand that the Romans traded and threatened (and were threatened by) other societies. Vulnerable to attack from the sea, Britain was invaded by Northern European Angles, Saxons and Jutes, and Scots from Ireland. Invasion, migration and settlement introduced social and cultural, including religious, change. Settlements developed along fertile river valleys or at the mouths of rivers. Place names suggest the origins or nature of the settlement: *ing* (people of) suggests an early settlement, named after a chieftain; *wic*, a dairy farm. By the early seventh century, rival kingdoms developed, some kings converted to Christianity.

Artefacts, including burial goods, suggest a period of transition from pagan beliefs to Christianity. Apparently, Christian burials took place in locations that would have been ritually significant during pre-history. Portable high-status goods and jewellery combined scenes and symbols from Christianity with pagan images. Over time, influential monasteries were established, often near the coast, by significant individuals, including noble women. Renowned, particularly in the North East, for Christian art, including illustrated manuscripts, monasteries had an important social role, caring for the poor and homeless. Table 6.16 identifies investigations.

Table 6.16 Anglo-Saxon settlement

How did the invaders know about the Roman withdrawal from Britain and the fall of the Roman Empire? Where did the invaders come from?	Did the invaders settle in our region?
Which kingdom would we have lived in?	Did daily life change?
What do stories, including mythology, tell us about the invaders?	How would you recognise an important settler?
Did Christianity change society?	What were the roles of women across society?

THE VIKING AND ANGLO-SAXON STRUGGLE

Pupils who are aware of the wealth of the Anglo-Saxon monasteries will understand that the coastal religious communities were known to Scandinavian traders. They will understand why they attracted sea pirates. Viking raids threatened large areas of Europe. People were seized, with valuable portable religious art, including manuscripts and richly jewelled artefacts. While some people were enslaved or killed, many of status were held hostage and ransomed, as were artworks. The *Anglo-Saxon Chronicle* (AD/CE 890) describes the AD/CE 793 raid on Lindisfarne in dramatic language. The report includes fire-breathing dragons, but no mention of the horned helmets depicted in nineteenth-century artwork and Hollywood films. Versions of the *Chronicle*, with other sources, can be found on the British Library website.

As power shifted between the Saxon kingdoms, Viking activity continued. Pupils should investigate the nature of the emerging kingdoms and the struggle for ultimate control, ending in 1066 (Table 6.17). Legacies include English towns and counties, the development of laws and justice, and the Royal Mint.

Table 6.17 The struggle for England

What was the Anglo-Saxon response to the raids and settlement?	How did the struggle shape England?
What was the role of women across society? Is there any evidence of leadership by women?	Why did some leaders convert to Christianity?
Did the Vikings settle in our area?	Why is King Alfred known as the great? What might he have looked like?
How did Edward the Confessor contribute to the end of Saxon rule?	Was William the Conqueror a Viking?

PRE-1066 LOCATIONAL KNOWLEDGE

Ensure that pupils use globes and mapping to identify locations across Britain, the Roman Empire, Germany, Denmark, the Netherlands, Scotland, and Ireland. Ordnance Survey and historical mapping highlight the relevance of physical geography.

LOCAL HISTORY

Local archaeology companies, museums and history groups can support teaching. Historical mapping identifies changes in land use and infrastructure, and the function or disappearance of significant buildings. Using evidence from the census and directories to investigate the background and importance of significant local individuals, buildings and inscriptions on gravestones provides opportunities (Table 6.18) to diversify and decolonise enquiries.

Table 6.18   Local studies

Who owned this large house?	What does this gravestone tell us? Did the family move into the area? Did the children attend school? Why did they die?
Why has the railway line disappeared?	Was this area always a football ground? Has this building always been a supermarket?

POST-1066

Making connections to pre-1066 studies extends prior learning. As KS3 introduces the Reformation, the Industrial Revolution, the world wars and the Holocaust, Table 6.19 focuses on social issues.

Table 6.19 Post-1066

What was the social significance of Henry VIII's closure of the monasteries?
How did the Industrial Revolution and the introduction of railways change lives locally, nationally and globally?
War memorial: what happened to (name)? How did the wars affect lives locally and nationally?
What is the legacy of Greek and Roman architecture in our local area? Why do we still read Greek and Roman myths today?
How did changes in social legislation affect the daily lives of Jewish children in Nazi Germany? What was the Kindertransport?
How did evacuation change some children's lives in Britain during the Second World War? Were children evacuated to/from our region?

THE EARLIEST CIVILISATIONS

Enquiries into the first civilisations (Table 6.20) should identify the significance of locational and physical geography. Parallel timelines suggest possible trading networks.

Table 6.20 Comparing civilisations

What significant physical features did the civilisations have in common?	How did the climate help farmers?
Did the civilisations know about each other?	Where did people live? Was there a social hierarchy?
How did written communication contribute to the development of these civilisations?	What did people believe?
Did children go to school?	Who invented the wheel?

Develop the depth study through an archaeological or biographical lens. Increase diversity by including the female pharaoh, Hatshepsut, or the Shang Empress, Fu Hao.

ANCIENT GREECE

Reference locational and physical geography to identify the main city states and the significance of the sea to travel and trade. Investigate social and military differences between the rival power bases of Athens and Sparta. Use classical literature, mythology and artefacts to investigate society, including slavery, beliefs, advances in technology and the subsequent cultural impact on the Western world. Consider the impact of later Western interest.

NON-EUROPEAN SOCIETIES

Ensure that pupils can locate the society. Draw on prior learning to make comparisons with British history.

EARLY ISLAMIC SOCIETY

Around AD/CE 900, Baghdad was a large, influential capital city. The focus of an extensive empire, the Circular City developed on the fertile River Tigris, accessing global trade. The House of Wisdom drew scholars from across the world. Before being sacked by the Moghuls in AD/CE 1258, the city influenced the development of medicine, philosophy, finance, architecture, and maths, including algebra.

Investigate the global significance of Islamic culture during the period and up to life today.

THE MAYA, *C.* AD 900

The Maya lived in hierarchical city states across climate zones, including the highlands, lowlands and rainforests of south-east Mexico and central America. Religion was important across society. Royal families were linked to blood-thirsty nature gods – even football had a ritual significance. Clothing showed status, with educated scribes and priests at the centre of the ruling classes. Hieroglyphs recorded elite lifestyles. Mathematics was important, contributing to the building of painted stone temples and pyramids. An accurate calendar, incorporating the cycles of the planets, is believed to be unique. In rural areas, farmers cultivated crops, including maize, avocado and tomatoes. These were traded for minerals from the highlands.

While the cities declined, stone buildings, including the stepped pyramids and artefacts, provide evidence today of the former civilisation. Investigate reasons for the decline.

BENIN, *C.* AD/CE 900–1300

Physical geography was important to the Benin Empire. Ruled by divine royal dynasties, Benin City was protected by tropical rainforest and hills. Traders had to navigate a river and swamp to access the fortified city. Prior to the arrival of Portuguese traders in the late fifteenth century, Benin, now part of modern Nigeria, was a wealthy kingdom, rich in resources. Crops, including yam, palm oil and peppers, were bartered with ivory and leather goods, and pottery locally and across Africa. Skilled craftsmen who created a range of goods, including sophisticated bronze artwork, were organised into guilds.

Benin was an oral society. Official storytellers reported the past and passed on beliefs, myths, legends and proverbs across society.

The decline of Benin is linked to the expansion of British trade, particularly an interest in rubber. Investigating why Benin bronzes are in British institutions and why people campaign for their return, as well as why the British wanted to acquire the rubber, will highlight the colonial legacy.

PART 3: UNDERSTANDING THE DEVELOPMENT OF CHILDREN'S KNOWLEDGE IN HISTORY

ENQUIRIES

Well-structured enquiries create apprentice historians. Pupils move from the previous memorisation of often disconnected facts to activities that *enable (them) to demonstrate their historical understanding* (Maddison, 2014, p7). Analysing sources and artefacts encourages pupils to research, discuss and record their findings in ways that help them to *think for themselves* (Maddison, 2014, p6).

SUBSTANTIVE CONCEPTS

Sequencing concepts repeatedly as threads enables future learning by drawing meaningfully on prior learning (Jenner, 2021a). Pupils who recognise the significance of trade to the Roman Empire are likely to understand the importance of trade across pre-history, the ancient civilisations and to the Anglo-Saxons and Vikings. Themes should not be delivered in isolation; their meaning should always be taught in context (Fidler, 2020). Substantive concepts will continue to be developed at Key Stage 3, adding 'new layers of meaning' (Fordham, 2017, p2).

Table 6.21 *Examples of substantive concepts or themes*

Border	Civilisation	Empire	Invasion
Parliament	Peasantry	Power	Religion
Ritual	Settlement	Society	Trade

DISCIPLINARY CONCEPTS OR SKILLS

These are key to developing historians (Lomas, 2019). Allowing pupils to *frame historically-valid questions*, they underpin enquiries, *written narratives and analyses* (DfE, 2013, p188).

CHRONOLOGY

Planning to teach vocabulary associated with chronology, a critically important disciplinary concept, develops chronological understanding progressively across the key stages (Fidler, 2020). Moving from 'A long time ago' through a recognition of dates, decades and centuries, to the accurate use of BC/BCE, AD/CE secures understanding.

Table 6.22 Chronological understanding

Historical vocabulary and terminology The use of identified historical vocabulary to discuss and record historical events.	Sequenced events across time Establishing strong mental timelines, enabling pupils to secure a sense of how periods and events fit together in sequence.

Duration
 	
Forming dates *into patterns* (Dawson*).
 	
Scaled timelines to emphasise the duration of eras.
	Creating a sense of period
	
	Continuity and change:
	• What remained the same?
	• What changed? When?
	  o Within an era.
	  o Across periods.

Table 6.23 Historical skill

Reasons and results Continuity Change Cause Consequence	Interpretations Similarity and difference. Different perspectives of events, including diversity and decolonisation.
Historical evidence Constructing a knowledge of the past by: • identifying sources and artefacts; • analysing the value of the evidence; • interpreting the evidence. How do archaeologists and archivists do this?	Significance Did a person or event: • change events; • affect or change lives; • have a lasting impact locally, nationally or globally; • provide good/bad examples of how to live? (Dawson)

Second-order skills encourage pupils to gain historical perspective. Analysing evidence and asking relevant questions strengthens understanding, helping to identify connections between local, national and global developments (DfE, 2013).

*Ian Dawson confirms the complexity of securing chronological knowledge and understanding, observing that it involves planning across *several different but closely related understandings* (Dawson, n.d.). Other disciplinary concepts are outlined in Table 6.23.

Interrogating artefacts and written sources to secure knowledge is important. Jenner (2021b) emphasises the importance of avoiding anachronistic writing and superficial activities that distract from history.

Challenging pupils to use vocabulary accurately from word banks, particularly when compiled with pupils, scaffolds historical writing (Bruce, 2020). Feed-forward should develop historical knowledge or skills, identifying how pupils can improve their history. *A history piece of work deserves a history comment* (Maddison, 2020).

SUBJECT ASSESSMENT

Target setting and grading pupils summatively in history is complicated and time-consuming. Moving from pupil targets to monitoring the impact of teaching formatively, including low-stake, high-quality retrieval quizzes, secures connections. Doherty (2017) emphasises the value of well-planned closed and open questions. Using a structured quiz, evaluating pupils' prior knowledge of trade links during the Bronze and Iron Age periods, before introducing the importance of trade networks to the success of the Roman Empire, will inform teaching and encourage *connected, flexible thinking among learners* (Coe, 2022).

EVIDENCING PUPILS' UNDERSTANDING AND PROGRESS

Considering the same source or artefact at the beginning and end of enquiries shows what pupils know and understand more accurately than recounting facts in a writing task:

1. What I think: Image	2. What I now know: Image
Three things I would like to know: 1. 2. 3.	Answers to my three questions: 1. 2. 3.
	I will remember: 1. 2. I would still like to find out about:

Figure 6.2 Assessing pupil progress

Creating knowledge organisers or scripting and presenting a podcast are also useful-end-of-unit assessments. Allowing pupils to use vocabulary lists and criteria to evaluate their own knowledge and understanding, as well as that of their peers, encourages critical thinking.

The enquiry at Table 6.24 draws on prior learning to interpret artefacts and sources.

Table 6.24 *Referencing prior learning across a sequenced enquiry*

KS2 Anglo-Saxon Enquiry: How dark were the Dark Ages?			
Concepts: Settlement, trade and power			
Prior knowledge of Roman Britain			
Extensive trade networks across and beyond the Empire.			
Assessment 1			
What does this photograph (gold and gem artefact) tell you about the Anglo-Saxons? What would you like to know?			
Prior learning	**Learning outcomes**	**Questions to develop skills and understanding**	**Activities**
Role of imports in securing Roman influence. Permanent nature of Roman status: stone villas and monuments.	Anglo-Saxon trade networks were essential to the production and import of high status, portable goods.	How did the Anglo-Saxons acquire precious gems and metals?	Identify global trade networks.
Origins of garnets.	Importance of navigable rivers to trade networks.	How did the artefacts reach Britain?	Map the route digitally, including German rivers. Locate workshops in Germany and in Kent.
Importance of precious gems and metals to Saxon culture.	Significance of sources: • artefacts; • texts, including storytelling.	How do we know that Anglo-Saxons valued these artefacts?	Analyse evidence: • high-status Anglo-Saxon burials and hoards; • oral and written stories: *Beowulf*.
Assessment 2			
Can you now read the artefact? Can you answer your questions? What do you still want to know?			

Pupils should recognise:

- the importance of an extensive trade network to the Romans and the Anglo-Saxons;
- differences between representations of Roman and Saxon wealth.

This extends skills and promotes a deep historical understanding of the Anglo-Saxons as cosmopolitan traders (Aronovsky, 2017).

PART 4: DEVELOPING SUBJECT KNOWLEDGE

FURTHER RESOURCES

WEBSITES

British Library: www.bl.uk @britishlibrary

British Museum: www.britishmuseum.org/, @britishmuseum

Digimap for Schools: https://digimapforschools.edina.ac.uk/, @Digimap4schools

Historic England: https://historicengland.org.uk, @HistoricEngland

Historical Association: www.history.org.uk/, @histassoc

Ian Dawson: https://thinkinghistory.co.uk/, @BearWithOneEar

International Slavery Museum: www.liverpoolmuseums.org.uk/international-slavery-museum, @NML_Muse

National Archives: www.nationalarchives.gov.uk/, @UkNatArchives

National Trust: www.nationaltrust.org.uk/features/colonial-countryside-project/

PODCASTS

The Rest is History

You're Dead to Me

FACEBOOK

History Rocks – Creative Primary History @HistoryRocksUK

History/Geography Coordinators – Primary

Mr T does Primary History @Mr S Tiffany

Primary History Matters @HistoryPrimary

AUTHORS

Non-fiction

Corinne Fowler

David Olusoga

Janina Ramirez

Michael Wood

Fiction

Tony Bradman

Michael Morpurgo

Janina Ramirez

Hilary Robinson and Martin Impey

Rosemary Sutcliffe

REFERENCES

Ahlberg, J and A ([1981] 2011) *Peepo!* (30th edn). Thirsk: Dialogos.

Aronovsky, I (2017) A trail of garnet and gold: Sri Lanka to Anglo-Saxon England. *Primary History*, 76: 22–7.

Bradbury, A (2021) *The Early Years Foundation Stage*. London: Learning Matters.

Bruce, L (2020) Improving literacy, improving history. Practical Histories, 24 November. Available at: https://practicalhistories.com/2020/11/improving-literacy-improving-history/

Coe, R (2022) A model for great teaching. Available at: https://evidencebased.education/a-model-for-great-teaching/ (accessed 3 August 2022).

Crawford, H (2016) Using artefacts to develop young children's understanding of the past. *Primary History*, 72: 6–7.

DfE (2013) *The National Curriculum in England Framework Document*. London: HMSO. Crown copyright.

Dawson, I (n.d.) Introducing thinking history. Available at: www.thinkinghistory.co.uk/ (accessed 1 August 2022).

Doherty, J (2017) Skilful questioning: the beating heart of good pedagogy. *Impact*, 1. Available at: https://my.chartered.college/impact/issue-1-assessment/ (accessed 11 August 2022).

Downing, V and Boydell, S (2022) Integrating the local context into the curriculum to support students with the transition from 'understanding the world' in EYFS to history in Key Stage 1. *Impact*, 14: 65–8.

Fearn, H and Keay, J (2021) Curriculum: keeping it simple. Blog. Ofsted: schools and further education & skills (FES): 8 December. Available at: https://educationinspection.blog.gov.uk/2021/12/08/curriculum-keeping-it-simple/ (accessed 10 August 2022).

Fidler, A (2020) More than just a word list. *Primary History*, 84: 30–3

Fordham, M. (2017) Substantive concepts at KS2 & KS3: 9 November. Available at https://clioetcetera.com/2017/11/09/substantive-concepts-at-ks2-ks3/ (accessed 10 August 2022).

Jenner, T (2021a) *Ofsted Research Review Series: History*. Available at: www.gov.uk/government/publications/research-review-series-history/research-review-series-history (accessed 1 August 2022).

Jenner, T (2021b) Curriculum: history in outstanding primary schools (FES). Blog: Ofsted: schools and further education skills: 27 April. Available at: https://educationinspection.blog.gov.uk/author/tim-jenner-hmi-subject-lead-for-history/ (accessed 1 August 2022).

Lomas, T (2019) Getting to grips with primary history. *Primary History*, 82: 9–16.

Lyndon-Cohen, D (n.d.) Approaches to decolonising and diversifying the curriculum: secondary history. Available at: https://my.chartered.college/research-hub/approaches-to-decolonising-and-diversifying-the-curriculum-secondary-history/ (accessed 8 August 2022).

Maddison, M (2014) The National Curriculum for History from September 2014: the view from Ofsted. *Primary History*, 66: 5–7.

Maddison, M (2020) Ten things to remember when teaching history . . . Practical Histories: 1 November. Available at: https://practicalhistories.com/2020/11/when-teaching-history-remember-to/ (accessed 15 August 2022).

Ofsted (2019) *Education Inspection Framework Equality, Diversity and Inclusion Framework*. Available at: https://assets.publishing.service.gov.uk/government/uploads/system/uploads/attachment_data/file/821069/Education_inspection_framework_-_equality__diversity_and_inclusion_statement.pdf (accessed 8 August 2022).

Olusoga, D (2020) *Black and British: A Short Essential History*. Stuttgart: Macmillan Children's Books.

7

MATHEMATICS

NICK DAVIES

KEYWORDS: FLUENCY; REASONING; MATHEMATICAL LANGUAGE: GENERALISATIONS; MASTERY; CONJECTURE; PROOF; VARIATION; CONNECTIONS.

LINKS TO THE CORE CONTENT FRAMEWORK

How Pupils Learn (Standard 2): 2.1, 2.2, 2.6

Subject and Curriculum (Standard 3): 3.1, 3.4, 3.6

PART 1: EXPLORING MATHEMATICS

WHAT IS MATHEMATICS?

Mathematics is a human language like English, French or Chinese as it allows people to communicate with each other; however, unlike other languages, mathematics is universal. As a language, it means that we all have the ability to understand it. Through the medium of language, logic and reasoning can be fully developed – the factors at the heart of embedded learning in mathematics (Williams, 2008). However, if it is presented in a way that is not meaningful – that is, it fails to make 'human sense' and if unfamiliar language is used – problems almost certainly will arise (Atkinson, 1998, p17). With the ability to communicate mathematically comes the opportunity to understand, analyse, critique and take action regarding important social and political issues in our world, especially issues of injustice.

Mathematics is also an immensely practical subject and is essential to our daily lives to carry out everyday calculations at work; to understand our own finances, including mortgages, pensions and credit cards; and to interpret mathematical information we receive from the media. What it is not is simply a collection of facts to be memorised, with certain procedures or a set of seemingly arbitrary rules to follow to solve questions.

WHY IS MATHEMATICS IN THE NATIONAL CURRICULUM?

Mathematical understanding helps children make sense of the world around them and it is an essential part of our personal and working lives. Furthermore, as the national curriculum for mathematics states, it is *critical to science, technology and engineering, and necessary for financial literacy and most forms of employment* (DfE, 2013, p3). Developing a sound understanding of mathematics when we are young is essential and children's early mathematical understanding is strongly associated with their later school achievement. It has, therefore, a major impact on young people's educational progress and life outcomes (Duncan et al., 2007). As Epstein et al. (2010) posit, *Being unable to cope with mathematical ideas and thinking excludes people from such jobs in ways that produce and reinforce social inequalities* (p46).

HOW HAS KNOWLEDGE IN MATHEMATICS DEVELOPED OVER TIME?

Mathematics has developed throughout the world and no single culture has a monopoly on the subject (Evans, 2014). While there were remarkable developments in ancient Greece and throughout Europe in the Modern Era (late 1400s–1950s), these accomplishments would not have been possible without the contributions from various cultures such as the Babylonian, Indian and Islamic cultures.

Much of the mathematics taught today is named for, or attributed to, male European mathematicians of the nineteenth century (Barrow-Green, 2020), or, as some commentators put it, 'dead, white males'. As such, there appears little reference in mathematics teaching to show the rich diversity of contributions to mathematical development from a range of backgrounds.

Indeed, the national curriculum (DfE, 2013) makes a brief reference to this aspect in one Year 4 objective: *Children should be able to . . . know that over time, the numeral system changed to include the concept of zero and place value* (p24). The National Centre for Excellence in Teaching Mathematics (NCETMa, n.d.) outlined that this objective incorporates an understanding that the current Western numeral system is the modified version of the Hindu numeral system developed in India. Given that the Williams's review (2008) argued that *opportunities for children to engage with the cultural and historical story of both science and mathematics could have potential for building their interest and positive attitudes to mathematics* (p62), perhaps a wider focus on these aspects would be of benefit to children in school.

So why is historical knowledge about mathematics relevant today? Is mathematics not an objective subject with universal truths? For instance, is 1 + 1 = 2 not true everywhere? While some would argue that this subject is objective, others would say that as mathematics has been developed and interpreted by humans throughout the ages (thus, a subjective, social construct), it makes the study of its development a worthy goal (Evans, 2014). For instance, in European culture, mathematics was considered to be 'discovered' by the ancient Greeks, with Pythagoras and Euclid among the most prominent mathematicians of the time. However, Pythagoras' theorem was first developed in India, approximately 100–300 years prior to his theorem being used (Finashin, 2018). Furthermore, the concept of zero originated within Sumerian culture circa 3 BC and from there developed by the Babylonians; the circle that we use today to represent zero originated in Chinese writing around the eighth century, but in ancient Greek culture, zero only occasionally appeared (Kaplan, 2007). Thus, while it can be said that the ancient Greeks 'formalised' mathematics, many key concepts had been in existence long before then or were developed elsewhere.

So how has the curriculum changed in recent times and what, if any, assumptions should we challenge in relation to these changes? Since the national curriculum was established in 1988, the mathematics curriculum has arguably been quite prescriptive in what teachers are required to teach. Perhaps this was in part due to the weak school mathematics outcomes prior to this, when teachers and schools could decide what to teach; governmental policies therefore aimed to standardise mathematics across the nation.

However, prior mathematics curricula also focused more on 'instrumental' learning, considered by Skemp to be learning *rules without reason* (1976, p20) rather than 'relational' learning, which for Skemp meant *knowing what to do and why* (1976, p26). Debatably, this has contributed to many children and teachers lacking understanding in mathematics concepts as the focus was on rote learning and learning rules to solve questions. In turn, this can lead to a lack of confidence when teachers are aiming to explain concepts or how to apply procedural knowledge to solve problems, without having a full understanding themselves.

The current iteration of the mathematics criteria (DfE, 2013) is intended to move away from simply procedural learning, with an aim for pupils to *make rich connections across mathematical ideas to develop fluency, mathematical reasoning and competence in solving increasingly sophisticated problems* (p3). This change of focus is important as it gives children the opportunities to make sense of the subject, and with understanding can they enjoy it.

Aligned with the current curriculum is the government's promotion of 'mastery' teaching, with its focus on a *deep understanding of mathematics procedures, concepts and principles* . . . (Haylock and Manning, 2019, p6), with an aim of incorporating good practice from south-east Asian countries which have regularly performed well in the Programme for International Student Assessment (PISA) rankings.

MATHEMATICS NOW

The momentum for teaching for mastery has increased markedly since the introduction of the current national curriculum (DfE, 2013) and this approach is adopted in many English schools. Within research, mastery tends to have different meanings attached to it. For this chapter, teaching for mastery describes the elements of classroom practice and school organisation that combines to give pupils the best chances of mastering maths. Achieving mastery means acquiring a solid enough understanding of the maths that has been taught to enable pupils to move on to more advanced material (NCETMb, n.d.).

The key aspects to this approach (Figure 7.1) comprise the Five Big Ideas (NCETM, 2017): coherence, representation and structure, mathematical thinking, fluency and variation.

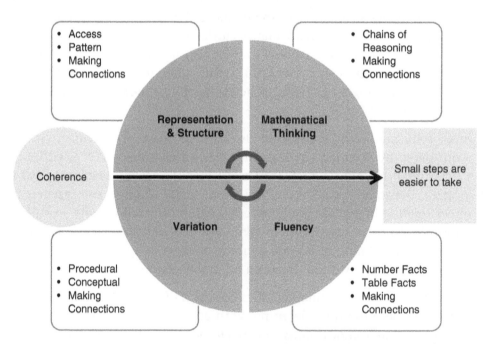

Figure 7.1 Teaching for mastery (NCETM, 2017)

Aligning with the national curriculum objective (DfE, 2013) that *the majority of pupils will move through the programmes of study at broadly the same pace* (p3), teaching for mastery involves teaching pupils through whole-class interactive teaching where the focus is on all pupils working together on the same lesson content at the same time, as happens in Shanghai and several other regions that teach mathematics successfully. This ensures that all can master concepts before moving to the next part of the curriculum sequence, allowing that no pupil is left behind, which sometimes appears to be in contrast to traditional teaching methods (Jerrim et al., 2015).

The development of mastery approaches in schools emphasises the need for teachers to possess a high level of subject knowledge, but has also highlighted that they understand the importance of working collaboratively with colleagues and to be continually involved in professional development (NCETM, 2019).

A theme absent from the teaching for mastery approach as well as from both the national curriculum and the Core Content Framework is that of attitudes to mathematics. This is considered to be an integral part of mastery teaching in south-east Asian countries. Given that many children and teachers often lack confidence in the subject and a significant number report having mathematics anxiety, it becomes an important aspect of learning. Indeed, the Singapore primary curriculum has three broad goals, one of which is for pupils to *develop positive attitudes towards mathematics* (p7). Furthermore, within the main syllabus, one of its aims is to *build confidence and foster interest in mathematics* (Ministry of Education Singapore, p8). A focus on attitudes is also present as one strand out of the five strands of mathematics proficiency in North America, where the term 'productive disposition' (National Research Council, 2001) is used. This refers to pupils perceiving mathematics as both useful and worthwhile, and that everyone is capable of learning the subject.

REFLECTION

What are your beliefs and attitudes towards mathematics?

How do these influence the way you teach children in this subject?

WHAT MIGHT KNOWLEDGE IN MATHS LOOK LIKE IN THE FUTURE?

Following the Covid-19 pandemic, as we know, much of teaching moved online. This in itself exposed a lack of research into online learning and how to make it more effective. It may be that there becomes a greater need to provide blended learning and to be able to offer sufficient depth to the learning, particularly from a mathematics point of view; creating online tasks and activities for mathematics which focus on problem-solving and reasoning, rather than just 'doing sums', will become important. Otherwise, should another pandemic appear, there is a risk that children will only be offered a limited diet of a more 'traditional' approach to learning – namely, a focus on calculations, abstract representations and the learning of methods to solve calculations.

Also, never has mathematics been more important than today, and the way the future looks, we need to prepare children for the digitalisation that is happening and the huge amounts of data that we are now presented with. As such, children today will need to be given greater opportunities to become mathematical thinkers, as opposed to teaching that focuses specifically on content. Being able to analyse, reason and problem-solve are likely to be at the forefront of the future in mathematics.

PART 2: FOUNDATIONAL KNOWLEDGE IN MATHEMATICS

The national curriculum for mathematics aims to ensure that all pupils:

- become fluent in the fundamentals of mathematics, including through varied and frequent practice, with increasingly complex problems over time, so that pupils develop conceptual understanding, and the ability to recall and apply knowledge rapidly and accurately;

- reason mathematically by following a line of enquiry, conjecturing relationships and generalisations, and developing an argument, justification or proof using mathematical language;

- can solve problems by applying their mathematics to a variety of routine and non-routine problems with increasing sophistication, including breaking down problems into a series of simpler steps and persevering in seeking solutions (DfE, 2013, p3).

Within these aims are a variety of terms (see Table 7.1) that may not be fully understood by all practitioners and, as such, may be beneficial to expand upon. Understanding these key ideas can prove helpful when developing foundational knowledge in mathematics and these are explored in Table 7.1, below.

Table 7.1 Key mathematical terms and interpretations

Term	Interpretation
Fluency	*A quick and efficient recall of facts and procedures and the flexibility to move between different contexts and representations of mathematics* (NCETM, 2017, para 5).

Term	Interpretation
Variation	*How the teacher represents the concept being taught, often in more than one way, to draw attention to critical aspects . . . It is also about the sequencing of the episodes, activities and exercises used within a lesson* (NCETM, 2017, para. 6).
Conjecture	A mathematical conjecture is made when one thinks something may be true (a theory) but has yet to prove it so; they arise when one notices a pattern that holds true for many cases, but this does not mean that it is true in all cases. For example, a child may notice a pattern that when a whole number is multiplied by 10, then a zero appears to be added to the starting number. However, this is not true when decimals are involved (e.g., 0.1 x 10 = 1, not 0.10).
Generalisations	Unlike conjectures, generalisations can be understood as the process through which we gain a general statement; an identified pattern remains true in all situations. For instance, when the sum of digits adds up to 3, 6 or 9, it will always be a multiple of 3 (e.g., 3 + 4 + 5 = 12; add the 1 and 2 digits in 12: 1 +2 = 3).
Proof	A mathematical proof is a logical argument that convinces other people that something is true. Children at primary school level are not expected to provide detailed proofs of their theories; however, they can still be encouraged to provide a compelling argument why a generalisation is true.
Mathematical language	Mathematical language is the means through which children can communicate meaning, either in words or verbally. We want children to be able to present their thinking and reasoning through the use of mathematical vocabulary.

This section now focuses on a more detailed look at these terms.

FLUENCY

As well as being a key aim of the national curriculum, it is also a central component of teaching for mastery. However, research in this field shows that the term can have multiple meanings. Different schools may interpret the term differently and can take the view that fluency only means a focus on recalling facts and learning techniques (McClure, 2019, para 2). However, fluency is generally considered to also involve an understanding of when to use a certain method and why it is appropriate to do so; it also involves developing conceptual understanding.

While Ofsted did not define the term in their research review (Ofsted, 2021), the terms they use to classify the mathematics curriculum content knowledge clearly link to what fluency entails: declarative knowledge ('I know that'); procedural knowledge ('I know how') and conditional knowledge ('I know when'); these terms also relate well to Skemp's (1976) notions of instructional and relational learning discussed above.

Table 7.2 A summary of mathematics curriculum content classifications (Ofsted, 2021)

Category	Summary	Content
Declarative: 'I know that'	Facts and formulae	Relationship between facts (conceptual understanding).
Procedural: 'I know how'	Methods	Relationship between facts, procedures and missing facts (principles/mechanisms).
Conditional: 'I know when'	Strategies	Relationship between information, strategies and missing information (reasoning).

When pupils learn and use declarative, procedural and conditional knowledge, their knowledge of relationships between concepts develops over time (Brown et al., 2003). As with teaching for mastery, it is important for teachers to develop a rich network of mathematical knowledge to include providing pupils with a varied range of activities, knowing which resources and manipulatives are the most effective for which topic and being able to model maths concepts using a variety of representations – e.g., bar model, number line, fraction walls, etc.).

REFLECTION

During your practice, think about which manipulatives you use:

Why did you select a particular representation?

What mathematical structure did you want to draw out?

Was this resource the most suitable way to identify this structure? How do you know?

VARIATION

To start, it is important to differentiate 'variation' from 'variety'. Variety in this context means providing children with a range of questions that focus on mechanical repetition only (e.g., practising column addition and just changing the numbers in the questions each time).

There are two aspects of variation: *procedural* variation and *conceptual* variation. The former aims to create a suitable avenue for practising the thinking through, noticing relationships between questions. Consider the two different sets of subtraction questions below (Askew, 2015), noticing how they are organised (Table 7.3).

Table 7.3 Two sets of subtraction questions (Askew, 2015)

Set A	Set B
120 - 90	120 - 90
235 - 180	122 - 92
502 - 367	119 - 89
122 - 92	235 - 180
119 - 89	237 - 182
237 - 182	502 - 367

If the focus was on children using formal subtraction methods, then either set could be used. However, if the learning centred on finding the difference, to identify the underlying mathematical structure, set B offers deliberate practice, as explained in Table 7.4 below. Questions are displayed one at a time, with the children encouraged to represent the calculations pictorially – for example, on a number line. This can then be extended into the notion of generalisations by asking the pupils: 'What could you do to convince me that the difference remains the same?'

Table 7.4 Examples of variation questions

Set B	Explanation of variation
120 - 90	The numbers are deliberately close together in range so that the focus can be on the difference, rather than needing a formal subtraction method; the difference is relatively straightforward for children to find.
122 - 92	Children can be asked to explain why the answers are the same; the question focuses children's attention to the critical aspect of the learning (the difference).
119 - 89	This question again focuses on the key aspect of the learning, but is perhaps not as obvious as in question 2.
235 - 180	A new starting point is given, with the values being further away than in example 1 but not so far away that a formal subtraction method is used.
237 - 182	Children are asked to explain how this relates to question 4, and to draw this representation on a number line to see the relationship between them.
502 - 367	Having being exposed to the underlying structure of finding the difference, the aim is for children to hopefully apply their learning from above, and to look closely at the numbers to notice that they could use 500 - 365 to find the difference. Children can represent their findings on a number line and explain their reasoning to another child.

It is important not simply to provide pupils with a worksheet of questions without the opportunities to share their thinking. Likewise, it is important to understand what type of questions provide focused variation and which do not, as illustrated through the examples in Tables 7.3 and 7.4 above.

Conceptual variation highlights a concept's key features by focusing on what it is and what it is not. For example, you may show pupils examples and non-examples of triangles (Figure 7.2). It is important to show all aspects being varied (in this case, length of sides, angles and orientations); if an object is presented in the same way each time, false generalisations may be made (e.g., a triangle has one side as a horizontal base and the vertex pointing upwards, as in the first shape).

Figure 7.2 Examples of triangles and non-triangles

It is also important to provide standard and non-standard examples in different contexts – for example, when learning about parallel lines. In Figure 7.3 below (Boaler et al., 2016), children were asked if lines *a* and *c* were parallel.

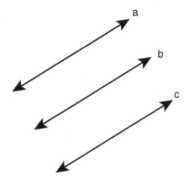

Figure 7.3 Images of parallel lines

Most children said that they are not parallel because line *b* was in the way. This is because parallel lines are almost always presented in a standard way (Figure 7.4)

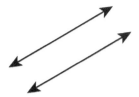

Figure 7.4 Traditional representation of parallel lines

The central idea of teaching with variation is to highlight the essential features of a concept or idea through varying the non-essential features.

When giving examples of a mathematical concept, it is useful to add variation to emphasise:

• What it is (as varied as possible).

• What it is not.

When considering questions or activities, it is valuable to think about what links the examples so the mathematical structures can be emphasised.

CONJECTURE

A conjecture is an assertion that is yet to be proved and is seen as an essential part of investigating and problem-solving; it can be viewed as making an educated guess and it is considered it to be a fundamental component of reasoning (Haylock and Manning, 2019).

Asking conjectures encourages thinking and it is the art of thinking that allows connections to be made. When carrying out an investigation, we want to look for patterns and structures. Once we have examined them, we can begin to form a hypothesis (conjecture). Offering pupils these types of activities can stimulate discussion and encourage reasoning, and the search for clues (patterns and structures) also promotes fluency.

A conjecture example could be to ask: make a conjecture about the next number in the pattern 2, 6, 11, 17 . . . The terms increase by 4, then 5 and then 6. Conjecture: the next term will increase by 7, so it will be 17 + 7 = 24.

Alternatively, it could involve an investigation, such as through a game of Nim. Essentially, it is a game for 2 players and a collection of 10 counters. Pupils take turns taking 1 or 2 counters from the pile. Whoever takes the last counter wins. Conjectures can arise through encouraging pupils to decide what a winning strategy might be.

- The person who goes first wins.

- The person who goes second wins.

- Who wins depends on how many counters there are.

- It doesn't matter what you do until there are 5 counters left.

- You win if there are an even number of counters on your turn.

- You win if there are an odd number of counters on your turn.

These conjectures can then be tested, counter-examples formed and new conjectures arrived at. Above all, it can promote deep thinking about mathematical structures and patterns.

GENERALISATIONS

In essence, a generalisation can be described as *an observation about something that is always true* (Haylock and Manning, 2019, p42) and is considered to be a fundamental aspect of mathematics; for Mason (1996), *A lesson without the opportunity for learners to generalise is not a mathematics lesson* (p65).

Generalisations are an integrated aspect of reasoning and problem-solving, both key objectives within the national curriculum. It can be useful to see the steps in the problem-solving process and how this leads to making generalisations (Table 7.5).

Table 7.5 The problem-solving process (Pennant and Woodham, 2018)

The Steps	The process
1. Getting started	• Select an example that is accessible to all • Represent using resources (manipulatives, pictorial)
2. Working on the problem	• Visualise • Reason logically • Work systematically • Work backwards • Conjecture • Identify patterns • Trial and improvement • Transfer learning to a new example
3. Digging deeper	• Generalise • Verify • Prove
4. Conclude	• Communicate findings • Evaluate

A key aspect of moving towards generalisations is enabling pupils to transfer their findings from one example to another new one. During this process, similarities and differences between the two examples may emerge. Exploring further examples means that strategies might appear which are *always* true, which is the essence of a generalisation (Pennant and Woodham, 2018).

To highlight this process, consider the following example:

Ask pupils to write down four consecutive numbers – for instance 4, 5, 6 and 7. Then ask them to identify what they notice about the relationships between the numbers. Possible responses may include:

- The difference between the first number from the second number is 1.

- The sum of the first and last numbers is always odd.

- The sum of the first and last numbers is a prime number.

- The sum of all the numbers is even.

To encourage transfer of learning, you could then ask the pupils to see if these statements are true for other consecutive numbers. From there, they can then begin to make generalisations. In the fourth step (Table 7.5 above), they can then draw their conclusions and, if necessary, adjust their generalisations. For example, it may appear that the sum of the first and last numbers are indeed prime. However, in the pattern, 6, 7, 8, 9, this generalisation would not be true, although it is true for several consecutive numbers. From here, they may revise their generalisations – for example, if a pattern starts with a multiple of 3, the sum of the first and last digits are not prime numbers:

6, 7, 8, 9

9, 10, 11, 12

12, 13, 14, 15

Children can then be encouraged to reason why this holds true: if you start a sequence of four numbers with a multiple of three, then the last number will also be a multiple of three. As such, the sum of the first and last digits will always have more than two factors, thus meaning that the sum cannot be a prime number. In short, being able to generalise a situation involves identifying its underlying mathematical structure.

Notice how the use of reasoning and mathematical language can be drawn out through such investigations. We return to mathematical language below, but first, we can see how generalisations lead towards proofs.

PROOF

In essence, at primary-school level, a proof refers to getting pupils to construct a credible argument as to why a generalisation must be true. Clearly, given the young ages of pupils at primary school, being able to articulate precisely can be challenging. As such, proof does not need to entail a cohesive, written explanation but can include concrete and/or pictorial representations too (Figure 7.5). For instance, pupils may use manipulatives to prove the statement: 'When you halve an even number, you always get a whole number.'

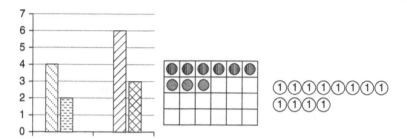

Figure 7.5 Images of representations of halving numbers

The use of manipulatives is also an effective way to demonstrate proof by counter-example – finding an example to disprove a conjecture:

- Statement: A multiple of 8 is also a multiple of 4.

16 is a multiple of 8 as there are two groups of 8 in 16; 16 is made up of four multiples of 4.

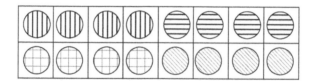

Figure 7.6a

- Statement: Therefore, multiples of four are also multiples of 8.

12 is made up of three multiples of 4; however, 12 is not a multiple of 8.

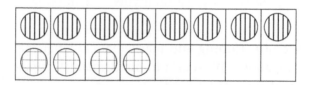

Figure 7.6b

In summary, pupils will need repeated opportunities to focus on generalising and proof, and will benefit from the opportunity to converse, reason and communicate what it entails frequently. In becoming fluent with proof, they are also becoming experts at reasoning and all this will contribute towards their mastering of mathematics.

MATHEMATICAL LANGUAGE

The accurate and regular use of mathematics vocabulary by teachers can develop pupils' understanding of the connections between the various mathematics concepts and the terminology associated with these concepts (Sprosty, 2018). As such, *a deliberate and careful attention to acquiring and using the vocabulary of mathematics, with its wondrously specific technical language, is a must* (Murray, 2004, p1). Children are not often exposed to mathematical language in their homes and social environments (Murray, 2004), highlighting the essential role of the classroom teacher.

Various approaches can support the mathematics-specific language acquisition and application. These include displaying them on the board and specifically referring to them throughout the lesson. Working walls are also useful in this regard and can contain definitions of key terms. However, these approaches do not necessarily ensure a conceptual understanding of the terms. Ways to address this include the use of a Frayer model (Figure 7.7), which has the benefit of being used as a formative assessment tool as they can reveal the extent of a pupil's understanding.

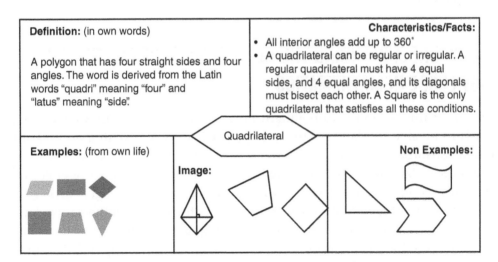

Figure 7.7 An exemplar of the Frayer model

Additionally, Sprosty (2018) identified several ways to integrate mathematics vocabulary into the classroom (Table 7.6).

Table 7.6 Mathematical vocabulary strategies (adapted from Sprosty, 2018)

Avoiding homonym and homophone confusion	Utilising linguistics to support understanding of mathematical terms	Creating graphic organisers	Using a variety of different ways to strengthen vocabulary
Identifying and discussing which words sound the same and are spelt the same (homonyms) but have different meanings - e.g., sign, term, difference, volume, sum, etc. Identify and discuss which words sound the same but are spelt differently (homophones) - e.g., root/route, way/weigh, to/too/two, etc.	Examine the source of a word (etymology) - e.g., quadri-lateral; hex-agon (Greek: *hex* = six; *gonia* = angle) Analyse word meaning through prefixes, suffixes and roots - e.g., dec-ade, dec-imal, centi-metre, etc.	Similar to the Frayer model (above), pupils can create concept maps, visual representations of words.	Use picture dictionaries as a visual learning strategy in which pictures are connected with written descriptions in the pupils' own words Drama - pupils dramatise a meaning of a mathematical word

In summary, due to the high frequency of mathematical words used in the classroom, regular and varied strategies are needed to develop pupils' conceptual understanding of these terms. This will aid their ability to reason, to make conjectures, and to formulate generalisations and proofs.

PART 3: UNDERSTANDING THE DEVELOPMENT OF CHILDREN'S KNOWLEDGE IN MATHEMATICS

The aim of this section is to highlight how essential subject knowledge acquisition is to be able to plan effectively sequenced units of teaching and learning. Perhaps unsurprisingly, Fennema et al. (1989) observed that teachers who were more knowledgeable about the topic they were teaching were more effective in these areas compared to topics in which they had less knowledge. Furthermore, Hill et al. (2005) found that pupils of teachers with stronger mathematical knowledge for teaching made greater progress than pupils whose teachers had relatively weaker knowledge. For ideas on how to develop your subject knowledge further, please see Part 4 below. Before then, to highlight how subject knowledge is important when planning a learning sequence, an example of these steps is shown below (Table 7.7) within place value for Years 4–6.

Table 7.7 *Illustrating how a sequence of lessons can be developed on place value*

Year group	Learning outcomes	Activities to develop the skills and understanding	Next steps
4	Order and compare numbers beyond 1,000.	You could ask children to compare different sets of dienes, place value counters and numbers using the > or < or = symbols (see Figure 7.8 below).	Ask children questions that develop their mathematical talk – for example: When comparing numbers, which column do you start with? Why? Which strategy did you use to compare two numbers? Is this the same as or different from your partner? Which approach was more effective, do you think?
5	Read, write, order and compare numbers to at least 1,000,000 and determine the value of each digit,	You could give the children a set of digit cards and ask them to make and read large numbers following instructions that you call out such as these: make 34 now 234, now 2,348, 23,487, 123,487, 9,123,487. Identify the cards that show how many hundreds, tens, millions, thousands, etc. there are.	Develop mathematical thinking by asking questions such as: If I add 4 hundred to 69,642, which numbers will change? What will be my new number?
6	Read, write, order and compare numbers up to 10,000,000 and determine the value of each digit.	Present children with seven-digit cards – e.g., 0, 2, 2, 6, 6, 4, 6. Ask them to use the digits cards and the statements written below to work out the number: • The millions and ones have the same digits. • The ten thousand digit is double the hundreds digit. • The hundred thousand digit is three times smaller than the tens digit. • Is there more than one solution? Now make up your own set of statements for someone else to solve.	Develop problem-solving and reasoning skills by asking questions such as: Eva has ordered eight 6-digit numbers. The smallest number is 345,900. The greatest number is 347,000. All the other numbers have a digit total of 20 and have no repeating digits. What are the other six numbers? Can you place all eight numbers in ascending order?

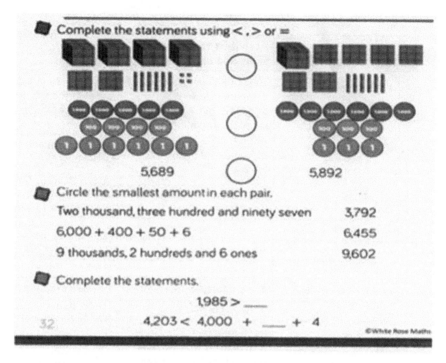

Figure 7.8 Images comparing different sets of dienes, place value counters and numbers using the or ‹ or = symbols (linked to Year 4 activities in Table 7.5 above) (Images with kind permission of White Rose Maths)

PART 4: DEVELOPING YOUR KNOWLEDGE OF MATHEMATICS FURTHER

Some reading to support your development:

Haylock, D and Cockburn, A (2013) *Understanding Mathematics for Young Children* (4th edn). London: SAGE.

This book, aimed at those who teach mathematics in the age range 3–7 years provides a detailed understanding of the mathematical ideas behind the subject matter they cover in the classroom.

Rowland, T, Turner, F, Thwaites, A and Huckstep, P (2009) *Developing Primary Mathematics Teaching: Reflecting on Practice with the Knowledge Quartet.* London: SAGE.

This book is aimed at teachers and trainee teachers of primary mathematics, and is aimed at encouraging a structured reflection of practice to help develop your mathematics teaching expertise.

Haylock, D and Manning R (2014) *Mathematics Explained for Primary Teachers* (5th edn). London: SAGE.

While the whole book is an excellent tool to support subject knowledge development, the first two sections consider key ideas about mathematical understanding, reasoning and problem solving as well as a discussion about mathematics anxiety.

Hanson, A, Drews, D, Lawton, F and Surtees, L (2020) *Children's Errors in Mathematics*. London: SAGE.

This book is a resource to help you develop your knowledge and understanding about how children learn mathematics, and how errors and misconceptions are not only a natural part of learning mathematics, but are an essential requisite to effective learning.

WEBSITE RECOMMENDATIONS

The National Centre for Excellence in Teaching Mathematics (NCETM) provides a plethora of support, resources, videos and research articles for trainee and in-service teachers. The NCETM is at the forefront of promoting and developing teaching for mastery in schools and offers a range of resources to develop your expertise in mathematics: www.ncetm.org.uk/

NRICH provides a wealth of resources to embed rich mathematical tasks into everyday classroom practice as well as offering a store of research articles to support your own professional development: https://nrich.maths.org/

White Rose maths provides a vast bank of resources to support planning and teaching in the classroom. Many of the resources are free, although there is a small yearly charge for accessing further planning and developmental tools: https://whiterosemaths.com/

SPECIALIST ORGANISATIONS

The Association of Teachers of Maths (ATM) is an association dedicated to the teaching and promotion of mathematics. Member benefits include professional support, a monthly journal, CPD opportunities and access to an online back catalogue of publications and interactive resources links. There is a small cost involved: www.atm.org.uk/

OTHER HELPFUL NATIONAL RESOURCES

Maths Hubs, coordinated by the NCETM, comprise a partnership of schools, colleges and other organisations working together to provide support for maths teaching in a particular region of England. They are free to join and provide a range of CPD opportunities that enable teachers to work collaboratively with the support of local leaders of maths education: www.ncetm.org.uk/maths-hubs/about-maths-hubs/

REFERENCES

Askew, M (2015) *Transforming Primary Mathematics*. Abingdon: Routledge.

Atkinson, S (1998) *Maths With Reason*. London: Hodder & Stoughton.

Barrow-Green, J (2020) *Decolonising the Curriculum Through the History of Mathematics* Openlearn. Available at: www.Open.Edu/Openlearn/Science-Maths-Technology/Mathematics-Statistics/Decolonising-The-Curriculum-Through-The-History-Mathematics (accessed 1 September 2022).

Boaler, J, Chen, L, Williams, C and Cordero, M (2016) Seeing as understanding: the importance of visual mathematics for our brain and learning. *Journal of Computational and Applied Mathematics*, 5 (5): 1–6.

Brown, M, Askew, M and Millett, A (2003) How has the national numeracy strategy affected attainment and teaching in Year 4. *Proceedings of the British Society for Research into Learning Mathematics*, 23: 13–18.

Duncan, GJ, Dowsett, CJ, Claessens, A, Magnuson, K, Huston, AC, Klebanov, P, Pagani, LS, Feinstein, L, Engel, M and Brooks-Gunn, J (2007) School readiness and later achievement. *Developmental Psychology*, 43: 1428.

Department for Education (DfE) (2013) *Mathematics Programmes of Study: Key Stages 1 and 2. National Curriculum in England*. Manchester: Department for Education. Crown copyright.

Epstein, D, Mendick, H and Moreau, M-P (2010) Imagining the mathematician: young people talking about popular representations of maths. *Discourse Studies in the Cultural Politics of Education*, 31: 45–60.

Evans, B (2014) *The Development of Mathematics throughout the Centuries: A Brief History in a Cultural Context*. Hoboken, NJ: John Wiley & Sons.

Fennema, E, Carpenter, T and Peterson, P (1989) Teachers' decision making and cognitively guided instruction: a new paradigm for curriculum development. In K Clements and N Ellerton (eds) *Facilitating Change in Mathematics Education*. Geelong, Australia: Deakin University Press.

Finashin, S (2018) History of maths. Available at: www.Studocu.Com/En-Us/Document/Temple-University/Basic-Concepts-Of-Math/History-Of-Math-Concepts/20434835 (accessed 2 September 2022).

Hill, HC, Rowan, B and Ball, DL (2005) Effects of teachers' mathematical knowledge for teaching on student achievement. *American Educational Research Journal*, 42: 371–406.

Jerrim, J, Austerberry, H, Crisan, C, Ingold, A, Morgan, C, Pratt, D, Smith, C and Wiggins, M (2015) *Mathematics Mastery: Secondary Evaluation Report*. London: Education Endowment Foundation.

Kaplan, R (2007) What is the origin of zero? How did we indicate nothingness before zero? *Scientific American*. Available at: www.Scientificamerican.Com/Article/What-Is-The-Origin-Of-Zer/#:~:Text=The%20first%20recorded%20zero%20appeared,The%20end%20of%20the%20eighth (accessed 2 September 2022).

Mason, J (1996) *Expressing Generality and Roots of Algebra: Approaches to Algebra*. Dordrecht: Springer.

McClure, L (2019) Developing number fluency – what, why and how? Nrich. Available at: https://Nrich.Maths.Org/10624 (accessed 2 September 2022).

Ministry of Education Singapore (2013) Maths Syllabus Primary One to Six. Available at: www.Moe.Gov.Sg/-/Media/Files/Primary/Mathematics_Syllabus_Primary_1_To_6.Pdf (accessed 12 September 2022).

Murray, M (2004) *Teaching Mathematics Vocabulary in Context*. Portsmouth, NH: Heinemann Educational Books.

National Research Council (2001) *Adding it Up: Helping Children Learn Mathematics*. Washington, DC: National Academies Press.

Ncetma (n.d.) National curriculum resource tool, Year 4 – number and place value. Available at: www.Ncetm.Org.Uk/In-The-Classroom/National-Curriculum-Resource-Tool/?Topic=1693&Year=1757 (accessed 1 September 2022).

Ncetmb (n.d.) School leaders: information for school leaders about free professional development. Available at: www.Ncetm.Org.Uk/Professional-Development/School-Leaders (accessed 1 September 2022).

Ncetm (2017) Five big ideas in teaching for mastery. Available at: www.Ncetm.Org.Uk/Teaching-For-Mastery/Mastery-Explained/Five-Big-Ideas-In-Teaching-For-Mastery/ (accessed 1 September 2022).

Ncetm (2019) Teaching for mastery: what is happening in primary maths, and what next? Available at: www.Nwmathshub3.Co.Uk/News/Wp-Content/Uploads/2019/10/Ncetm_Thematic_Report.Pdf (accessed 1 September 2022).

Ofsted (2021) *Research Review Series: Mathematics*. London: Ofsted. Crown copyright.

Sprosty, K (2018) 'I forgot that quotient meant to divide so I added instead and got the wrong answer': the link between math vocabulary and problem-solving. Available at: www.Otterbein.Edu/Wp-Content/Uploads/2018/10/Sprosty.Pdf (accessed 1 September 2022).

Pennant, J and Woodham, L (2018) Mastering mathematics: the challenge of generalising and proof. Nrich. Available at: https://Nrich.Maths.Org/11488 (accessed 1 October 2022).

Skemp, RR (1976) Relational understanding and instrumental understanding. *Mathematics Teaching*, 77: 20–6.

Williams, P (2008) *Independent Review of Mathematics Teaching in Early Years Settings and Primary Schools*. Nottingham: Department for Children, Schools and Families. Crown copyright.

8

MUSIC

JON AUDAIN, SARAH LLOYD AND HELEN MEAD

KEYWORDS: MUSICAL SKILLS; SINGING; LISTENING; IMPROVISING AND COMPOSING; PLAYING AND PERFORMING; INTERRELATED DIMENSIONS OF MUSIC; CREATIVITY; TACIT KNOWLEDGE; DECLARATIVE KNOWLEDGE; PROCEDURAL KNOWLEDGE.

LINKS TO THE CORE CONTENT FRAMEWORK

High Expectations (Standard 1): 1.2

Subject and Curriculum (Standard 3): 3.2, 3.3, 3.4, 3.5, 3.6, 3.7

Classroom Practice (Standard 4): 4.3, 4.4

Managing Behaviour (Standard 7): 7.1

PART 1: EXPLORING MUSIC

WHAT IS MUSIC?

[Music] is all around us. It is the soundtrack to our lives. Music connects us through people and places in our ever-changing world. It is creative, collaborative, celebratory and challenging. In our schools, music can bring communities together through the shared endeavour of whole-school singing, ensemble playing, experimenting with the creative process and, through the love of listening to friends and fellow pupils,

performing. The sheer joy of music making can feed the soul of a school community, enriching each student while strengthening the shared bonds of support and trust which make a great school.

(DfE, 2021, p3)

Unlike many other curriculum subjects, no child will start school as a blank canvas when it comes to musical experiences. They already come hardwired to music, which gives you as an educator a huge wealth of experience to tap into.

Music can unlock both intrinsic and extrinsic skills. There is *science* to music; how sounds are created and how they travel; music is made up of *numbers*, patterns and fractions; music itself is a universal *language* that crosses *cultural barriers*; the whole body is *physically engaged* with music, from controlling the vocal cords and diaphragm when singing, to dancing, to fine motor control of playing an instrument with beaters; music is art – an *emotional reaction* and outpouring that is individual but can create a community.

REFLECTION

What does music mean to you?

How do you interact with music in your daily life?

WHY IS MUSIC IN THE NATIONAL CURRICULUM?

Music is a universal language that embodies one of the highest forms of creativity. A high-quality music education should engage and inspire pupils to develop a love of music and their talent as musicians, and so increases their self-confidence, creativity and sense of achievement.

(DfE, 2013)

This opening statement in the national curriculum reinforces the importance of music being a fundamental part of every child's learning journey. Allowing children time and space to be creative and develop their imagination is vital, along with developing a life-long love of music (Paynter, 1982). At the heart of the music curriculum are creativity, curiosity and excitement and children who are developing increased self-confidence, self-esteem and collaborative skills. Music offers opportunities to support children's mental health and allows them time to express their emotions. It is a unique subject. One with its own challenging set of skills and procedural knowledge for children to acquire but also a subject which is very powerful across the curriculum. Music has the ability to open doorways to other worlds and times, provides creative opportunities to respond with artistic and dance skills, and the ability to support acquisition of powerful declarative knowledge in other subject areas.

REFLECTION

What are you excited about exploring and sharing from the national curriculum with your class?

What does being musical mean to you?

What worries you? How will you overcome those worries or fears?

HOW HAS 'KNOWLEDGE' IN MUSIC DEVELOPED OVER TIME?

The concept of music is layered with meaning and absorbed through a variety of our senses (Elliott, 1991; Swanwick, 1994). Sometimes it is acquired, while sometimes it is learnt.

DEFINING THE THREE TYPES OF KNOWLEDGE WITH MUSIC

Children need to:

- experience sound: you do this when the children are part of a wide range of musical experiences. They are *part* of the music. They are *absorbed* by the music. They are *emotionally connected* to the music. In essence, only a wide musical 'menu' will facilitate this;

- develop skills: you do this when you teach the specific skills needed – for example how to create and manipulate instrumental sound;

- understand and recall facts: you do this when you provide information about composers and genres and musical terminology – for example:

  Florence Price (1927–53) was the first African American woman recognised as a symphonic composer; The Beatles were an English rock band, formed in Liverpool in 1960 and got the idea for their name from Buddy Holly and The Crickets).

The *Ofsted Research Review for Music* (Ofsted, 2021) provided a perspective on how musical knowledge is developed through these activities and experiences. The *Research Review* highlighted the three types of knowledge (Table 8.1).

Table 8.1 Forms of knowledge based on the Ofsted Research Review (2021)

Experiential (knowledge of)	
Tacit: tacit knowledge refers to the knowledge gained through experience that is often difficult to put into words.	This is the implicit rather than formal knowledge gained through experiencing, listening to and performing music. This includes personal feelings and responses to music.
Procedural (knowledge how)	
Procedural: procedural knowledge is the knowledge exercised in the performance of a task.	These are the skills the children learn - for example, how to keep a steady beat, how to play notes on a recorder, how to play accurately with two beaters.
Facts (knowledge about)	
Declarative: declarative knowledge refers to facts or information stored in the memory.	This is a recall of facts - knowledge about music such as composer, dates, genre, names of instruments.

DIVERSITY AND REPRESENTATION IN MUSIC

The Black Lives Matter movement raised the awareness of decolonisation within education. Within music, Professor Nate Holder (www.nateholdermusic.com) is challenging the 'antiquated ideas of a great composer'. The idea of the 'great composers' has dominated the musical repertoire in schools, giving more 'value' to dead, white, male composers. We now need to redress the balance and ensure that all children experience a broad and balanced musical canon. Think of it like a restaurant menu. Children need to be offered a rich and varied musical diet from a young age so they experience a full, well-rounded canon. How do you know what you like if you haven't tried it?

An open and honest discussion around diversity and representation is essential with your children. Acknowledging that female composers on your timeline don't appear until a certain point in time is important. Ask the challenging questions so children probe around the complexities of the subject: 'Do you think that there weren't female composers at this time? Why is this?'

REFLECTION

How do I start thinking about diversity in music?

- Watch and reflect: BBC Four: *Black Classical Music: The Forgotten History* (2020).

- Are you representing male and female composers and musicians in your classroom?

- Are you representing music from across all periods of times fairly?

- Does diversity only sit in Black History month in October or are you integrating this throughout each lesson, month and year? These are moments to think about and challenge your own thinking.

- Could you represent this on a timeline in your classroom? Perhaps you could add musicians and composers as you meet them in your teaching and learning to refer to and add to as a working wall for your children.

- Classroom resources: BBC *Trailblazers, Listen & Celebrate*.

MUSIC NOW

Music education has been shaped very differently over the past few years with the key drivers being knowledge (see Table 8.1) and progression through the skills development. Ofsted (2021) themselves acknowledge the breadth and diversity of music available and are keen for schools to be aware that they cannot cover everything. The national curriculum statements (DfE, 2013) lend themselves to being applied in a variety of ways. Choosing the most important and meaningful knowledge for your children in your school is up to you and your music subject leader.

Each school will have found its own approach to the music curriculum which you will need to familiarise yourself with. Some of the initiatives and approaches adopted now are outlined below.

WIDER OPPORTUNITIES OR FIRST ACCESS PROJECTS

These projects are often delivered by a local music hub or specialist teachers. The projects will introduce Key Stage 2 pupils to the skills of playing an instrument as a whole class and can last between one term and one year. The aim of this is to ensure that every child, regardless of family income or circumstances will have the opportunity to learn to play an instrument. A diverse range of instruments can be used in these projects, but common choices are recorder, ukulele, djembe, pbuzz and more traditional orchestral instruments such as violin, flute and trumpet.

MODEL MUSIC CURRICULUM (2021)

The *Model Music Curriculum* (MMC) was published by the DfE in March 2021 and aimed to *introduce the next generation to a broad repertoire of music from the Western Classical tradition, and to the best popular music and music from around the world* (DfE, 2021, p2). The MMC aims to assist schools in developing a clearly sequenced and ambitious curriculum, but is not a statutory document and therefore can be adapted and revised by schools.

OTHER PERSPECTIVES AND APPROACHES TO MUSIC EDUCATION

Internationally, music can be approached in a variety of different ways. Some teachers have been influenced by the thoughts of well-known composers about what music education should look like. Some are approaches to music and some are specific methods. You may be in a school that adopts one of these methods: Zoltán Kodály, Émile-Jacques Dalcroze, Orff Schulwerk, Edwin Gordon, Shinichi Suzuki, Reggio Emilia. Sarrazin (2016) provides a further summation of these methods and sees one school's adoption of the Kodály approach in action.

WHAT WILL MUSIC EDUCATION LOOK LIKE IN THE FUTURE?

In June 2022, the direction for music in the future was introduced in the form of the second National Plan for Music (NPME2). The National Plan for Music Education establishes a vision by 2030 to enable all children within England to *learn to sing, play an instrument and create music together* and *have the opportunity to progress their musical interests and talents* (DfE, 2022, p5).

It emphasises the importance of partnerships between education settings, music hubs, music organisations working with young people and the music industry. It connected with the *Model Music Curriculum* and the original *National Plan for Music Education* (DfE, 2011).

The NPME2 outlines the key features of high-quality school music provision as:

- Timetabled curriculum music of at least one hour each week.

- Access to lessons across a range of instruments and voice.

- A school choir/vocal ensemble.

- A school ensemble/band/group.

- Space for rehearsals and individual practice.

- A termly school performance.

- Opportunity to enjoy live performance at least once a year.

PART 2: FOUNDATION KNOWLEDGE IN MUSIC
WHAT DOES MUSIC MEAN FOR ME AS A TRAINEE?

That wasn't as bad as I thought it was going to be!

The children responded so well.

I didn't think it was going to work but it provided my class with a way of making music.

I was so glad I gave it a go no matter how nervous I was. It is easier teaching children than your peers.

These are just a few comments from trainees after they have planned and taught music. The confidence of trainees to teach music is a continual research focus (Seddon and Biasutti, 2008); that red-faced feeling when sometimes a subject is perceived as specialist in its nature (Hennessy, 2000). However, from reading above, music is the playful expression of sound. Being musical as a teacher means being able to facilitate the experimentation and structuring of that sound with the principal aim of improving the quality of the children's musical response or their understanding. It involves careful modelling, questioning and scaffolding of musical concepts that are all daily aspects of teaching you already use. Music is one of those practical subjects that has many activities, games and techniques that you can try out during the course of the day. So, as a trainee you can easily take a small amount of time to develop your music toolkit and build a bank of activities you then feel confident delivering with your class.

WHAT DOES KNOWLEDGE IN MUSIC SOUND LIKE?

Music is multi-layered; a highly creative subject best experienced first-hand through your senses. Musical learning is rooted in sound. When you are teaching music, the purpose is to develop children as musicians.

Learning is a change in long-term memory. In music, these changes occur through the acquisition of tacit, procedural or declarative knowledge.

To successfully teach the music national curriculum (2013), there is some declarative and procedural knowledge you need to have yourself. This section will ensure that you know the main areas of learning, understand the musical skills and foundation knowledge in music. It will provide examples for you to use to enhance your own knowledge and support you to deliver this with confidence and expertise. Some of this knowledge you may need to read in smaller chunks, digest and return to later. Some you may use as a guide and to prompt your own memory. Music is unique in the way it is shared across three types of identified knowledge (tacit, procedural and declarative) and needs careful planning and consideration. This section will support your development as a trainee.

MUSICAL SKILLS

- Singing
- Listening

- Improvising and composing
- Playing and performing

These intrinsic skills are drawn from the key points in the national curriculum for music. Although your focus may be on one skill in particular, most quality music lessons involve some element of all the skills – you can't play or sing without listening, most composition begins with improvisation. Over a unit of work, all these skills will have been developed and will in turn develop the child's overall musicianship and understanding. Over the course of their primary education, these skills will be revisited and developed in a spiral curriculum (Boyce-Tillman and Anderson, 2022; Fautley and Daubney, 2022; Swanwick and Tillman, 1986).

REFLECTION

Tell the children which skill or skills you are focusing on in that lesson - you can use a display to highlight the skills in your class or music room.

SINGING

Singing is using your voice to create music, including singing, chanting, rap, on your own or with a group. It should form the basis for all music-making skills as the golden thread to linking your learning. Try to build the other skills from this.

Singing as a class is a joy. It brings a communal sense of well-being and togetherness, and has been shown to improve your sense of overall well-being, (Clift and Morrison, 2011).

Top tips:

- Everyone can sing, but some of us with more confidence than others. And remember, you are *leading* the singing – this doesn't mean you are the lead singer. Enthusiasm and effort go a long way.

Keeping it simple is the key. Songs in the classroom need to be simplistic and memorable – beneficial to the teacher and the children.

Some singing vocabulary to get you started:

Table 8.2 Singing vocabulary

Posture	The position in which someone holds their body when performing.
Diction	Making the words clear to hear.
Expression	Showing moods, thoughts or feelings with your voice.

Solo	Performing or singing alone.
Unison	Everyone playing or singing the same thing together.
Round	A song where one group starts and the next starts after a line of singing - e.g., row, row, row your boat.
Call and response	A song where the leader sings a line and the rest of the group sings another line in response.
Chant	A song that is spoken rather than sung - e.g., raps and chants.

Table 8.3 Developing your subject knowledge in singing

Developing your subject knowledge in singing	
Resource to explore	**How it will help to develop your subject knowledge**
The Singing School Handbook: https://shop.singup.org/the-singing-school-handbook.html	This comprehensive guide developed by SingUp provides detailed guidance on planning singing and further resources.
Buddulph, J and Wheeler, J (2017) Singing the primary curriculum. In P Burnard and R Murphy (eds) *Teaching Music Creatively* (2nd edn). London: Routledge, pp69–84.	Use Chapter 6 to identify where singing can fit within the primary curriculum, as well as how to plan for creative song making and how to sing creatively with children.
Gareth Malone: Tips for teaching singing. BBC Bring the Noise	These films will increase your understanding of how to warm up for singing, ways you can teach a song, tips for how you as the leader can support and develop singing for performances.
Go and try	
Teach the song Kye Kye Kule, which is a call-and-response song from Ghana. Add actions to the song, then reflect on the questions on the prompts on the right.	What did the children learn? Declarative: children will know the structure of a call-and-response song. Procedural: children will sing in unison with control of pitch. Tacit: children will embed a steady beat through physical actions
Further resources to explore	
• SingUp • Out of the Ark • Everybody Sing • Song Source • Singing Sherlock Books	A range of different websites with singing resources. Some of these require further subscriptions as a school and some of these resources can be individually purchased with their accompanying backing tracks.

LISTENING

Listening is when you are giving a sound your attention. Listening as a musician means observing the music closely and looking for the elements of music in the piece. It is really important that children have an opinion or an emotional response about the music they have listened to and that they have an opportunity to share this. Offering your children rich diverse listening experiences will open their ears to a world of sound.

REFLECTION

What live listening experiences could you offer your children? Are there parents that could come into school and perform? Could local secondary schools bring in ensembles? Is the local music hub offering free children's concerts?

Consider how you ask your children to respond and reflect on what they are hearing. How can the other art forms support this? How will they share their musical thoughts?

Some listening vocabulary to get you started:

Table 8.4 *Listening vocabulary*

Ensemble	A large group of musicians playing together.
Genre	The style of the music. Some examples of musical genres would be pop, heavy metal, blues, house, jazz, etc.
Major and minor	The key of a piece of music can be major or minor. Music in a major key can sound brighter and happier, whereas music in a minor key can often sound darker – e.g., Mozart *Horn Concerto No. 1 in D major*, and Mozart *Concerto for Piano in D minor*.

Table 8.5 *Developing your subject knowledge in listening*

Developing your subject knowledge in listening	
Resources to explore	**How it will help to develop your subject knowledge**
• Nate Holder and Helen MacGregor: *Listen and Celebrate*.	Providing a selection of pieces from a range of time periods, countries and styles, this book celebrates the people who wrote the music. It deepens our understanding of a wider range of composers and offers an immersive experience through active listening and composing activities.
• Helen MacGregor: *Listening to Music* series. https:// collins.co.uk/collections/ music-express-extra	This series engages children in listening to music. It provides a basis for a range of listening, composing and performing opportunities

Go and try	
Listen and draw	What did the children learn?
Here are two contrasting pieces of music.	Declarative: children will know the name of a composer, piece, and their place and time in musical history.
The Storm: Britten	Procedural: children will listen with sustained attention.
Albatross: Fleetwood Mac	Tacit: children will create a personal response to a piece of music.
Play the music to your class and ask them to respond using art materials. They may choose to create a scene or more abstract lines and shapes. Use their artwork as a basis for class discussion.	
Further resources to explore	
• Minute of listening • Classical 100 • Classical 200	Banks of wide-ranging listening examples to support your understanding of musical elements and genres. Classical 200 has activities to try out with your children to develop their understanding further.

IMPROVISING AND COMPOSING

Improvising is creating music on the spur of the moment. For young children, this 'musical play' is the first step in composition. Composing is creating your own music, making musical decisions and selecting sounds with purpose. Composing is intrinsically linked to improvising.

REFLECTION

Ensure your classroom is a safe space for taking musical risks. There are no right or wrong answers; encourage creativity and having a go.

To start with, give children a frame for composing creatively within. This can be altered and removed as they become more confident over different units of work.

THE USE OF QUESTIONING DURING COMPOSITION ACTIVITIES

At times, it can feel daunting to help guide and support your children when they are composing. The sound, experimentation, improvisation and discussion can all seem like there are multiple aspects happening, and, in a way, there are! Try to use the Watch, Wait and Wonder approach shown in Figure 8.2 to give yourself time and space before you engage with the musicians:

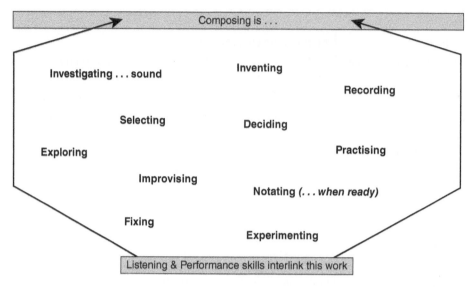

Figure 8.1 Composing is . . .

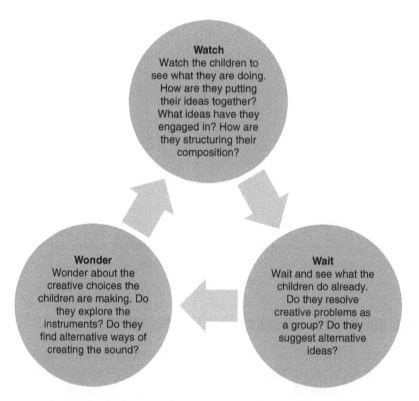

Figure 8.2 The teacher's role during composition using the Watch, Wait and Wonder approach

When you adopt an approach like this, your use of questioning becomes essential for deepening and progressing the children's musical understanding and knowledge and on occasions to introduce creative ideas when groups develop a block or struggle with generating ideas. This technique is referred to as 'possibility thinking' (Craft, 2001; Craft et al., 2007) whereby you suggest different ideas to help continue to fuel the creative spark of the group. These question starters (Table 8.6) are a useful guide to use generally across all areas of music, as well as to help your children to develop their ideas and support them with any composition challenges they are facing.

Table 8.6 Question starters

What is happening ... ? (descriptive, affective, opinions)	How will you ... ? (reflective, opinion)	How might it have ... ? (reflective, opinion)	How could you do this differently? (opinion, reflective)	How do you feel about ... ? (affective, opinion, reflective)
What do you think ... ? (opinion, evaluation)	Why did you do that or use that sound? (exploration, description, opinion, affective)	What do you think the problem is? (opinion, descriptive, evaluation)	What could you do to solve this problem? (opinion, exploration, descriptive)	Tell me about ...

In their study, Major and Cottle (2010) identify five phases of questioning throughout the composition process.

Phase 1

'Tell me what is happening in your picture?'

'Sound grid? Fanfare? Planet piece?'

Phase 2

'Why did you choose that instrument?'

Phase 3

'What did you think about while you were making the music?'

'What do you like about it?

'What would you change?'

Phase 4

'Was there anything you found difficult?'

'How did you solve it?'

Phase 5

'Tell me about the process you went through.'

Table 8.7 Developing your subject knowledge in composing

Developing your subject knowledge in composing	
Resources to explore	**How it will help to develop your subject knowledge**
Read Burnard, P with Boyak, J and Howell, G (2017) Children composing: creating communities of musical practice. In P Burnard and R Murphy (eds) *Teaching Music Creatively* (2nd edn). London: Routledge, 37–54.	This chapter will support you in moving into the role of facilitator and guide while your children are composing. Case studies develop your understanding of how this might look in school and your role within composing activities.
Composing Doodling Improvising Encouraging Children's Own Music in Primary Schools: www.ism.org/professional-development/webinars/composing-doodling-improvising-encouraging-childrens-own-music-in-primary-schools	This film, presented by Dr Alison Daubney, develops confidence and understanding in facilitating and promoting children's exploration of music through improvising and composing.
Explore the BBC 10 pieces: www.bbc.co.uk/teach/ten-pieces	These resources will support your understanding of how classical music can be used as a springboard for creativity with children. Detailed schemes of work will show how musical learning can be developed from these starting points.
Go and try improvising	
Create a soundscape with a group of children. • Show the children a picture such as Van Gogh's 'Starry Night'. Ask the children to find and create sounds inspired by the image.	What did the children learn? Declarative: children will know that music can represent image. Procedural: children will choose sounds to describe an image. Tacit: children will respond to art through music.
Go and try composing	
Compose the journey through the storm with Benjamin Britten, BBC 10 pieces: www.bbc.co.uk/teach/ten-pieces	What did the children learn? Declarative: children will know how to use structure in a composition. Procedural: children will compose a sequence of sounds. Tacit: children will explore and select appropriate sounds for a purpose.

PLAYING AND PERFORMING

Playing is using voices, bodies and instruments to create music. Performing is playing in front of an audience.

REFLECTION

Think of ways to create performance opportunities with your class. This could be informally to the Senior Leadership Team or another class, or inviting parents in.

Ensure that your children play both tuned and untuned instruments throughout their year with you.

The following is some playing and performing vocabulary to get you started.

Table 8.8 Playing/performing vocabulary

Tuned or untuned percussion	Percussion means any instrument that is struck to make a sound. • Drums, triangles, claves and tambourines are all untuned percussion, meaning that their sounds may have higher or lower tones, but they do not match a given note on a keyboard. Although they can have pitched sounds, they cannot play a melody. • Glockenspiel, chime bars, Boomwhackers and xylophones are all examples of tuned percussion. Each bar or tube on the instrument has a given pitch. You can see this with the letter that they are usually marked with.
Phrases	Musical sentences.
Conductor	The person who directs the musicians and keeps them together.
Accent	Emphasising one note or word.
Ostinato	A repeating musical pattern. These can be rhythmic or melodic. In popular music, they are often referred to as riffs or licks.

Table 8.9 Developing your subject knowledge in playing and performing

Developing your subject knowledge in playing and performing	
Resources to explore	How it will help to develop your subject knowledge
• *Agogo Bells to Xylophone*: https://collins.co.uk/pages/ primary-music	You need to be confident with the instruments you are using with your children. This book has detailed images and information to ensure you are playing and naming instruments correctly.

(Continued)

Table 8.9 (Continued)

Go and try	
Eine Kliene Nachtmusik for percussion: https://youtu.be/ETSdeb-YK4s	What did the children learn? Declarative: children will know about the instrument they are playing – its name, where it's from, etc. Procedural: children will know the techniques in playing instruments – e.g., using two beaters, fingering, chord shapes. Tacit: children will develop confidence and a sense of pride performing as part of a group.
Further resources to explore	
Websites	**YouTube channels**
BBC 10 pieces: www.bbc.co.uk/teach/ten-pieces *Body Beats* by Ollie Tumner: www.beatgoeson.co.uk/ *Kaboom Percussion*: www.kaboompercussion.com/ *Bobby Shaftoe Clap your Hands* by Sue Nicholls: https://collins.co.uk/products/9780713635560	*Musication*: www.youtube.com/c/musication Mr F: www.youtube.com/channel/UCO2jMHHbKVJxj8YtsFaMOuA Music with Mr Grey: Ukulaliens: www.youtube.com/c/UkulaliensUkuleleClub/videos

INTERRELATED DIMENSIONS OF MUSIC

The following table refers to the 'interrelated dimensions' of music. These are the basic building blocks for all music. Terms such as these simply reinforce that they should not be taught in isolation and that the elements are interwoven with each other. It is important that you know about the musical language that exists and ensures discussions are held using this language when talking about music with your class. Using the technical terms is not vital – volume instead of dynamics is fine. It is more vital that children understand the concepts that these words represent. Your children may become happy using the musical terms or they may be confident talking about them without using the exact term. Either of these are OK as long as your teaching focuses around them.

Table 8.10 What are the interrelated dimensions of music?

Interrelated dimension	What it means	Key words
Pitch: Donkey – Saint-Saens: www.YouTube.com	High and low	Melody: a sequence of notes that make a tune. Pentatonic: a scale with only five notes – e.g., CDEGA (no F and B). Scale: a set of musical notes ordered by pitch – e.g., CDEFGABC = C major scale, CDEGA – pentatonic scale.

Interrelated dimension	What it means	Key words
Dynamics Bjork – 'Oh so quiet': www.YouTube.com	The volume of sounds – loud and quiet	Italian terms to describe dynamics: f = forte (loud) p = piano (quiet) crescendo (getting louder) ‹ diminuendo (getting quieter) ›
Tempo: Edward Grieg: 'In the Hall of the Mountain King': www.YouTube.com	The speed of the sounds – fast and slow, getting faster, getting slower.	Italian terms to describe tempo: largo: a slow tempo andante: a walking pace presto: a quick tempo
Texture: Steve Reich: 'The Four Sections' www.YouTube.com	How many sounds you hear at once. Thin texture, thick texture.	Solo or whole orchestra, duet, trio, ensemble.
Timbre: Mozart: Horn Concertos classical100.org	The sound quality produced by individual instruments and voices.	There are no specific terms used for timbre, and children will find their own adjectives to describe sound. Encourage discussion around sound by talking about sound quality using words such as: bright, sparkly, scratchy, smooth, sharp, dull.
Duration: Johann Strauss II: 'The Blue Danube Waltz': classical100.org	The length of the sound: long and short sounds.	Ostinato: a repeating musical pattern; in popular music, they are often referred to as riffs or licks. Pulse or steady beat: the heartbeat of a piece of music, it can be fast or slow, it can speed up or slow down. Rhythm: a mixture of long and short sounds.
Structure: The Beatles: 'Yellow Submarine' www.YouTube.com	How the music is organised: repetition, patterns, etc.	Some examples of structure could be: verse and chorus call and response 12-bar blues rondo form: ABACA

NOTATION

Being creative with sound and expressing through playing, singing and composing is the first step in musical learning. However, having the ability to write down your musical ideas creates opportunities for revisiting and editing, as well as simply remembering what you were doing. The first steps to notation will be the linking of sound to a simple picture or symbol (graphic notation). This can then develop into a more standard notation such a Western stave notation.

Table 8.11 Graphic notation

Graphic notation

What it looks like

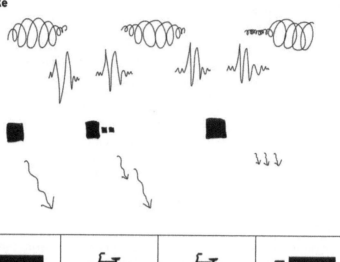

What do we mean by graphic notation?	Examples
Graphic notation uses a wide range of personal symbols of varying sizes and colours made up of different pictures, shapes and squiggles. It is the first link between the essence of sound represented in a symbolic form.	Kandinsky on Chrome Music Lab allows the children to draw and then hear the sounds:
Pictures can be used as the beginning to this journey. As a class, you can decide the sound that matches a picture or image.	musiclab. chromeexperiments.com
As children progress in their notation, they will begin to show the interrelated dimensions in their own way –	Other examples of how sound can be represented through graphics:
e.g., I = in KS1, pitch may be shown by drawing the sound higher or lower on the page. Moving to KS2, the colour chosen may represent the coloured Boomwhackers, or chime bars, or the note name is written next to the symbol.	Alex Chorley: 'Thunderstorm', a graphic notation composition.
Dynamics could be represented by drawing symbols larger and smaller. Timbre can be represented by using different colours for the symbol depending on how the children feel about the sound. Children may decide the colour of the sound or use smooth or jagged lines.	Debussy: 'Clair de lune': www.youtube.com
Graphic notation is perfect for children to use and create when composing. It allows them to notate their own musical thoughts and formalise their ideas. Returning to their graphic notation means they can edit and revise ideas in order to move on their learning. This is a fundamental difference between improvising (in the moment) and composing.	

Table 8.12 Formal notation

Formal notation	
Rhythm notation	**Pitch notation**
Key words: Crochet Quaver Semi-quaver Minim Rest	Key words: High Low Scale Melody
What it looks like: Mu - sic is fun! 	What it looks like:

What do we mean by rhythm notation?	What it looks like in the classroom	What do we mean by pitch notation?	What it looks like in the classroom
How the notation looks alters its length.	Rhythm Level 1: https://youtu.be/3v5REqCKOOo	Where the notation sits alters its pitch.	Melody maker: chrome music lab: https://musiclab.chromeexperiments.com/melody-maker/

Stave notation

What it looks like:

(Continued)

Table 8.12 (Continued)

Formal notation
Stave notation uses five lines called the stave (or staff in America). Musical notes and symbols are placed on the lines to mean a musical effect. Different pitches are represented by each line and rhythmic notation tells the musician how to read the music. It is worth noting that this is a Western musical tradition dating back to medieval times. Other cultures use differing forms of notation.
For some children, notation makes total sense and enhances their understanding. It needs a great deal of understanding before you can truly be creative with stave notation. Consider the amount of exposure to words and letters children need before and during their journey towards reading and writing independently. This is the same for learning to read and write musically, and the additional challenge we face here is that children often are not exposed to this language outside of their music lesson or the music environment. It is important that children learn to read and write music, but should always be taught using musical sound and within a musical activity. Consider it as an extra tool you have to use, not as the sole focus for your teaching.

THE MUSICAL ENVIRONMENT

Creating the right learning environment is key for musical learning. You may be fortunate to have a dedicated space in school which is always ready for music. This may be a carpeted room to help deaden sound with no tables or chairs and a large open space on the floor for working. If this is not the case, then you will need to consider how you can best re-create this for your children. Could you teach music after playtime or lunchtime so you can move tables and chairs to the side?

REFLECTION

Consider what resources will best support your children and how you could display these.

- Skills display: these words could have arrows that you use to show the focus skills of the lesson.

- Interrelated dimensions display: pictorial representations and simple words.

- Examples of graphic notation ideas.

- Rhythmic notation: this could be the school system that is used, minibeast words, tea/coffee words language (see notation for further examples).

- Working wall to refer to current learning.

- A music history timeline: add composers and musicians you are listening to with their dates in sequential order.

Also, try to consider what practical resources might your children need access to?

- Quality instruments/sound makers: these are best labelled with their correct name and a picture so that your children and other adults talk about them correctly and can put them away.

- Paper and pencils (HB and coloured).

EARLY YEARS MUSIC

Children learn best through exploration, play and creativity and in any Early Years setting you need to be offering them invitations to explore and develop through sound and music making. Children's curiosity needs to be engaged with inventive and open-ended activities and at the core the learning should be led by the child. Children need to be provided with positive relationships and an enabling environment.

Early Years teachers and support staff are highly skilled in spotting spontaneous moments as well as observing the planned ones. Adults can partner children in musical play – for example, you may notice a child singing or chanting as they play. Join in with their song, echo it back, or you could join in as children are tapping on instruments or other noise makers. Match their speed and patterns, echo back. There will be times when it is more appropriate to stand back, listen and observe, and take notice of what the children are doing with sound. Some great examples can be found here: www.youtube.com/watch?v=vCdh1XDsydA.

As part of a carousel of activities or during free-flow invitations for children to explore, sound should be made. This could be as simple as plastic bottles filled with different materials (sand, rice, water, dried peas) or kitchen utensils tied to railings. There should also be opportunity for children to explore more sophisticated percussion instruments, such as drums and tambourines. Children must also have the opportunity to experience tuned instruments – e.g., glockenspiels, chime bars, Boomwhackers.

Untuned instruments are equivalent to monochrome lead pencils which children are more than happy to use in many highly creative and satisfying ways. Tuned instruments, on the other hand, like colour pencils, add a whole new realm of possibilities to this monochrome world, thus expanding the creative process through the introduction of pitch.

(Greenhalgh, 2018, p47)

REFLECTION

- What sound makers are on offer in your setting?

- How do children access them?

- Is there a mixture of tuned and untuned instruments?

In addition to independent sound-based activities, it is valuable to have designated music time within the EYFS classroom. Over time, build up to a 25–30-minute session per week to make sure that children are able to experience a range of musical activities together. For these sessions, sit in a circle with your children, making sure you and the other adults in the room are part of the music making. To help the children develop their confidence in these sessions, try to keep to the same format each week. An example is provided in Table 8.13. You may even want to repeat the same or similar activities each week for a half term. You will find that more children join in with the songs and activities each time you repeat them as their confidence builds.

A simple music time session could be structured like this:

Table 8.13 How a music session in EYFS might look

Timings	Activity	Links to Early Learning goals
5 minutes	Hello chant: *Hello, Abigail. How are you? Who's your friend sitting next to you?* Ask Abigail to tell you the name of the child to her left and repeat the chant for the next child, and so on around the circle.	Communication and language. Personal, social and emotional development.
3 minutes	Sing your 'Song of the Week'. Maybe children can suggest actions for it or learn Makaton signs. This could include counting songs and songs with patterns such as five little speckled frogs or ten fat sausages.	Literacy. Physical development. Expressive arts and design. Mathematics.
10 minutes	Introduce some instruments. Play 'What's in the bag?' Hide four or five instruments or sound makers in a large sack. Ask the children to listen carefully as you play the instrument in the bag. Ask them what they hear. They may be able to tell you the name of the instrument or they may describe the noise.	Communication and language.

Timings	Activity	Links to Early Learning goals
15 minutes	Allow children to select an instrument each. This may seem chaotic, but it gives the children the chance to explore the instruments. Use this time to observe what the children are doing. Make sure you have a clear 'stop signal' established before attempting this. Try some simple instrument games: Chant: *We play and we play and we STOP.* *We play and we play and we STOP.* *We play and we play and we play and we play.* *And we play and we play and we STOP!* Exaggerate your stop, perhaps adding a 'stop' hand signal. Try again at different speeds. Praise those children who stop quickly. Traffic lights: show children a red and green card circle. Red means they stop; green means they can play their instruments. Again, exaggerate showing the green card. Mix up whether you change quickly or slowly. In time, children could be in control of the traffic lights. Finally, ask the children to play along with a recorded piece of music. Try to choose something with a strong, clear, steady beat and ask the children to 'play along'. Model how you might play along with the steady beat of the song or play your instrument in different ways. The children may copy you or find their own moves and sounds. If you spot a child doing something great, encourage others to follow them. This could develop into a 'follow-the-leader' game.	Personal social and emotional development. Understanding the world. Communication and language. Physical development.
5 minutes	Choose a piece of music that the children can get up and move to. You may want to judge whether you need an upbeat energetic piece, or perhaps something slower and calming. Props for movement can be useful like ribbons or silks. Diversify your listening repertoire using tracks the children will know, such as a Disney songs, but also feeding in classical music and music from other cultures.	Understanding the world. Physical development. Expressive arts and design.
3 minutes	Finish with a known song to end the session, or share a story song together - e.g., Barefoot Books.	Communication and language. Literacy. Expressive arts and design.

Visual and sensory aids such as props, puppets, parachutes, lyras and scrunchies can enhance a session. These sessions can easily be shared with parents at the end of a half term, asking them to come in and join in with the children. These early, low-key performances are great for building confidence with the children for more formal performances.

Music in the Early Years is a powerful tool. In addition to learning discrete musical skills such as singing in pitch and keeping a steady beat, music enhances learning across the Early Learning goals. It can support language development, literacy and numeracy, fine and gross motor skills and social skills. It can engage and inspire children, allowing them to show skills that otherwise may have been hidden. But best of all, music with young children is creative, playful, expressive and joyful.

Further resources to explore:

- Cotton, M (2005) *Agogo Bells to Xylophone: A Friendly Guide to Classroom Percussion Instruments*. London: Collins.

- Greenhalgh, Z (2018) *Music and Singing in the Early Years*. London: Routledge.

- Making music meaningful in the Early Years: www.teachearlyyears.com/learning-and-development/view/making-music

- Music in the round: Soundplay Resource Pack: https://studylib.net

- Musical development matters: https://network.youthmusic.org.uk/musical-development-matters

- Nicholls, S and Hickman, S (2021) *Early Years Foundation Stage: Ages 3–5* (Collins Primary Music). Collins: London.

- Singing circles: singing activities for 'schrunchies' (stretchy fabric rings), Lycra sheets and parachutes: www.musicmark.org.uk/wp-content/uploads/Book-SINGING-CIRCLES-definitive.pdf

- Young, S (2008) *Music 3–5*. London: Routledge.

PART 3: UNDERSTANDING THE DEVELOPMENT OF CHILDREN'S KNOWLEDGE IN MUSIC

Being a primary teacher is tricky. You have to be ready to develop skills in a range of subjects and ensure that children are learning more, remembering more and knowing more.

PROGRESSION WITHIN MUSIC

Musical learning falls into three different types of knowledge, as outlined at the beginning of this chapter. Good musical learning is rooted in knowing and understanding the musical elements and using these throughout the skills. For example, could you play chords on tuned percussion with three beaters without understanding the layout of notes on the instrument, how to hold the beaters correctly and how to use two? Building the skills in small, incremental steps in learning is integral for musical learning. By ensuring that the skills build in the right order at the right pace and at the right time, your children will amaze you with what they are capable of.

In order to plan for musical learning, it is important to ensure that you 'know' enough about the content at the appropriate level. As you plan for your children's learning, focus on the skills you wish to develop. Check that you are mapping these against a skills progression document and ensure that you are building on prior learning. Never be afraid to ask for help when there is a skill that you need to master or understand, there will always be an adult (or possibly older child) in school who can help you. Understanding what you are teaching is so important for true musical learning to take place with your children.

HOW DO CHILDREN DEVELOP AS MUSICIANS?

Musical progression comes with the development of each skill rooted in an understanding of the knowledge of each interrelated dimension. The range of skills to develop means that teaching through a spiral curriculum where each skill is frequently revisited, revised and improved upon is vital for the child to develop as a musician. This in turn means that, at times, it can be difficult to hear progression as a few skills overlap and develop in turn.

As you become increasingly more confident in teaching music, you will begin to explore how to enhance the quality of the children's music understanding and knowledge. In essence, you will look at how to deepen the musical learning and how children progress.

There are a number of different approaches to thinking about how children progress. One way is to consider is that when you teach an area of music, you can do one of three things to progress the children's learning (Ofsted, 2012, p139). Within a task, you could:

1. Increase the *range* of an activity by making the task longer, such as adding another verse or extending a composition.

2. Increase the *demand* by adding complexity to what you are asking the children to do – for example, you might add actions to song, play with two beaters

instead of one, or improve the *quality* of the musical behaviour the children are demonstrating. Can the children use an increasing array of dynamics such as a *crescendo* instead of just *piano* or *forte* sounds?

Another way of viewing progression is by focusing on the three interlinking 'pillars of progression' (Ofsted, 2021). Together, these pillars contribute to musical understanding.

Table 8.14 Ofsted: three pillars of progression

Technical	Constructive	Expressive
• Competence in controlling sound (instrumental, vocal or with music technology). • Use of a communication system, such as staff notation or guitar tab.	• Knowledge of the musical elements/ interrelated dimensions of music. • Knowledge of the components of composition.	• Musical quality. • Musical creativity. • Knowledge of musical meaning across the world and time.

Within composition, Swanick and Tillman's (1986) spiral model of musical development was monumental in the way that it explored how children composed. Tillman analysed hundreds and hundreds of different examples of children's compositions and identified common characteristics that she then developed into a spiral model. This is a model over the past thirty-five years that has been explained (Mills, 2009, pp97–101), reviewed (Anderson, 2022) and celebrated in the *British Journal of Music Education* (39 (1)).

REFLECTION

Locate a skills progression document

This document can illustrate how musical skills can be broken down across each of the school years and what would be expected for each year group. A child achieving at the expected level would be achieving these musical skills in each year group.

Explore the example from the Music Mark website: www.musicmark.org.uk/wp-content/uploads/peer-to-peer_progression_framework.pdf. In addition, your local music hub is likely to have their own framework you may wish to use. The *Model Music Curriculum* (2021) illustrates one example of what progression looks like.

HOW DO YOU NOTICE PROGRESSION IN MUSIC?

It can be hard to notice the progress across a year for an individual child. Making film/audio recordings at significant points during your teaching can be really informative. Recordings allow the children to reflect on their musical journey and hear ways they can make improvements through critical reflection. Films allow you time to reflect, see and hear children who may need further support or challenge, and to set small areas for improvement. Fundamentally, as the films/audio recording build as a bank, they enable you to hear the progress that children are making with different areas of musical learning and see how their technical skills with instruments are improving. These films allow you time to reflect on musical learning that is much harder to spot in the moment when you are leading or part of the musical process.

SPOTTING MUSICAL TALENT AND POTENTIAL

How does a child show that they are 'outstanding' in music? How do you know if a child in your class has musical talent? You may think that this might mean they play a musical instrument, sing in tune or read musical notation. What about the children who have had little or no musical input? What about those children who compose and create music at home using technology? As a class music teacher, you are in a privileged position to see all the children taking part in musical activity – not just those who have been lucky enough to get music tuition out of the classroom. How can you spot the musical potential of every child in the room? The NPME 2 highlights the need for talent to be identified so that *all* children can progress their interest and potential.

Awards for Young Musicians (ATMs) has been researching how best to support teachers in identifying musical potential in the classroom and has developed eight facets to look for:

1. Enjoyment.

2. Active listening.

3. Absorption in the music.

4. Commitment to the process.

5. Inclination to explore.

6. Inclination to lead.

7. Memory.

8. Expression.

You can find out more about these facets and AYM training and research at: www.a-y-m.org.uk/how-we-help/identifying-talent/

Ensure that you step back from the music making and make time to observe the children's musical behaviours and note those that show potential and talent. Your music lead or local hub should be able to point you to pathways for progression for those children.

PART 4: EXPLORING MUSIC FURTHER

Ensuring that you are up to date with the latest musical developments will be really important once you are teaching your own class. Simple updates by email can sometimes make all the difference to keeping your finger on the pulse. Most of these organisations have a newsletter or a way you can sign up without paying for membership, although you may decide that this would be beneficial.

Periodically check through the online seminars they offer, often for free, and hear the latest debates or talks by HMI Ofsted Music Leads and other leading figures in music education. There may be sessions that keep you up to date with what you need to be doing in school, sessions of personal interest and ones that really challenge the way you think about certain aspects of music education. Podcasts offer an alternative that may fit your schedule better. However you choose to improve your own musical knowledge, the following are the associations, individuals, books and podcasts we would suggest you check first.

SUBJECT ASSOCIATIONS FOR MUSIC

MUSIC MARK: WWW.MUSICMARK.ORG.UK/

Music Mark is a superb organisation for keeping you up to date with what's going on and keeping your knowledge up to date. They hold a range of online live seminars you can join to hear a range of speakers, including current Music HMI and other influential figures. Membership is free for students with a reduction for recent graduates. Music hubs around the country identify schools that are eligible to become a Music Mark school, which gives the school free access to the resources and online seminars.

THE INCORPORATED SOCIETY OF MUSICIANS: WWW.ISM.ORG/

This is the UK's professional body for musicians and subject association for music who give music educators access to a wealth of CPD, planning and resources (paid subscription).

THE MUSIC TEACHERS' ASSOCIATION: WWW.MUSICTEACHERS.ORG/

With the aim of Connecting–Inspiring–Leading, Music Teachers' Association offers membership to join together with our music teachers in an online community alongside a wealth of resources.

MUSIC EDUCATION COUNCIL: HTTPS://MEC.WHITEFUSE.NET/

The Music Education Council draws its membership from across the entire music education and music industry sectors. It provides online seminars and monthly newsletters.

MUSICIANS' UNION: HTTPS://MUSICIANSUNION.ORG.UK/

MU work to maximise the employment and overall income of musicians as well as protecting and improving working conditions. They offer advice, support and legal assistance.

REFLECTION

Locate your local music hub and ensure you are on their mailing list. They are funded to support you and your teaching in school, and will be more than happy to help with planning and supporting musical learning – all you need to do is ask!

FURTHER RESOURCES TO SUPPORT YOUR DEVELOPMENT

Books to deepen your musical understanding:

- Beach, N, Evans, J and Spruce, G (eds) (2010) *Making Music in the Primary School: Whole Class Instrumental and Vocal Teaching*. London: Routledge.

- Burnard, P and Murphy, R (eds) (2017) *Teaching Music Creatively*. London: Routledge.

- Daubney, A (2017) *Teaching Primary Music*. London: SAGE.

- Hallam, S and Creech, A (eds) (2010) *Music Education in the 21st Century in the United Kingdom: Achievements, Analysis and Aspirations*. London: Institute of Education Press.

Websites to explore:

- ISM Primary Music Toolkit: www.ismtrust.org/resources/primary-toolkit

- The Music Education Podcast

- Oak Academy (unit and lesson plans with supporting videos): https://classroom.thenational.academy/

- Teaching Notes: Music Teachers Association's Podcast

REFERENCES

Anderson, A (2022) The Swanwick/Tillman spiral of musical development: impacts and influences – guest editorial, *British Journal of Music Education*, Cambridge University Press, *39* (1): 1–43.

Boyce-Tillman, J and Anderson, A (2022) Musical development then and now: in conversation with June Boyce-Tillman, *British Journal of Music Education*, Cambridge University Press, *39* (1): 51–66.

Clift, S and Morrison, I (2011) Group singing fosters mental health and wellbeing: findings from the East Kent 'singing for health' network project, *Mental Health and Social Inclusion*, *15* (2): 88–97. Available at: https://doi.org/10.1108/20428301111140930

Craft, A (2001) An analysis of research and literature on creativity in education. London: QCA. Available at: www.researchgate.net/profile/Anna_Craft/publication/237469169_Report_prepared_for_the_Qualifications_and_Curriculum_Authority/links/0deec5398845f4bb43000000.pdf

Craft, A, Cremin, T, Burnard, P and Chappell, K (2007) Developing creative learning through possibility thinking with children aged 3–7. In A Craft, T Cremin and P Burnard, (eds) *Creative Learning 3–11 and How we Document It*. London: Trentham. Available at: http://oro.open.ac.uk/12952/2/

Department for Education (DfE) (2011) The importance of music: a national plan for music education. Available at: www.gov.uk/government/publications/the-importance-of-music-a-national-plan-for-music-education

Department for Education (DfE) (2013) *The National Curriculum: Music Programmes of Study: Key Stages 1 and 2*. Available at: https://assets.publishing.service.gov.uk/government/uploads/system/uploads/attachment_data/file/239037/PRIMARY_national_curriculum_-_Music.pdf

Department for Education (DfE) (2021) *The Model Music Curriculum: Key Stages 1 to 2: Non-statutory Guidance for the National Curriculum in England*. Available at: https://assets.publishing.service.gov.uk/government/uploads/system/uploads/attachment_data/file/974358/Model_Music_Curriculum_Key_Stage_1__2_FINAL.pdf

Department for Education (DfE) (2022) The power of music to change lives: a national plan for music education. Available at: www.gov.uk/government/publications/the-power-of-music-to-change-lives-a-national-plan-for-music-education. *A short summary of this document has been produced by the Music Teachers Association* available at: www.musicteachers.org/wp-content/uploads/2022/06/NMPE2-Summary-for-Schools.pdf

Elliott, D (1991) Music as knowledge. *The Journal of Aesthetic Education, 25* (3): 21–40. Available at: www.jstor.org/stable/3332993

Fautley, M and Daubney, A (2022) Curriculum considerations in music education in England: spiral thinking, spiral planning and its impact on contemporary thought. *British Journal of Music Education*, Cambridge University Press, *39* (1): 131–40.

Greenhalgh, Z (2018) *Music and Singing in the Early Years*. Abingdon: Routledge.

Hennessy, S (2000) Overcoming the red-feeling: the development of confidence to teach music in primary school amongst student teachers. *British Journal of Music Education*, Cambridge University Press, *17* (2): 183–96.

Major, A. and Cottle, M. (2010) Learning and teaching through talk: music composing in the classroom with children aged six to seven years. *British Journal of Music Education*, Cambridge University Press, *27* (3): 289–304.

Mills, J. (2009) *Music in the Primary School* (3rd edn). Oxford: Oxford Music Education.

Ofsted (2012) Music in schools: wider still, and wider. Available at: https://assets.publishing. service.gov.uk/government/uploads/system/uploads/attachment_data/file/413347/Music_in_schools_wider_still__and_wider.pdf

Ofsted (2021) *Research Review for Music*. London: Ofsted. Available at www.gov.uk/government/publications/research-review-series-music/research-review-series-music (accessed 15 December 2022).

Paynter, J (1982) *Music in the Secondary School Curriculum: Trends and Developments in Classroom Teaching*. Cambridge: Cambridge University Press.

Sarrazin, N (2016) *Music and the Child. Open SUNY Textbooks*. Available at: https://open.umn.edu/opentextbooks/textbooks/283

Seddon, F and Biasutti, M (2008) Non-music specialist trainee primary school teachers' confidence in teaching music in the classroom. *Music Education Research, 10* (3): 403–21. Available at: http://dx.doi.org/10.1080/14613800802280159

Swanwick, K (1986) *Musical Knowledge: Intuition, Analysis and Music Education*. Abingdon: Routledge.

Swanwick, K and Tillman, J (1986) The sequence of musical development: a study of children's compositions. *British Journal of Music Education, 3* (3): 305–9.

9

PRIMARY FOREIGN LANGUAGES
CATHY BURCH

KEYWORDS: COMMUNICATION; VOCABULARY; GRAMMAR; PHONICS; LANGUAGE STRUCTURES; INTERCULTURAL UNDERSTANDING; INCIDENTAL CLASSROOM TARGET LANGUAGE.

LINKS TO THE CCF

High Expectations (Standard 1): 1.2

How Pupils Learn (Standard 2): 2.2, 2.4, 2.7

Subject and Curriculum (Standard 3): 3.2, 3.5, 3.7

Classroom Practice (Standard 4): 4.8, 4.9

PART 1: EXPLORING PRIMARY FOREIGN LANGUAGES
WHAT IS PRIMARY FOREIGN LANGUAGES?

Learning a foreign language has been part of the national curriculum in England at KS2 and KS3 since 2014, for all pupils aged 7 to 14. At KS2, the foreign language taught can be either a modern foreign language such as French or Spanish, or an ancient language such as Latin or Ancient Greek (DfE, 2013). Ancient languages do not require the same oral practice or presentation, and this is clearly marked in the national curriculum for languages at KS2. At KS3, the foreign language taught must be a modern language. However, secondary schools may offer ancient languages in addition. A foreign language is not the same as a 'home' language, which is a language learned in childhood in the home environment (UNESCO, 2022).

A total of 99 per cent of all primary schools in English state that they teach a foreign language at KS2 (Tinsley and Board, 2016). French is currently the most commonly taught foreign language in English primary schools by far, accounting for around 76 per cent of all teaching at KS2. Spanish is currently taught in about 29 per cent of English primary schools at KS2, with some schools teaching both languages. Only a small minority of primary schools teach other languages such as German or Mandarin Chinese (Collen, 2022).

Although not currently part of the national curriculum until KS2, 42 per cent of KS1 teachers state that they also teach foreign languages (Tinsley and Board, 2016). In order not to interfere with learning how to read and write in the first language, English, the teaching of this age group tends to focus on the oracy skills of speaking and listening only. Primary Foreign Languages at KS2 focuses on all four 'language skills' of communication: speaking, listening, reading and writing.

At KS2, foreign languages are increasingly being taught by the class teacher rather than a 'specialist' languages teacher, often following either a published scheme or one created in-house. Therefore, as Jones and Coffey wisely state of Primary Foreign Languages, *the teacher is the greatest resource of all* (2017, p31). This chapter looks at the subject and pedagogical knowledge required by trainee teachers relating to foreign language teaching in KS2, so that they may teach foreign languages to the best of their abilities. References are made to examples in French and Spanish in order to illustrate the main ideas, but the principles may equally apply to any foreign language.

WHY IS PRIMARY FOREIGN LANGUAGES IN THE NATIONAL CURRICULUM?

Over twenty years ago, EU heads of state agreed on the importance of improving basic skills, in particular by *teaching at least two foreign languages from a early age* (Barcelona European Council, 2002, p19). As a result, learning at least one foreign language has been compulsory from the age of 8 to 18 in most EU countries since 2003 (European Commission, 2017). In England, learning a foreign language finally became compulsory at both KS2 and KS3 (for pupils aged 7 to 14) in September 2014 (DfE, 2013).

The referendum on the United Kingdom's European Union membership in June 2016 led to the UK's withdrawal from the EU. The Confederation of British Industry commented that education and skills would play a vital role in the future relationship with the European Union and underlined the fact that foreign languages and cultural understanding would be vital in order deliver the government's vision of 'Global Britain' (CBI/Pearson, 2019). In a similar vein, the 'National Recovery Programme for Languages', formulated by the All-Party Parliamentary Group on Modern Languages in 2019, stated that the UK's languages deficit is holding the country back *economically, socially and culturally* (APGML, 2019). The report asserts that the UK's lack of language skills costs an estimated 3.5 per cent of GDP and that languages are needed to grow an export-led economy. In response to this situation, the programme's first strategic objective is to *develop and implement an inclusive languages policy from age 5 to 18 with clear pathways to qualifications in a wide range of languages.*

The national curriculum languages programmes of study for KS2 and KS3 (DfE, 2013) highlights the importance of language learning in the global context in its opening sentence: *Learning a foreign language is a liberation from insularity and provides an opening to other cultures.* According to the Purpose of study, *Language teaching should provide the foundation for learning further languages, equipping pupils to study and work in other countries.* The government's ambition that the vast majority of mainstream state school pupils should be currently studying a language at GCSE has been clearly documented for several years, but has not yet been achieved (Ofsted, 2021, p5). Noting that less than half of all pupils were studying a language at GCSE, Her Majesty's Chief Inspector (HMCI) observed that it seemed clear that for the government's ambition to be met, *primary schools will need to lay the foundations in these subjects before their pupils move on to study them at secondary school* (HMCI, 2016). This makes clear Ofsted's view that primary foreign language learning is required to enable pupils to achieve a GCSE and beyond.

REFLECTION

What do you think should be included in foreign language learning by primary school pupils?

Why is it important for young children to learn foreign languages?

What, and how, exactly should young children be taught in this subject?

HOW HAS 'KNOWLEDGE' IN PRIMARY FOREIGN LANGUAGES DEVELOPED OVER TIME?

Judging from the stated 'aims' of the national curriculum for languages for KS2 and KS3, 'knowledge' in Primary Foreign Languages centres on pupils learning how to communicate using the four language skills of listening, speaking, reading and writing. With specific reference to subject knowledge in KS2, the document states that pupils should learn *to understand and communicate ideas, facts and feelings in speech and writing, focused on familiar and routine matters, using their knowledge of phonology, grammatical structures and vocabulary* (DfE, 2013). Learning about culture is mentioned only briefly at the beginning of the current Purpose of study (DfE, 2013).

Before the national curriculum came into being, the KS2 Framework for Languages formed non-compulsory guidance from the government on their commitment to all pupils in KS2 having the 'entitlement' to learn a foreign language (DES, 2005, p1). Intercultural understanding formed one of the three core strands of the KS2 Framework for Languages, along with Oracy and Literacy, in conjunction with two cross-cutting strands, Language Learning Strategies and Knowledge of Language (DES, 2005, p6): at this stage, then, intercultural understanding was considered of great importance in studying a foreign language. The KS2 Framework stated the following rationale:

> *Language competence and intercultural understanding are an essential part of being a citizen. Children develop a greater understanding of their own lives in the context of exploring the lives of others. They learn to look at things from another's perspective, giving them insight into the people, culture and traditions of other cultures.*

(DES, 2005, p8)

The current lack of importance attributed to intercultural understanding as one of the cornerstones of language learning in primary schools may be problematic in terms of presenting pupils with a decolonised curriculum. If, as teachers, we do not refer to culture at all and just teach the foreign language, we may unwittingly be encouraging a culturally ignorant or even 'Anglocentric' view of the world in our pupils. Through the inclusion of intercultural understanding in our teaching, pupils may be encouraged to adopt a respectful approach towards other cultures. For young children, this might include how children from another culture live their lives on a daily basis – for example, where they live, what their school is like or how they spend their time. We could consider how this differs or is similar to how we live our lives and emphasise to children that it is important not to judge others – that no one culture is better or worse than another.

Even if we include culture, a false view or representation of 'the other' may still persist. In our attempt to decolonise our language teaching, as teachers, we may ask pupils where French is spoken outside France, or where Spanish is spoken outside Spain. However, if we do not ask pupils and discuss *why* other countries speak those languages, or indeed, English, we miss discussing the catastrophic effect of colonisation globally, and the resulting loss of many indigenous languages. Similarly, we should be wary of presenting stereotypes when we represent any nation, but rather aim to promote inclusion of all peoples across the globe.

REFLECTION

How far is critical thinking about race/ethnicity present in our curriculum?

How far do the materials and resources we use promote voices and perspectives that come from beyond a 'Eurocentric' core?

(Adapted from Panford and Irvine, 2021.)

PRIMARY FOREIGN LANGUAGES NOW

Current themes in the teaching of Primary Foreign Languages are many and varied. As such, below are just a few examples that cause much discussion, including the choice of language taught, issues around transition from KS2 to KS3, and the increasing prominence in the three pillars of progression – phonology, vocabulary and grammar.

THE CHOICE OF LANGUAGE TAUGHT

Due to its dominant status as a 'global language' (Graham et al., 2016), English is the foreign language most commonly taught at primary and secondary schools in nearly all European countries (European Commission, 2017). In England, on the other hand, there is no one obvious choice of foreign language, although French, German and Spanish remain the top preferences year on year (Joint Council of Qualifications, 2018).

French is by far the most common foreign language taught at primary level, possibly because it is the foreign language that most people in the UK say they are able to speak well enough to hold a conversation (British Council, 2017, p11). However, the second most taught language in primary schools, Spanish, has a shallower orthography than French, meaning that the letters and sounds (the Sound–Symbol Correspondences or 'SSCs') of the writing system are more closely aligned. This may make the Spanish language easier for children to learn. Spanish is also spoken by more people across the world than French and is seen by the British Council as the most important language for the UK, followed by Mandarin, French, Arabic and German (British Council, 2017, p4).

The national curriculum for languages programme of study maintains that language teaching should provide the foundation for learning *further languages* and focuses on the need for pupils to make *substantial progress in one language* (DfE, 2013), without specifying further. The question of which language to teach at primary school also needs to take into account the expertise of those teachers teaching the foreign language (Ofsted, 2021), along with the training they receive, and the support and guidance from their secondary counterparts (Burch and Vare, 2020).

REFLECTION

Why is it important for young children to learn foreign languages?

TRANSITION FROM KS2 TO KS3

Challenges hindering successful transition from KS2 to KS3 in foreign languages may include inadequate training of teachers, insufficient liaison between primary and secondary schools, and a lack of continuity in language learning between primary and secondary school (Hunt et al. 2008). Secondary school languages teachers report that primary school children receive a 'mixed experience' of foreign language teaching at KS2 (Tinsley and Board, 2017, p45), and this wide variety of provision at primary level poses challenges for successful transition at KS3. The variability in the amount and quality of language teaching provision at primary school in the UK is considered more profound than in other subjects (Graham et al., 2016, p683). Consequently, some secondary schools take a 'clean slate' approach and start foreign language teaching from scratch with all Year 7 pupils, regardless of their prior knowledge (Pachler, 2014, p97). Not surprisingly, this repetition of known content may have negative effects on both progression and learner motivation (Courtney, 2017, p3).

Although part of the national curriculum, it is only in recent years that Primary Foreign Languages has begun to form part of Ofsted inspections more generally as part of the 'broad and balanced' curriculum. This lack of attainment benchmarking may be seen as exacerbating the current issues relating to the 'mixed experience' of language teaching at KS2 and the impact that this has on transition and KS3. The Department for Education is reported to be planning to provide non-statutory guidance for languages education for 7- to 14-year-olds on these issues in the next year (Schools Week, 2022).

WHAT MIGHT KNOWLEDGE IN PRIMARY FOREIGN LANGUAGES LOOK LIKE IN THE FUTURE?

Since the publication of the national curriculum for languages in 2013, there has been an ever-increasing importance placed on the teaching of vocabulary, phonology and grammar at all stages, including KS2. Therefore, this represents the foundation knowledge required of all primary school teachers teaching foreign languages, and the lens through which knowledge in Primary Foreign Languages may be viewed and assessed in the future. For this reason, these 'pillars of progression' will be covered in more detail in Part 2 of this chapter.

PART 2: FOUNDATION KNOWLEDGE IN PRIMARY FOREIGN LANGUAGES

THE THREE PILLARS OF PROGRESSION IN LANGUAGE LEARNING

The national curriculum for languages at KS2 states that teaching

> *should enable pupils to understand and communicate ideas, facts and feelings in speech and writing, focused on familiar and routine matters, using their knowledge of phonology, grammatical structures and vocabulary.*

(DfE, 2013)

In recent years, increasing attention has been focused on these three aspects, now referred to as the 'three pillars of progression':

- vocabulary, a chosen set of words in the language;

- grammar, a set of features that are the essential building blocks needed to put language together to make meaningful sentences, and

- phonics, the set of sound–symbol correspondences that represent the relationship between how the language sounds and how it is written (Hawkes, 2021).

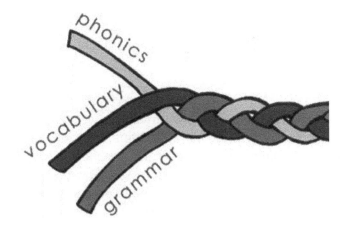

Figure 9.1 NCELP's visual presentation of the three pillars

As NCELP's (National Centre for Excellence for Language) metaphor of the braid indicates, knowledge is made stronger because of the interconnections between the strands of grammar, phonics and vocabulary. These strands are closely intertwined to suggest that each strand is important and affects the others (Hawkes, 2021).

Ofsted's Curriculum research review for languages (2021) provides explicit guidance on the three pillars, and as such merits the close attention of anyone considering what key foundational knowledge they might need to teach Primary Foreign Languages, particularly the sections specifically dedicated to phonics, vocabulary and grammar. Each section ends with an outline of the features which high-quality languages education may have, any of which may be considered possible areas of investigation in Ofsted inspections of foreign languages in the future.

As general guiding principles, Ofsted's Curriculum research review for languages (2021) suggests that:

- phonics, vocabulary and grammar are all essential aspects of foreign language learning;

- each requires explicit instruction (so teachers should draw explicit attention to language, rather than assuming that all pupils will notice patterns in grammar, vocabulary and phonics);

- each requires planned practice and review;

- a step-by-step explicit approach is required to ensure logical planning for progression, moving from simple to more complicated aspects;

- curriculum planning of vocabulary, grammar and phonic knowledge and progression should go hand in hand, as they are all related and connected.

Taking into account guidance from the national curriculum for languages, the Curriculum research review for languages related to the key themes, next we consider what trainee teachers need in terms of foundational knowledge for each pillar.

PHONICS

Phonology is not mentioned in the KS3 curriculum for modern foreign languages, but is mentioned specifically in the KS2 curriculum. Logically, in order for children in KS2 to learn foreign language phonology, KS2 teachers need to teach the phonics of the foreign language. If you are not quite sure how to, the good news is that there are lots of excellent resources to help you, and you will find these listed in Part 4 of this chapter under Recommended phonics resources. We will look at one such example by way of illustration.

Table 9.1 What trainees need to know in terms of phonics

Related links taken from the KS2 national curriculum	What do pupils need to learn by the end of KS2?	What do trainees need to know?
Explore the patterns and sounds of language through songs and rhymes and link the spelling, sound and meanings of words.	They need to learn common Sound Spelling/Symbol Correspondences (SSCs) in the foreign language.	They need to know the common Sound Spelling/ Symbol Correspondences (SSCs) of the foreign language.
Develop accurate pronunciation and intonation so that others understand when they are reading aloud or using familiar words and phrases.	They need to learn to pronounce words accurately in the foreign language. They need to learn how to use intonation correctly – for example, when asking a question or making an exclamation.	They need to know how to pronounce words accurately in the foreign language, so they can model this for the children. They need to know how to use intonation correctly, so they can model this for the children.

Figure 9.2 The main SSCs in Spanish (Hawkes and Avery, 2019)

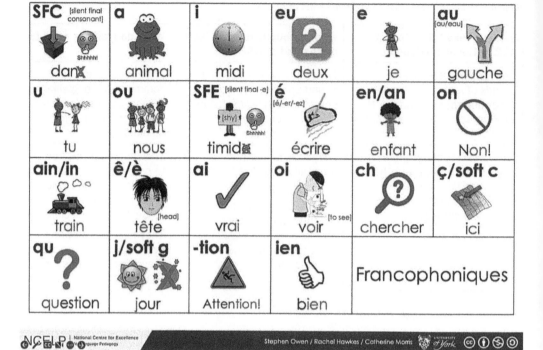

Figure 9.3 The main SSCs in French (Owen et al., 2019)

Both resources in the figures above are freely available from the NCELP website, and contain embedded links to audio clips that will help you learn/revise how to pronounce both the key words and the SSCs (Sound–Symbol Correspondences) they contain in the foreign language: just click on the letter(s) to hear the SSC sound alone, and then either the picture or the word to hear the source word itself. Links to these resources and others are available in Part 4 of this chapter.

Practise saying the SSCs and key words for each SSC aloud until you know both on sight. Using the links to vocabulary resources at the end of this chapter, you can then begin being a 'language detective', investigating foreign words and seeing whether they fit these patterns of sounds. If you are ever unsure about how a word is pronounced, then you can check it via a good pronunciation website like https://forvo.com/ which has audio clips of native speakers pronouncing the word for you to listen to.

In terms of how to teach foreign language phonics to KS2 pupils, the TSC (2016, p12) recommend that teachers familiarise themselves with L1 English phonics techniques and apply those to the teaching of phonics of the new foreign language, and that this takes place during the first year of language learning. For example, this might include assigning a gesture and/or image to a SSC and practising saying this and key words with the SSC. Once this knowledge is secure for this

SSC, pupils can be 'language detectives' to look out for this sound in new words they learn. For more ideas, please see the list of phonics teaching resources in Part 4 of this chapter.

VOCABULARY

Over the four years of KS2, it is estimated that primary school children will learn around 450 words of primary school, at an average of 3-4 words per week (Hawkes, 2022).

When planning, the Curriculum research review for languages recommends that teachers:

- prioritise high-frequency words;

- choose topic-based vocabulary carefully;

- ensure that learners use these words across different contexts/topics;

- plan revisiting vocabulary to ensure that words are retained in long-term memory;

- make sure that words are included in comprehension (listening and reading) and production (speaking and writing).

Table 9.2 represents some ideas of possible themes that teachers could focus on to achieve the national curriculum requirements for vocabulary, based on 'age and stage'-appropriate interests of KS2 pupils.

In summary, vocabulary themes might include: me, my family, friends and pets; sports and hobbies; food; school subjects and classroom items, time and routines; my home and home town. Other useful vocabulary might include: numbers; days of the week; months of the year; weather; descriptions of colour, size, personality. Of course, more vocabulary might be needed, but this is a good basis for any trainee.

It might be that you already know this vocabulary from your own school days or you may need to learn or revise these words and phrases. Under Recommended vocabulary resources in Part 4 of this chapter, you can find a list of suggestions to help you.

GRAMMAR

Grammatical structures that might be useful for trainees to know are listed below. These include how to ask and answer questions; sentence formation; basic language structures; feminine, masculine (and neuter) forms in singular and plural; basic conjugation of verbs; and word order of sentence, including adjectival placement and agreement (masculine/feminine/singular/plural).

Table 9.2 Possible themes linking to national curriculum outcomes

Related links taken from the national curriculum outcomes by the end of KS2	Some possible themes based around children's interests	Some examples
To understand and communicate ideas, facts and feelings in speech and in writing, focusing on *familiar and routine matters, speak in sentences, using familiar vocabulary, phrases and basic language structures.*	Me – what their name is and how old they are, but also how they are feeling. Family – siblings, parents and their descriptions (age, personality). Pets – descriptions (colour, size, personality). Sports/hobbies – what they do or what they like/don't like in terms of playing different sports or hobbies: reading, watching television, listening to music, etc. Food – what they like/don't like, what they would like to eat (e.g., for a café role play). School – classroom items (pencil, ruler), subjects they study and likes/dislikes, school routines, time (e.g., walk to school, arrive at X). Home – whether they live in a house/flat, in the countryside/town, the different rooms in their home. Home town – what their town is like, what buildings it has. Dates – today's date, birthday.	My name is Alex. I am 10 years old. I am very well. I am tired. I have one brother. He is called Jamie and he is 15 years old. He is kind. I have a white dog. He is big and he is nice. I love swimming, but I don't like reading. On Saturdays, I play football. I like apples but I don't like bananas. I would like an orange juice, please. I have a ruler. I don't have a pencil. I love history but I hate maths. I walk to school. I arrive at 8.30. I live in a flat in the town. I live in Cheltenham. In Cheltenham there is a theatre, a cinema and lots of cafés. Today is Thursday, 21 January. My birthday is on 8 February.
Engage in conversations; ask and answer questions; *express opinions and respond to those of others; seek clarification and help.*	Greetings. Getting to know someone else – sharing basic information about yourself (as above: name, age, where you live, family and who you live with, pets, hobbies, likes/dislikes). Asking and answering questions – e.g., asking opinions on a subject and responding with opinions. Clarifying and asking for help.	Hello! How are you? What's your name? How old are you? (As above) Sharing name, age, family, pets, hobbies, etc. Do you like swimming? I love swimming. Excuse me. Can you help me? Where is. . . . ?

Related links taken from the national curriculum outcomes by the end of KS2	Some possible themes based around children's interests	Some examples
Broaden their vocabulary, including through using a dictionary.	Learning how to use a bilingual dictionary	
Describe people, places, things and actions orally and in writing.	As above – e.g.: People – family, friends. Places – home, hometown. Things – classroom items, pets, food. Actions – sports, hobbies, going to school. Descriptions of these aspects – e.g., adjectives relating to people – personality, physical size of places, colour of classroom items, pets, etc.	

NB: A basic language structure enables us to take an item of vocabulary such as 'a dog' and form a sentence using it, like a sentence starter – e.g., 'I have . . . a dog'. Other common language structures include: I am, I like, there is, it is . . .

Table 9.3 below provides examples for each grammatical structure. Again, this list is not exhaustive, but will give you a good basis for teaching KS2 foreign languages. Suggested recommended resources are provided in Part 4 of this chapter to help you learn or revise this knowledge.

Table 9.3 Examples of grammar KS2 pupils need to know

Related links taken from the national curriculum	What do pupils need to know by the end of KS2?	Some examples
Ask and answer questions.	To ask a question: Second person singular (you) conjugation.	Are you . . . ? Do you have . . . ? Do you like . . . ?
	To answer a question: first person singular (I) conjugation.	I am . . . I have . . . I like . . . I don't like . . .

(Continued)

Table 9.3 (Continued)

Related links taken from the national curriculum	What do pupils need to know by the end of KS2?	Some examples
Speak in sentences, using familiar vocabulary, phrases and basic language structures.	Sentence formation – e.g., in Spanish, you don't normally need to include subject pronouns like 'I' (unless it is not clear who you are talking about).	I have a dog. In Spanish: *tengo un perro*
	Basic language structures: these allow children to put vocabulary into a sentence.	I am (tired). I have (two sisters). I like (dogs). I don't like (apples). There is/are (a pen). It is (hot).
Basic grammar appropriate to the language being studied, including (where relevant): feminine, masculine and neuter forms.	Feminine, masculine and neuter forms in singular and plural.	A girl, a boy. In Spanish: *una chica, un chico.* The girl, the boy. In Spanish: *la chica, el chico.* The girls, the boys. In Spanish: *las chicas, los chicos.*
Conjugation of high-frequency verbs.	Conjugation of verbs (in present tense): (singular) I am You are They are (plural) We are You are They are	To be To have To like To live
Key features and patterns of the language; how to apply these – e.g., to build sentences, and how these differ from or are similar to English.	Word order of sentence – e.g., adjectival positioning; adjectival agreement (masculine/feminine); adjectival agreement (singular/plural).	I have a nice brother In Spanish: *tengo un hermano simpatico.* I have a nice sister. In Spanish: *tengo una hermana simpática.* I have two nice rabbits. In Spanish: *tengo dos conejos simpáticos.*

INCIDENTAL CLASSROOM TARGET LANGUAGE

It is common practice for primary foreign languages teachers to use the foreign language not just to teach key vocabulary in the foreign language, but to use the foreign language for classroom interactions such as instructions and praise. In this way, teachers act as a role model in pronouncing simple words and phrases in the foreign language for young children, embedding basic communication in the language throughout the lesson, and ideally throughout the day. The KS2 national curriculum for languages places great emphasis on using languages for communication, so encouraging this communication in the foreign language with children using incidental classroom language is essential.

On the use of the target language, the Curriculum research review for languages comments:

> *Of course, we want learners to be exposed to the language they are learning… using the target language is an essential part of practice and reinforcement, including building familiarity with rhythms, sounds and intonation.*

(Ofsted, 2021)

However, the Curriculum research review also acknowledges that there is some debate concerning the use of the target language, which may relate to concern that some pupils may feel overwhelmed by a teacher speaking lots of complicated foreign language that they do not understand. One way of making classroom language comprehensible and accessible from the beginning is to keep it simple and to add a gesture that shows the meaning clearly. You could use the same gestures as you would do when using instructions and praise in English. For example, you might cup your hand behind your ear to indicate the instruction 'listen' or you might count down from five in the foreign language with a finger to your lips which will reinforce the meaning behind the instruction 'silence'. Some pupils will naturally be able to guess what you mean and follow your instruction, and with encouragement and praise (both verbal and a thumbs up and nodding gesture) you will soon find the rest of the class following suit. This combination of simple foreign language and gesture encourages pupils to work as 'language detectives' to decipher meaning. Talking about how pupils worked out meaning is also good to do, so that children can share how they worked out meaning with others. However, it is important not to overwhelm pupils, so introduce the pupils to more and more classroom language gradually over the course of a few lessons rather than all at once.

Table 9.4 Classroom instructions and praise

English	French	Spanish
Instructions		
Come in!	Entrez!	¡Entrad!
Sit down!	Asseyez-vous!	¡Sentaos!
Silence, please!	Silence, s'il vous plaît!	¡Silencio, por favor!
Look!	Regardez!	¡Mirad!
Listen!	Écoutez!	¡Escuchad!
Repeat!	Répétez!	¡Repetid!
Hands up!	Levez la main!	¡Levantad la(s) mano(s)!
In pairs!	Avec un/une partenaire!	¡En parejas!
All together!	Tout le monde ensemble!	¡Todos juntos!
Stand up!	Levez-vous!	¡Levantaos!
Let's go!	On y va !	¡Vámonos!
Praise		
Excellent!	Excellent!	¡Excelente!
Great!	Fantastique!	¡Fantástico!
Very good!	Très bien!	¡Muy bien!
Good!	Bien!	¡Bien!

Source: Adapted from the ALL-Connect KS2 Language Co-ordinator's Handbook

The table above provides examples of key phrases that are useful for all trainees to know and use when teaching. Don't forget to check your pronunciation with a good pronunciation website if you are unsure. Then practise saying the words with a gesture you would use with KS2 pupils to make the meaning clear. (More phrases are available from the source, the ALL-Connect *KS2 Language Co-ordinator's Handbook*, a link to which is found in Part 4.)

INTERCULTURAL UNDERSTANDING

As well as the three pillars of progression, knowledge relating to intercultural understanding acts as a fantastic 'hook' to learning, appealing to pupils' natural curiosity and interest in other children. This could include watching videos to learn about what a school in the foreign language speaking country looks like, what children might eat for breakfast or how festivities are celebrated. Intercultural understanding enables young children to learn about other children's lives and to reflect on the similarities and differences that exist between people across the globe. In order to encourage that respectful approach we discussed in Part 1, it is important that discussion of any intercultural differences is always consistent in its aim to decolonise the languages curriculum and not to judge another culture. One way to achieve this is to be clear with children that any perceived differences could be due to any number of reasons such as tradition, history, climate, religion, etc., and to question why it is that we do things differently in our country. It is also important to avoid stereotypes and remember to emphasise that you are learning about one example, but that doesn't mean that everyone in the country has the same experience or lives their lives in the same way.

To provide good knowledge of intercultural understanding to pupils, you need to learn this first yourself. It may be that you have experience or knowledge of another country already, but Part 4 provides some other ways you can gain this knowledge. In addition to doing your own research, one way could be to make a link with a similar school abroad via the British Council, or via your town or city's twinning organisation. This will help pupils learn about the chosen country through its people themselves. Remember there is a whole world for pupils to learn about and you don't just have to learn about European countries: you could choose a country in Africa or the Americas to promote voices and perspectives from beyond the 'Eurocentric' core, as we saw in Part 1 that Panford and Irvine (2021) suggest.

PART 3: UNDERSTANDING THE DEVELOPMENT OF CHILDREN'S KNOWLEDGE IN PRIMARY FOREIGN LANGUAGES

The time afforded to Primary Foreign Languages in primary schools is sadly quite limited. Although both the National Recovery Programme for Languages (APGML, 2019) and Graham et al.'s (2016) research suggest that an hour a week should be allocated to PFL, the average is nearer to 30–45 minutes per week at best (Tinsley and Board, 2017, p28).

REFLECTION

Given this very limited time even in supportive schools, how can we best develop children's knowledge in foreign languages?

There are some key principles that should be followed:

- learning should be memorable;

- new knowledge should be taught little and often;

- choose carefully what you teach to achieve quality rather than quantity (e.g., teach useful vocabulary rather than just teaching lots of words);

- prior knowledge should be reviewed and recycled in different contexts regularly;

- learning should be appropriate to the 'age and stage' of the young children learning it;

- learning should include an 'appropriate balance' (DfE, 2013) of the four skills: listening, speaking, reading and writing.

TEACH, PRACTISE, REVISIT AND 'RECYCLE'

Various techniques can be used to make learning memorable in even a short amount of time. These include assigning an appropriate gesture (Porter, 2012) and/or an image to a new item of vocabulary to be learnt. Using these visual or physical expressions can act as an aide-memoire and also link the word to its meaning – for example, children are more likely to remember the word for dog in a foreign language if they are looking at an image of a dog and acting out wagging their tails while saying the word. They also tend to enjoy pretending to wag their tails, too, and will happily repeat the word several times while doing so. This repetition is important as it is thought that words need to be repeated sixteen times before they are retained in the working memory. Repetition can be achieved through a variety of activities – not just 'listen and repeat' with the teacher, but also all-important pair work to practise the vocabulary in a more natural and relaxed environment – for example, playing picture or word pair games. Other ways include larger group games, singing songs, conducting whole-class surveys, etc.

Introduce carefully selected new knowledge gradually, little and often, so that pupils enjoy the process, but are not overwhelmed by the number of new words to learn. Once pupils are confident with some new vocabulary, it is essential to practise the words and phrases using the four language skills of listening, speaking, reading and writing in order to secure this knowledge in their long-term memory. Reviewing prior knowledge regularly will help children retain it in their memory, otherwise it will quickly be forgotten. One highly beneficial way of reviewing words that children already know is by reapplying or 'recycling' words from one context to another. For example, if pupils have learnt how to say 'I have' in the context of classroom items such as the phrase 'I have a pencil', they can use the same language structure in a myriad of different contexts, such as family – 'I have a sister' – or pets – 'I have a dog'.

The following table gives an example of how planning may be structured to go over prior learning, with language in italics below denoting where existing prior knowledge has been revised and/or 'recycled'.

Table 9.3 Learning outcomes and activities by year group

Year group	Learning outcomes – to be covered during the year	Activities to develop the skills and understanding	Next steps
Year 3	**Intercultural understanding:** • Basic intercultural awareness of the chosen country of study covering how people live their lives linked to topics covered – e.g., the classroom, food such as popular dishes/fruit (try some if possible); how key holidays are celebrated – e.g., Christmas, Epiphany. **Vocabulary** covered and practised regularly over the year: • Basic communication, including greetings. • All about me: name, age. • Colours, my favourite colour, flags. • The classroom and items: pencil, etc., plus I have: I have a pencil. • Description of classroom items (items + colour): I have a red pencil. • Numbers gradually introduced up to 31. • Months of the year. • Today's date and birthdays (to practise numbers and months). • Food items from the country. • Likes and dislikes, introducing the negative form: I like/I don't like plus food items. • Incidental classroom instructions and praise. **Phonics** covered and reviewed during the year: • Basic SSCs encountered during the year. **Grammar:** • Articles: a/the/some. • Feminine, masculine (and neuter) forms; singular and plural. • 1st person singular conjugation: I am, I have, I like/I don't like. . . • Conjunction: and.	Phonics word clouds on display: as you introduce new SSCs, put a phonics cloud for each up on display. As you learn new words, you can add some to the appropriate cloud display. Picture/word games to practise knowledge, but at a basic phrase/word level to provide short statements. Singing songs together, listening to native speakers' pronunciation and practising the language. Playing simple listening games like 'Simon Says' or speaking/reading games like Snap, Find the Pair. Pair work to practise speaking and listening; class surveys; role plays. Reading and written practice also at basic phrase/word level – e.g., today's date, a profile all about me (my name, age, birthday). Enjoying reading a simple book/poem together – e.g., using 'call and response' to practise reading it together with gestures.	You could perform a song you enjoy singing together at an assembly (with gestures to show meaning and understanding). You could look into making a classroom poster about your chosen country, adding information that you have found out about it through the year.

(Continued)

Table 9.5 (Continued)

Year group	Learning outcomes – to be covered during the year	Activities to develop the skills and understanding	Next steps
Year 4	**Vocabulary:** • My family + I have. • Pets + I have + colour. • Sports/hobbies + I like. • Birthdays (using months and numbers to 31). • Food + I like, I would like. • Larger numbers gradually introduced (up to 80/100, depending on difficulty in the foreign language). Further incidental classroom language used, in addition to Year 3. **Phonics:** • Additional SSCs encountered during the year; working as 'language detectives' to apply phonics knowledge to try to pronounce new words. **Grammar:** • 1st person singular: I love, I like, I hate. • Negative – e.g., I don't like, I don't have. • 2nd person singular for question formation: Do you like? Do you have? • Adjectival agreement and positioning for descriptions: I have a black dog. • Conjunctions: and/but. • Useful language structures such as 'It is/It is not', 'There is/there is not'. **Intercultural understanding:** • Linked to the vocabulary topics covered during the year, relating to how people in the chosen country live their lives, important celebrations during the year.	Continue adding to your phonics word clouds on display. Continue singing songs and watching short video clips, listening to native speakers' pronunciation, and practising the language. Continue playing verbal/written games to practise the language. Use pair work to practise speaking and listening; class surveys – e.g., on favourite hobbies; role plays – e.g., at the café or at the market to buy food, introducing a new friend to your family. Reading and written practice also at basic sentence level – e.g., a profile all about me (my name, age, birthday, my family and pets, my favourite hobbies/sports). Reading and writing activities in general could include more descriptions to revise Years 3 and 4 knowledge – e.g., the number of siblings, the colour of a pet, conjunctions such as 'and' and 'but'. This will naturally extend the level of written sentences. Enjoying reading simple books/poems together. Using a written template provided, pupils can produce their own adapted versions	You could have a whole afternoon dedicated to a particular role play, transforming the classroom into a café (with music, tablecloth, menus and real food) or a market with stalls and props (ideally with fake currency) for children to enjoy practising and using the language for a more extended period. You could look into making a classroom display of the children's work – e.g., their extended profiles about themselves, or their simplified versions of books or poems.

Part 4 provides a link to more examples available in the ALL Connect *KS2 Language Coordinator's Handbook*.

REFLECTION

Having now read a little more about primary foreign languages, what are your answers to the same questions posed at the beginning of this chapter?

What do you think should be included in foreign language learning by primary school pupils?

Why is it important for young children to learn foreign languages?

What, and how, exactly should young children be taught in this subject?

If you would like to keep on learning about primary foreign languages, then look at the recommended resources in Part 4.

PART 4: DEVELOPING YOUR KNOWLEDGE OF PRIMARY FOREIGN LANGUAGES FURTHER

GENERAL TEACHING RESOURCES

- The website of the subject association, the Association for Language Learning, has a wide range of guidance documents, information and links to extremely useful resources, plus links to online handbooks, wikis, etc., at: www.all-languages.org.uk

- The ALL-Connect *KS2 Language Co-ordinators' Handbook* covers many useful topics, including classroom Target Language on pp47–51: https://allconnect-blog.wordpress.com/category/ks2-coordinators-handbook/

- The National Centre for Excellence for Language Pedagogy (NCELP) has created a vast number of resources and schemes of work freely available at: https://ncelp.org

LEADING TEACHER-PRACTITIONER WEBSITES

These teacher-practitioners are the 'leading lights' in primary languages teaching:

- www.bbc.co.uk/bitesize
- www.cavelanguages.co.uk

- www.lightbulblanguages.co.uk

- www.rachelhawkes.com

- See also links to further resources at: www.frenchteacher.net/links/primary-schools/

RECOMMENDED PHONICS RESOURCES

- NCELP has created the 'Spanish SSC Phonics Poster Audio' seen on page 209 which can be found at the following link: https://resources.ncelp.org/concern/resources/dv13zt305?locale=en

- Also from NCELP, the Year 7 French SSC Phonics Poster Audio seen on page 210 is found at: https://resources.ncelp.org/concern/resources/nk322d35b?locale=en

- The Cave Languages website has lots of French phonics resources, including how to teach phonics. Many of the ideas can be applied to other languages. The resources can be accessed via the following link: www.cavelanguages.co.uk/french-phonics

- See also: www.rachelhawkes.com/Resources/Phonics/Phonics.php

RECOMMENDED GRAMMAR RESOURCES

- The National Association of Language Advisers (NALA) has created a detailed and comprehensive grammar resource that links English grammar to that of French, Spanish and German. The resources are available through a free download by registering at the following website: www.nala.org.uk/grammar-project/

- The subject association, the Association for Language Learning, has created the following resources and wiki based on KS2 grammar: https://allconnectblog.wordpress.com/2015/01/06/all-connect-ks2-grammar/ and http://all-grammar.wikidot.com

RECOMMENDED VOCABULARY RESOURCES

Many of the resources already mentioned include vocabulary, but if you prefer a book, you could choose:

For Spanish: Barton, A and McLachlan, A (2016) *Bloomsbury Curriculum Basics: Teaching Primary Spanish: Everything a Non-specialist Needs to Teach Primary Spanish*. London: Bloomsbury Education.

For French: Barton, A and McLachlan, A (2016) *Bloomsbury Curriculum Basics: Teaching Primary French*. London: Bloomsbury.

INTERCULTURAL UNDERSTANDING

There is a list of links to various intercultural understanding resources available from the Association of Language Learning at: www.all-languages.org.uk/primary-2/primary-resources/

Under the 'Global learning' section of this website, you can find links to resources like 'Hola Peru' and 'Take Mali', which have been specially designed to enhance intercultural understanding as well as language learning, at: www.globalcentredevon.org.uk/

PLANNING RESOURCES

For further planning examples, see Chapter 7 of the ALL Connect's *KS2 Languages Co-ordinator's Handbook* at: https://allconnectblog.files.wordpress.com/2016/01/all-connect-ks2-languages-coordinator-handbook1.pdf

Chapter 8 of this resource deals with individual lesson planning and examples are found in the related appendices.

RESOURCES, GAMES AND ACTIVITIES

For lots of resource ideas, see Chapter 8 of the ALL Connect's *KS2 Languages Co-ordinator's Handbook* at: https://allconnectblog.files.wordpress.com/2016/01/all-connect-ks2-languages-coordinator-handbook1.pdf

More resource ideas are available from the Association of Language Learning at:

www.all-languages.org.uk/primary-2/primary-resources/

Join the Facebook page, Languages in Primary Schools (LIPS), which provides a community of support for the teaching of languages in primary schools.

REFERENCES

ALL Connect (2016) ALL Connect *KS2 Languages Co-ordinator's Handbook*. Available at: https://allconnectblog.files.wordpress.com/2016/01/all-connect-ks2-languages-coordinator-handbook1.pdf

All-Party Parliamentary Group on Modern Languages (ALPGML) (2019) *A National Recovery Programme for Languages: A Framework Proposal from the All-Party Parliamentary Group on Modern Languages*, 4 March. Available at: www.britishcouncil.org/organisation/press/mps-and-peers-urgent-call-national-recovery-programme-revolutionise-language-skills-uk

Barcelona European Council (2002) Presidency conclusions: part 1. Available at: http://ec.europa.eu/invest-in-research/pdf/download_en/barcelona_european_council.pdf

British Council (2017) Languages for the future: the foreign languages the United Kingdom needs to become a truly global nation. Available at: www.britishcouncil.org/sites/default/files/languages_for_the_future_2017.pdf

Burch, C and Vare, P (2020) Stepping up in modern foreign languages: professional development across the primary to secondary school transition. *Language Learning Journal*, 48 (5): 613–27. Available at: https://doi.org/10.1080/09571736.2019.1642942

CBI/Pearson (2019) Education and learning for the modern world: CBI/Pearson Education and Skills Survey Report. Available at: www.cbi.org.uk/media/3841/12546_tess_2019.pdfn-education.

Collen, I (2022) Language trends 2021/2: the state of language learning in primary and secondary schools in England. *British Council*. Available at: www.britishcouncil.org/sites/default/files/language_trends_report_2022.pdf

Courtney, L (2017) Transition in modern foreign languages: a longitudinal study of motivation for language learning and second language proficiency. *Oxford Review of Education*, 43 (4): 462–81. doi: 10.1080/03054985.2017.1329721

Department for Education and Skills (DES) (2005) *The Key Stage 2 Framework for Languages*. Available at: http://dera.ioe.ac.uk/id/eprint/5830

Department for Education (2013) *The national curriculum in England: key stages 1 and 2 framework document*. Available at: https://www.gov.uk/government/publications/national-curriculum-in-england-primary-curriculum

European Commission (2017) *Key Data on Teaching Languages at School in Europe – 2017 Edition. Eurydice Report*. Luxembourg: Publications Office of the European Union. Available at: https://webgate.ec.europa.eu/fpfis/mwikis/eurydice/images/0/06/KDL_2017_internet.pdf

Graham, S, Courtney, L, Tonkyn, A and Marinis, T (2016) Motivational trajectories for early language learning across the primary–secondary school transition. *British Educational Research Journal*, 42 (4): 682–702. doi: 10.1002/berj.3230

Hawkes, R (2021) Session 1: Curriculum Design: intent, implementation and impact in languages 8.6.21 (PowerPoint presentation). *Curriculum Design, Phonics, Vocabulary and Grammar*. Available at: https://resources.ncelp.org/concern/resources/cr56n1940?locale=en

Hawkes, R (2022) Phonics, vocabulary, grammar: culture, creativity– Let's have it all at KS2! (PowerPoint presentation). *MFL SOS: a series of webinars hosted by Languagenut*. Available at: www.youtube.com/watch?v=4WqmWT1PcpI

Hawkes, R and Avery, N (2019) NCELP Resource Portal, Spanish SSC poster. Available at: https://resources.ncelp.org/concern/parent/dv13zt305/file_sets/np193925m (accessed 30 November 2022).

HMCI (2016) Monthly commentary: May. Available at: www.gov.uk/government/speeches/hmcis-monthly-commentary-may-2016

Hunt, MJ, Barnes, A, Powell, B and Martin, C (2008) Moving on: the challenges for foreign language learning on transition from primary to secondary school. *Teaching and Teacher Education*, 24 (4): 915–26. doi: 10.1016/j.tate.2007.08.005

Joint Council of Qualifications (2018) GCSE (full course) results summer 2018. Available at: www.jcq.org.uk/examination-results/gcses/2018/main-results-Table9.s

Jones, J and Coffey, S (2017) *Modern Foreign Languages 5–11: A Guide for Teachers* (5–11 series) (3rd edn). London: Routledge, Taylor & Francis.

Ofsted (2021) *Research Review Series: Languages*. Available at: www.gov.uk/government/publications/curriculum-research-review-series-languages/curriculum-research-review-series-languages

Owen, S, Morris, C and Hawkes, R (2019) *NCELP Resource Portal, Y7 French SSC poster*. Available at: https://resources.ncelp.org/concern/parent/nk322d35b/file_sets/vh53ww515 (accessed 30 November 2022).

Pachler, N, Evans, M, Redondo, A and Fisher, L (2014) *Learning to Teach Foreign Languages in the Secondary School: A Companion to School Experience* (4th edn). London: Routledge.

Panford, L and Irvine, M (2021) What does an antiracist, decolonised MFL lesson look like? ALL Languages World Conference 2021. Available at: www.all-languages.org.uk/about/community/special-interest-groups/de-colonising-the-curriculum/

Porter, A (2016) A helping hand with language learning: teaching French vocabulary with gesture. *The Language Learning Journal*, 44 (2): 236–56. doi: 10.1080/09571736.2012.750681

Tinsley, T and Board, K (2016). Language trends 2015/16: the state of language learning in primary and secondary schools in England. *British Council*. Available at: www.britishcouncil.org/sites/default/files/language_trends_survey_2016_0.pdf

Tinsley, T and Board, K (2017) Language trends 2016/17: the state of language learning in primary and secondary schools in England. *British Council*. Available at: https://www.britishcouncil.org/sites/default/files/language_trends_survey_2017_0.pdf

TSC (2016) *Modern Foreign Languages Pedagogy Review: A Review of Modern Foreign Languages Teaching Practice in Key Stage 3 and Key Stage 4*. Available at: https://ncelp.org/wp-content/uploads/2020/02/MFL_Pedagogy_Review_Report_TSC_PUBLISHED_VERSION_Nov_2016_1_.pdf

UNESCO (2022) Home language: definition. Available at: http://uis.unesco.org/en/glossary-term/home-language

Walker, A (2022) Languages 'attainment benchmarks' proposed to boost GCSE take-up. *Schools Week*, 31 October. Available at: https://schoolsweek.co.uk/languages-french-german-spanish-attainment-benchmarks-proposed-to-boost-gcse-take-up/

10

PHYSICAL EDUCATION

ANGELA WHITEHOUSE AND VICTORIA RANDALL

KEYWORDS: PHYSICAL EDUCATION; HEALTH; PHYSICAL ACTIVITY; SPORTING CULTURE; MOVEMENT COMPETENCY; TEACHING STYLES; FUNDAMENTAL MOVEMENT SKILLS; MODELS-BASED PRACTICE.

LINKS TO THE CORE CONTENT FRAMEWORK

How Pupils Learn (Standard 2): 2.7

Subject and Curriculum (Standard 3): 3.2

Classroom Practice (Standard 4): 4.2

Adaptive Teaching (Standard 5): 5.3

PART 1: EXPLORING PE

Learning to move and understand the body is essential for all living beings. It is important for health, engagement with the social world and for undertaking functional daily tasks. Movement occurs at the point of conception and remains with us throughout our whole life. Schools are important sites for children to engage with a range of movement skills and to nurture a love of movement that becomes habitual. Although movement is ubiquitous in the curriculum, and evident through play, mark making, travel and balance (consider the challenge for some children to be able to sit on a chair), Physical Education (PE) is unique as it is the only curriculum subject to place movement at its core. This can often worry many generalist teachers and trainee teachers who believe that they require specialist knowledge to provide children with valuable learning experiences in PE.

In this chapter, we aim to show how PE is much like any other curriculum subject in that it has core content and underpinning pedagogical approaches. This foundational knowledge will help support any teacher of primary PE to develop lessons that are inclusive, safe and enjoyable.

WHAT IS PE?

PE is a statutory subject within the national curriculum taught from Key Stages 1–4. The nature of the word 'physical' prominently placed within the subject title makes it a crucial area of a child's development.

In trying to establish what PE is, we begin with what it is not. Many misconceptions exist around primary PE and these are often fuelled by our own experiences at school. For example, PE in the primary stage should not be constructed as playing sport or experienced through competitive games that mimic adult bodies. Its success should not be restricted to how much children move in a given period of time or assessed by measurements of fitness. Our responsibility as teachers is to ensure that all children make progress regardless of their starting point.

Traditionally taught through different activity lenses of dance, gymnastics, games, athletics, swimming and outdoor and adventurous activities, PE has become highly contested as to what the subject's purpose is. We position in this chapter that effective PE teaching must consider the 'E' as well as the 'P'. In other words, it is about the physical within 'education'. Learning should be structured to enable children to develop cognitively, creatively, socially and emotionally, and be experienced through a range of different contexts and environments, promoted through equitable, inclusive and socially just practices.

WHY IS PE IS IN THE NATIONAL CURRICULUM?

The Purpose of Study for PE (DfE, 2013) requires pupils *to become physically confident in a way which supports their health and fitness* and is supported by the aim for all pupils to *develop competence to excel in a broad range of physical activities*. While the subject's aims also require pupils to *engage in competitive sports and activities, and lead healthy, active lives* teachers must be clear about what this looks like within high-quality PE teaching. The purpose of study and aims collectively refer to high levels of sustained activity and opportunities to develop socially and emotionally – for example, by being respectful and taking part fairly. Ofsted's (2022) *Research Review for Physical Education* supports this through their depiction of three Pillars of Progression: motor competence; rules, strategies and tactics, and healthy participation. The learning journey for each pupil should focus on *learning to move and moving to learn* (Doherty and Brennan, 2014), developing fundamental movement skill competencies, and using movement within the creative, social, emotional and cognitive domains.

HOW HAS KNOWLEDGE IN PE DEVELOPED OVER TIME?

For decades, the content of the PE curriculum has remained largely unchanged. Dominated by Eurocentric traditions established by colonialism and empire, much-loved activities such as tennis, cricket, Association football and Rugby Football Union have dominated, and with it gained global popularity. But do these types of activity fully represent the multicultural, multi-race and multi-faith diversity from within our schools? By not including activities from a broad range of cultures, are we depriving pupils of the opportunity to explore and apply their learning in ways that challenge, extend or motivate, while at the same time alienating other children who feel disconnected from the PE curriculum they are experiencing?

Banks (2016) argues that the notion of decolonising the curriculum must involve transformation. This means going beyond tokenistic changes of a curriculum's activity content and to delve deeper into questioning the values, concepts and pedagogy that enshrines the curriculum. Reflecting upon the learning environment, looking at policies, structures, procedures and processes will also come into play as part of this transformation (Race et al., 2022).

When reviewing the PE curriculum, school leaders, curriculum leaders and teachers might ask:

- Why do we teach the curriculum in the way that we do?

- What is the history of our curriculum and who was it written by?

- Who is invested in our curriculum?

- Who is our curriculum for and what voice do they have?

Decolonising what we teach is part of a much larger social justice movement in PE as we strive towards greater equality and enrichment in our schools. Lynch et al. (2020) argue that due to the lack of diversity within the profession, PE continually replicates a curriculum that is elite, individual, masculine and competition orientated.

Earlier in this chapter we briefly outlined the Purpose of study for PE, as stated in the national curriculum; this is the statement of importance for the subject and why it forms a crucial part of a child's broader education. Non-statutory guidance for 'what' is taught reinforces a dominance of traditional British sporting activities – e.g., cricket, football, hockey, netball, rounders and tennis – that are believed to help shape character and develop a competitive mentality (Lumpkin, 2011). However, the term 'non-statutory' means that a school has agency to decide what the best interpretation of that curriculum should be for its pupils and with it the discretion to decide what, why and how it is taught.

Griggs (2022) explains that from country to country and from era to era the dominance of what drives the content of a PE curriculum can change, as a culture becomes seduced by different powerful narratives. For example, from as early as the 1850s, the health benefits of PE have been a prevailing discourse, which became more explicit in the formation of the first national syllabus for 'Physical Training' (Board of Education, 1905). The focus on health, exercise and fitness remains a feature of our current day programme of study. In other countries, PE has been reimagined with health strongly aligned within it, such as in New Zealand and Australia where it is now called Health and PE, and in Wales where PE has been consumed within Health and Well-being. However, the ways in which health and fitness are realised have shifted over our curriculum's history from one of Swedish gymnastics and drill to therapeutic movement and outdoor play (Doherty and Brennan, 2014). The presence of culturally dominant sport in the curriculum as a vehicle for developing character, toughness, competitiveness and physical dominance prevailed in the Victorian era (Griggs, 2022). This 'sporting' version of PE moved from the public schools into state curricular around the early part of the twentieth century still persists to this day. Now taking on a tripartite approach to PE (health, sport and education), sport is still considered a highly valuable mechanism for promoting physical activity and health-orientated benefits, while at the same time developing character through competition.

While taking a look back through history can help us to understand why certain activities exist in the modern curriculum, it doesn't highlight what might be missing. Questioning what's not there or what is not visible can initially be challenging, particularly if what is being offered to children is accepted and not indicating any immediate concern. The process of unpicking a curriculum and the traditions that have shaped it (such as the activities being taught) can be an uncomfortable process that might call our own values and experiences into question.

The collective known as 'PhysEquity' in their blog Decolonising the PE Curriculum: A Case Study (https://physequity.wordpress.com/2021/08/06/decolonising-the-pe-curriculum-a-case-study/), a curriculum leader's experience of decolonising her own school's PE curriculum is shared. After engaging colleagues and students in a collaborative voice around curriculum content, different cultural activities were trialled. Her students reported that *they felt more engaged learning something completely different, that they enjoyed learning about sports/activities from other cultures and/or that they were so pleased to be playing something that reminded them of being at 'home'.*

Exploring different cultural activities alongside the children, families and colleagues within a school that reflect the school's community is a positive start in moving towards an equitable, inclusive and engaging PE curriculum. Lynch et al. (2020, p8) offer five steps to help support this process:

1. Take time to know your students.

2. Provide opportunities for ownership of the curriculum.

3. Allow students to create class expectations.

4. Practise democratic principles – e.g., implement opportunities for children to provide feedback on their experiences of the curriculum.

5. Move away from the teacher being an authoritative figure to a class facilitator.

If you are unable to make large-scale changes to the curriculum but would like to explore and then evaluate how different activities can impact upon engagement and learning, the following activities may offer your pupils some variation. The origins of these activities are from countries outside the UK but have a synergy to other familiar activities that children may have already experienced – e.g., Futsal and football or Capoeira and dance.

Table 10.1 *A range of culturally and globally diverse activities that have their own traditional and cultural history*

Activity	Overview	Learning focus
Futsal	A variation of football originating from South America. It is played inside and with a smaller ball. Each team comprises of five players (goalkeeper, winger, pivot, universal, defender). This version of football has become a popular version of street football: www.englandfootball.com/play/futsal	Develops foot-eye skills as well as agility and accuracy. Small-sided game with fluid rolling subs, requires good team communication and support among peers. Can be faster paced as it is played in doors on a hard surface.
Capoeira	Capoeira is a Brazilian martial art that combines elements of dance, acrobatics and music. Its history is steeped in the slavery of Africans. It is an evolving art form and has now received protected status for cultural heritage from UNESCO. A year of culture: Capoeira Dance from Brazil - Jumpstart: https://primaryschooldance.co.uk	The dance is experienced through the cooperation of two people working together. Using a series of fluid striking and defending moves. Decision making actions are in response to actions made by their partner. This activity draws upon creativity, strong but agile movements and quick thinking. The values of this activity promote respect of self and others, confidence and strength of community.

(Continued)

Table 10.1 (Continued)

Activity	Overview	Learning focus
Wallball	A fast-growing sport globally. With simple rules and few resources needed, this activity can be played anywhere and with anyone with a wall and a ball: https://ukwallball.co.uk/	This activity is a great pre-cursor to other net/wall games. Using the hand in replacement of a racket, children can focus on mastering hand-eye skills in a fun and competitive high scoring way. This is an inclusive game that can be played by, or with, anyone and can be easily adapted to suit learner needs.
Korfball	A variation of handball, basketball and netball originating from The Netherlands. The game is traditionally made up of equal numbers of boys and girls on a team playing in two zones. It is different from netball as it doesn't have a 3ft rule, but remains a non-contact activity. It doesn't allow dribbling the ball as in basketball: englandkorfball.co.uk	Korfball prides itself on promoting gender equality. It's a team-based game, requiring social skills such as cooperation and communication. Physical skills include passing, shooting, defending, travelling with changes of direction and intercepting.

As with all activities used within a PE curriculum, the teacher, alongside the children, have autonomy to adapt activities to suit the needs, age and developmental stage of the children and the resources available. Outside of the lesson, children could be encouraged to research these activities, their cultural and historical origins.

REFLECTION

What has been your most recent experience of PE?

What activities did this include?

How did you and others experience these activities?

What rationale for the activity was shared?

Consider what other culturally diverse activities could have also been used as a vehicle for learning in that same lesson.

PE NOW

Even in the most recent iteration of the national curriculum (DfE, 2013), PE continues to reflect the dominant societal, political and cultural interests of our time. The London 2012 Olympic and Paralympic Games is an example of a key moment in the subject's recent history that has influenced public thinking on how it can be part of a much wider narrative of sport and health through education (see Figure 10.1).

For primary PE in particular, significant investment has been made since the London 2012 Games, now exceeding over £2 billion (Randall and Griggs, 2022), the aim of which is to provide opportunities for more young people to be physically active and engage in high-quality PE (DfE/DHSC, 2014). The Primary PE and Sport Premium, also commonly referred to as the 'Premium', has been a cross-department investment from government, in areas of health, digital culture, media and sport and education to ensure that the legacy of the London 2012 Games transcends to future generations. As such, the revised PE curriculum that followed in 2013 placed a more prominent role on competitive sport than before, as millions of people globally experienced the power of sport in transforming lives and bringing communities together. At the same time, the perceived health benefits associated with sport participation amid a backdrop of rising obesity levels among children and adults, placed PE strategically to impact upon the future direction of the nation's health.

However immersive or impressive world-class sport is, its applicability to the primary PE curriculum is not easily translatable, appropriate or accessible to all; nor is placing PE as a solution to complex health epidemics such as obesity. Policies such as the *School Sport Action Plan, The Childhood Obesity Action Plan*, the *Primary PE and Sport Premium* and *Healthy Pupils Capital Fund*, continue to name PE within a sporting and health context (Long and Roberts, 2022), but little evidence exists on how impactful such strategies are on young people's health in the long term.

Figure 10.1 below draws upon Griggs's (2022) overview of PE over time and depicts PE as a pinball, moving between sport, health and educational discourses. As we move into the modern era, the placement on PE for health is seen once more and continues to fuel debate over the subject's aims and purpose.

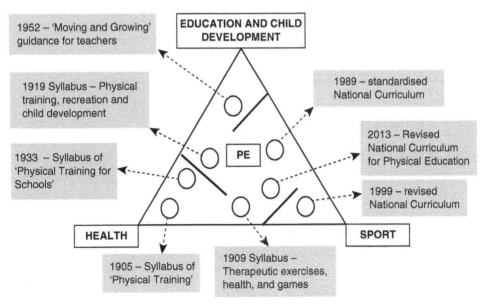

Figure 10.1 PE pinball within Health, Sport and Education (Griggs. 2022)

WHAT MIGHT PE LOOK LIKE IN THE FUTURE?

As the world recovers from the impact of the COVID-19 pandemic and continues to grow ever fearful of the global crisis in children's mental and physical health, it is likely that PE will remain within a space of health and well-being for the foreseeable future. However, Coulter and Ni Chroinin (2022) argue for primary PE to be reimagined in different ways and what its potential might be. One suggestion is to locate PE as a 'hub for all physical activity engagement', where children are connected to other forms of physical activity within and beyond the school walls. Alternatively, a second suggestion is for PE to become something bigger than PE and to act as a platform where global priorities, such as the environment, are directly explored through the child's physical engagement with them – e.g., respect for different environments, considering sustainable travel through physical activity, etc.).

Coulter and Ni Chroinin's (2022) suggestions offer much food for thought as schools review how PE may sit within a wider school curriculum context and in doing so, offer a new dimension to PE's history. PE will not be able to satisfy all the elements depicted in Figure 10.1 and other new dimensions all at once; therefore, locating the PE pinball in the exact centre may result in no dimension being effectively addressed at all.

REFLECTION

In your ideal conceptualisation of primary PE, where would you place the pinball within the dimensions of PE depicted in Figure 10.1?

What are your reasons for this?

Would you add a different aspect to the sport, education or health dimensions?

PART 2: FOUNDATION KNOWLEDGE IN PE

The knowledge required to become a competent teacher of primary PE can initially seem overwhelming, especially when you consider the many possible ways of knowing there are. However, the process of understanding what PE is – what should be taught and how it can be taught – is a career-long endeavour that can be gained from many different sources, perspectives and experience over time. In this chapter so far, we have argued that the aims and purpose of PE has been contested over the subject's history and is still a site of much debate. However, there is broad consensus that anyone learning to become a primary physical educator should be aware of some broad areas of knowing, including:

- fundamental movement skill development;

- pedagogical approaches to teaching PE;

- safe and inclusive principles of practice;

- physical activity contexts for learning.

In this section, we will address each of these areas to help support what Randall (2020) depicts as 'emerging' areas of knowledge in primary PE. This is the stage where a teacher develops a foundational understanding of what to teach, through an understanding of movement skill learning. The place of fundamental movement skills in PE is central to knowledge of the subject, as it is widely understood to form the basis of other more recognised forms of physical activity (Lawrence, 2021).

FUNDAMENTAL MOVEMENT SKILL DEVELOPMENT

While it can be helpful to know different sporting activities to support children to become more physically competent, it should not be *the* most important thing to know and prioritised over the children's needs. In other words, the lesson should be less about *how* to perform certain activities and more about what the child can learn *through* physical engagement with these activities. Central to participation in any forms of physical activity are knowledge of the fundamental movement skills that underpin them. For example, in athletic activities this might be a focus on just one skill at a time, such as throwing, or in contrast, a game like tennis will require the child to select and execute multiple movements in quick succession, such as run, stop, strike and side-step and in response to an ever-changing environment.

Before thinking about 'activities', we suggest first becoming familiar with the types of movement in which children should become competent. Gallahue et al. (2019) refer to three categories of movement skill: stability, locomotor and manipulation skills, where children will progress according to their developmental stage.

Stability skills – for example, posture, stopping, landing, cross-laterality, stretching/curling, twisting/turning, spinning, sinking/falling, body rolling, dodging.

Locomotor skills – for example, walking, running, galloping, skipping, hopping, jumping, climbing, swinging.

Manipulation skills – for example, throw, catch, kick, punt and strike.

The movement skill themes listed above explain the range of technical skills that a child can develop during the primary age phase, but alone does not explain the variety of ways a skill can be performed. Graham et al., (2020) further present three movement concepts that depict how the movement skills can be performed and experienced. These are:

Space: *where* the body moves – e.g., location, direction, pathways, levels and extensions.

Effort: *how* the body moves – e.g., timing, force and flow.

Relationships: *with* whom or with what the body moves – e.g., body parts, people, objects.

Combined, the movement skills (stability, locomotor and manipulation skills) and the movement concepts (space, effort, relationships) produce an array of movement competencies and form the foundational knowledge of what children will do in PE. The possibilities for movement exploration are endless. For example, consider the skill of running and how it can be adapted:

1. **Combining one movement skill with one movement concept** – e.g., running forwards; running backwards; running fast; running slow; running high; running next to someone; running with a racket; running clockwise; running zigzag.

2. **Combining one movement skill with multiple movement concepts** – e.g., running forwards, fast and clockwise.

3. **Combining multiple movement skills with one movement concept** – e.g., run, stop, jump, catch and land with a partner.

4. **Combining multiple movement skills with multiple movement concepts** – e.g., run, stop, jump, catch, land with a partner, at speed and following a curved pathway.

As children become more competent in their movement capabilities, their confidence should also increase to allow them to explore complex combinations of movement. Try to encourage children to be creative with the movement as much as you would reinforce good control and technique. Developing proficiency in their movement will be as much about exploration as it will be about practice.

PEDAGOGICAL MODELS OF LEARNING IN PE

Holistic learning within the national curriculum (DfE, 2013) is evident with reference to opportunities for pupils to communicate and collaborate, evaluate their learning and recognise their success. A 'one-size-fits-all' teaching style for PE, therefore, would not give pupils the opportunity to develop across all the physical, cognitive, social and affective domains.

Traditionally, primary PE is taught through an activity lens, but the teachers should use creativity and knowledge of their class to develop fundamental movement skills through engaging and collaborative experiences.

Models-based practice has been extensively written about, researched and applied within PE. Each model enables the teacher to plan meaningful experiences that support learners with a different purpose, be it exploratory, creative or collaborative, and can guide each child through a unique learning journey. The 'Cooperative Learning' model would be used to challenge pupils in the social context of their physical learning, working collaboratively in small mixed groups, developing not only their physical skills, but building social relationships and positive interdependence (Dyson and Casey, 2016). However, the 'Teaching Games for Understanding' model might be adopted when a more constructivist approach to learning is needed, challenging and developing a child's metacognitive abilities through decision making and problem solving through modified games (O'Leary 2016).

Mosston and Ashworth (2008) suggest that teaching behaviour is a chain of decision making. One style is not considered more or less beneficial than another, but everything that we teach is grounded in conscious decisions and certain behaviours which are evident in those decisions. For example:

- how teachers organise planning, pupil groupings and activities;

- management of time, space and equipment;

- creation of an inclusive and motivating environment;

- employing metacognitive processes to make connections in learning.

Mosston and Ashworth (2008) present 11 teaching styles that transition from being teacher led at one end of the spectrum to child centred at the other. Switching between these different styles during a lesson often leads to higher quality learning outcomes for pupils, but factors such as subject knowledge, experience of teaching or the school's policy can impact on the confidence of a teacher to do this. Importantly, the purpose of the lesson and the aim of learning will direct the type of style(s) to be used. Table 10.2 illustrates each of Mosston and Ashworth's (2008) teaching styles alongside an example of how the skill of jumping could be experienced by pupils through each one.

Table 10.2 The 11 teaching styles illustrated through the skill of jumping

Mosston and Ashworth Teaching style	Interaction	Example through the skill of jumping
Command (A)	Practitioner makes decisions. Participant copies and complies with instructions.	Teacher demonstrates how to perform five jumping techniques in turn. Pupils copy. Teacher observes compliance to the correct technique.

(Continued)

Table 10.2 (Continued)

Mosston and Ashworth Teaching style	Interaction	Example through the skill of jumping
Practice (B)	Practitioner sets up opportunities giving feedback to participant who is working at own pace on tasks set	Teacher demonstrates the five jumping techniques. Pupils are then asked to explore each one in their own time.
Reciprocal (C)	Participants work together, receiving feedback from each other. Practitioner provides reference points for feedback.	In pairs. pupils experiment with the jumping techniques shown. They perform each one to their partner, with their partner providing feedback against the correct model.
Self-check (D)	Practitioner sets criteria for success. Participants check their own performance against these.	A checklist of correct technique points is drawn up for a jumping technique. The pupil self-assesses where they are in relation to these points.
Inclusion (E)	Practitioner sets out a variety of tasks/opportunities. Participants select which task is most appropriate for their abilities and/or motivations.	The teacher shows the pupils the five different jumping techniques. In pairs, they are then asked to identify which jumping technique gives the furthest jump.
Guided discovery (F)	Practitioner uses questions and tasks to gradually direct participants towards a predetermined learning target.	In pairs, pupils identify five different jumping methods for jumping for distance. Record each one and discuss with the teacher what they have found out.
Convergent discovery (G)	Practitioner sets or frames problems. Participant attempts to find most appropriate solutions.	Pupils measure their height in distance on the ground. What jumping technique can you identify that will allow you to jump as near to your height or beyond?
Divergent discovery (H)	Practitioner sets or frames problems. Participant attempts to create possible solutions.	Using a combination of only three jumps, what is the greatest distance you can achieve linking these jumps together?
Learner designed (I)	Practitioner decides on area of focus. Participants develop within this area, drawing on practitioners' expertise.	A theme of jumping for distance is given to the class. In groups of three, the group video each other performing their jumping technique and identify what it is that needs developing in their performance. They then design an activity to achieve this.

Mosston and Ashworth Teaching style	Interaction	Example through the skill of jumping
Learner initiated (J)	Participants decide on how and what they are aiming for. Practitioner drawn on for support as needed.	Around the theme jumping for distance, the pupil decides what they want to work on and how they will go about doing this.
Self-teach (K)	Participants engage in development on their own.	Pupils develop their understanding of jumping for distance outside the lesson in their own time.

REFLECTION

Consider a different fundamental movement skill other than jumping. When might a child need to use that skill in an activity? Think of different ways in which the skill could be developed. What different contexts and environments could that skill be used in?

CREATING A SAFE AND INCLUSIVE ENVIRONMENT

Under the Equality Act of 2010, schools have a duty to ensure that all children with special educational needs and disabilities (SEND) have reasonable adjustments made to their learning to prevent disadvantage and ensure equality of opportunity. Inclusive practice in primary PE should strive to go beyond this and for teachers to plan for all learners to be included, not only those children with SEND. When considering inclusive practice, being reflective about your intent is important.

Consider:

- Who are you planning adaptations for? (All learners)
- How will you adapt activities within lessons? (Pedagogy)
- What will these adapted activities look like? (Content)

Knowing what you can change, and how, is important in creating an inclusive PE environment. You cannot change the learners in your classroom – they will all have unique personalities, abilities and needs, but you are able to control how you adapt activities in your PE lesson in response to these.

Adopting the principle of the Graduated Approach from the SEN *Code of Practice* (DfE, 2015) enables the effective teacher to create that inclusive environment through the cycle of 'Assess, Plan, Do and Review'.

Models such as Black and Stevenson's (2011) 'Inclusion Spectrum' are useful tools to support teachers to scaffold learning and teaching. The model of everyone can play, modified and parallel activity, and disability sport enables teachers to adapt activities to meet the needs of all learners. The STEP model (Pickup and Price, 2008) is a widely accepted model used in PE to modify the Space, Task, Equipment and People to provide support or more challenge with an activity.

As important as it is to empower children to be part of planning for inclusive practice, so is empowering children to be aware of their roles and responsibility to keep them and others safe. Safe practice in lessons needs to be integral in the planning process, and children should be taught to understand about how to keep themselves safe in PE and beyond the curriculum within all physical contexts. Teachers therefore need good foundational knowledge of how to ensure that their PE learning environment remains safe at all times. Key points to note are:

- It is a teacher's responsibility to examine the environment and equipment before the lesson starts and continue to monitor this throughout the lesson.

- Teachers should understand and follow the school's reporting system for broken or damaged equipment or environment.

- Schools are required to have risk assessments for PE lessons and it is the individual teacher's responsibility to have read and understood these (see AfPE, 2020, Safe Practice: in Physical Education, School Sport and Physical Activity).

The Association for Physical Education's Prevent, Inform and Education (PIE) model (see www.afpe.org.uk/physical-education/wp-content/uploads/PIE_5_8.pdf) advocates for the delivery of safe practice in PE lessons by considering:

- What can be anticipated about the activities within the PE lesson? Plan and organise the learning to PREVENT accidents or incidents from happening.

- Include children in learning about safe practice and INFORM them about what might cause them harm.

- EDUCATE children about what is safe and unsafe in PE lessons.

Care should always be taken to consider the balance between physical challenge and risk in any lesson. Putting a child in immediate danger is never the intention of any teacher, but neither should ensuring that activities are totally risk free. Ultimately, a 0 per cent risk-adverse environment will prevent physical skills developing and could ultimately place a child at a greater risk later when they are in a new and challenging environment.

PART 3: UNDERSTANDING THE DEVELOPMENT OF CHILDREN'S KNOWLEDGE IN PE

Having good subject knowledge underpins the ability to plan carefully sequenced lesson in PE. Teachers should first consider their understanding of fundamental movement skills before securing an understanding of specific activities – e.g., knowing how to teach the skills of throwing and catching before placing children in specific games activities that would put both these skills under pressure due to the rules and expectations within the game.

As explored in the previous section, teachers should also consider what they understand by pedagogical knowledge. This is knowledge of the different strategies and approaches that can be used within a lesson to enable the child to engage with the content and make progress. As referenced by Ofsted (2022, np): *Expert PE teachers can draw on their own broad-ranging content and pedagogical content knowledge to communicate objectives clearly and organise learning that challenges all pupils to know more and do more.*

Table 10.3 demonstrates a sequence of six dance lessons for Year 3 pupils.

The first lesson starts with children exploring movements in response to a stimulus. Although in this example we specifically draw upon the context of dance, the same exploration of fundamental movement skills could be applied within all areas of PE. For example, in a games context, this might include children exploring different ways to handle a ball, or in gymnastics they might explore different shapes that their bodies can make.

Building upon prior learning across a sequence of lessons is instrumental for children to embed their learning. Ofsted (2022, np) further suggest that it is important for a curriculum sequence to *maximize the likelihood that all pupils will be able to connect the steps they have taken to know more and do more in PE.*

Table 10.3 Sequence of six dance lessons for Year 3 pupils

Dance: Year 3
National curriculum reference: Perform dances with a range of movement patterns.
Overall intended learning outcome: Pupils will choreograph and perform a short dance in groups from the stimulus of machinery.
Stimulus: machinery Visit a local science museum or watch videos of large and small machinery in action. Look specifically at the mechanics involved in the movement of different parts of the machine. Create a word bank of movement vocabulary that will be used to create dance actions. Examples might include: twist, whirr, jolt, flip, slide, pump, spin.

(Continued)

Table 10.3 (Continued)

Adaptive practice possibilities – STEP model:

Space – children can explore the amount of space and directions within the space as well as working at different levels.

Task – children may be guided when changing the dynamics of the movement or adding connections.

Equipment – models of moving machinery or movement word banks could be used to provide a scaffold for how to move.

People – pupils may continue to work individually or in pairs; others may need additional adult intervention to generate ideas.

Lesson	Learning outcome	Activities to develop skills and understanding	Key questions
1	To explore action words and create a short motif.	**Creating a motif linked to the stimulus** using the action words created, children individually explore these actions with their bodies. Children use action words to explore movement, experimenting with the order in which they want to perform them. Rehearse these actions until they can confidently remember and perform them. Present pieces of music with different tempos and ask children to perform their motif accompanying the music. Children record their 4 actions on a storyboard strip as words or stick drawings.	How did your body feel when you performed your actions to the slow/fast music? Explain why you chose to put your actions in that order.

| 2 | To develop a motif with a partner into a longer sequence of dance. | **Developing a motif** Play music examples from Lesson 1 and children recall and practise their motifs. Children work with a partner. Child 1 performs one of their actions, then child 2, continuing until all 8 actions have been performed. Repeat and then practise this until the pair can perform all 8 actions confidently together. Play machinery music throughout for the children to gain some rhythmic sense to their actions. | How could you work together with your partner to help each other remember all of the actions? What could you do as you move to give your body a 'machine like' quality? |
| 3 | To develop the dance by adding transitions that create a flow and movement within the dance space. | **Introducing transitions** Using the machinery music, children explore travelling in different ways, then explore turning in different ways, adding jumps as they explore travelling and turning. Children continue to work in their pairs to add transitions (travel steps, turns or jumps) to their motif. Pairs perform their dances to another pair and feedback on how well the dance flows and moves in the space. | Explain why you chose this transition movement. What different directions could you travel in within your dance space? |

(Continued)

Table 10.3 (Continued)

4	To explore and change the dynamics of movements.	**Developing dynamics** Play music with different tempos and children perform their actions. Discuss how the feel of the actions changed when the tempo changed. Children change the speed or effort of some of their actions in their 'machine'. Perform for another pair and reflect on the impact on the audience of their changes. Does it make the dance more 'machine like'?	How does your body feel different by changing the dynamic of that action? How does changing the dynamic make your dance look more machine like?
5	To connect with other performers within the dance and develop spatial awareness within the dance space.	**Connections** Play machinery music while pupils travel and move. At a signal, children connect by facing a partner to perform a machine action together. Pairs join to make a group of four. Pairs stand in close proximity to each other and perform their dances at the same time. Develop this by looking for opportunities to connect - this could be actual connections by physical contact or by movements under or between each other.	How can you make sure that you don't bump into anyone when performing your dance next to another pair? Explain how you created a connection in your dance with your group of 4.

| 6 | To work collaboratively to perform in unison.

To give relevant feedback to a partner, setting goals together for next steps in learning. | **Unison and performance**
Play music with a strong rhythmic beat. Use movement vocabulary from word bank and children move together in unison.
Children work in their 4s to add one new action that they perform in unison. Children decide where to include this in their dance and practise together.
Provide success criteria for performance; clear and controlled actions, unison working with partners and different dynamics.
Children perform for another group and feed back against the success criteria. | What could you do to ensure that you and your partner moves in unison?
Explain how you have achieved the different parts of the success criteria.
What goals would you set yourself next time you take part in dance lessons? |

Within this sequence of lessons, the learning is structured to enable children to develop creatively, cognitively, socially and emotionally within the physical context (dance). Adapted practice to support an inclusive curriculum is considered through the STEP model (Pickup and Price, 2008) and is integrated within lessons for all learners rather than a bolt-on for those pupils with SEND. It is important to remember that the child must have a voice when making adaptations to any activities. Asking children what they think they can do and not imposing limitations through perceived constraints will be pivotal in providing inclusive experiences within PE lessons.

PART 4: DEVELOPING YOUR KNOWLEDGE OF PE FURTHER

FURTHER RESOURCES

There are a number of organisations and professional bodies that exist to support teachers' ongoing professional development in primary PE.

Association for Physical Education (AfPE): www.afpe.org.uk/physical-education/ is the subject association for PE in England.

PE Scholar is an online resource that links to contemporary research, resources and offers a number of online training courses for teachers: www.pescholar.com/

Primary Physical Education Assembly (PPEA) is an online resource for anyone who wants to know, do or inspire in primary PE. This site includes links to reading, online events and connections to the wider primary PE community: www.ppea.org.uk/

Youth Sport Trust (YST) is a charitable origination supporting PE, health and well-being and youth sport: www.youthsporttrust.org

RECOMMENDED PRACTITIONER WEB-BASED RESOURCES

Disentangling Inclusive Primary Physical Education: www.dippe.lu/

Meaningful Physical Education: meaningfulpe.wordpress.com/

ProActive PE: https://proactivepe.co.uk/

Spectrum of Teaching Styles: www.spectrumofteachingstyles.org

BLOGS AND COMMUNITY PAGES

PEPRN (Physical Education Practitioner Research Network): www.peprn.com/

PhysEquity: https://physequity.wordpress.com/

RECOMMENDED BOOKS

Goodway, JD, Gallahue, DL and Ozmun, JC (2019) *Understanding Motor Development: Infants, Children, Adolescents, Adults* (8th edn). London: McGraw-Hill.

Graham, G., Holt/Hale, SA and Parker, M (2020) *Children Moving: A Reflective Approach to Teaching Physical Education* (10th edn). New York: McGraw-Hill.

Griggs, G and Randall, V (2022) *An Introduction to Primary Physical Education* (2nd edn). London: Routledge.

Howells, K, Carney, A, Castle, N and Little, R (2017) *Mastering Primary Physical Education*. London: Bloomsbury.

Lawrence, J (2017) *Teaching Primary Physical Education* (2nd edn). London: SAGE.

Pickard, A and Maude, P (2021) *Teaching Physical Education Creatively* (2nd edn). London: Routledge.

REFERENCES

AfPE (2020) *Safe Practice: In Physical Education, School Sport and Physical Activity*. Leeds: UK Coaching.

Banks, JA (2016) *Cultural Diversity and Education: Foundations, Curriculum and Teaching*. New York: Routledge.

Black, K and Stevenson, P (2011) *The Inclusion Spectrum*. Australia: Theinclusionclub.com

Board of Education (1905) *The Syllabus of Physical Exercise for Schools*. London: HMSO.

Coulter, M and Ní Chroinin, D (2022) The possibilities and challenges within primary physical education. In Griggs, G and Randall, V (2nd edn) *An Introduction to Primary Physical Education*. London: Routledge.

DfE (2013) *The National Curriculum in England Key Stages 1 and 2: Framework Document*. London: DfE. Crown copyright.

DfE/DHSC (2014) *SEND Code of Practice: 0–25 Years*. Available at: www.gov.uk/Government/Publications/Send-Code-Of-Practice-0-To-25 (accessed 26 June 2022).

Doherty, J and Brennan, P (2014) *Physical Education 5–11: A Guide for Teachers*. Oxford: Routledge.

Dyson, B and Casey, A (2016) *Cooperative Learning in Physical Education and Physical Activity: A Practical Introduction*. London: Routledge.

Gallahue, DL, Goodway, J and Ozmun, JC (2021) *Understanding Motor Development: Infants, Children, Adolescents, Adults* (8th edn). Burlington, MA: Jones and Bartlett Learning.

Graham, G, Holt/Hale, SA and Parker, M (2020) *Children Moving: A Reflective Approach to Teaching Physical Education* (10th edn). New York: McGraw-Hill.

Griggs, G (2022) Development of physical education in primary schools. In Griggs, G and Randall, V (eds) *An Introduction to Primary Physical Education* (2nd edn). London: Routledge.

Lawrence, J (2021) Debates in the teaching of primary physical education. In V Bower (ed.) *Debates in Primary Education*. London: Routledge.

Long, R and Roberts, N (2022) *Physical Education, Physical Activity and Sport in Schools*. Available at: https://Researchbriefings.Files.Parliament.Uk/Documents/Sn06836/Sn06836.Pdf (accessed 3 August 2022).

Lumpkin, A (2011) Building character through sports. *Strategies: A Journal for Physical and Sport Educators*, 24 (6): 13–15.

Lynch, S, Sutherland, S and Walton-Fisette, J (2020) The A–Z of social justice physical education: Part 1. *JOPERD: Journal of Physical Education, Recreation and Dance*, 91 (4): 8–13.

Mosston, M and Ashworth, S (2008) *Teaching Physical Education* (1st online edn). Available at: https://Spectrumofteachingstyles.Org/Assets/Files/Book/Teaching_Physical_Edu_1st_Online.Pdf (accessed 7 July 2022).

Ofsted (2022) *Research Review for Physical Education*. Manchester: Ofsted. Crown copyright.

O'Leary, N (2016) Learning informally to use the 'full version' of teaching games for understanding. *European Physical Education Review*, 22 (1): 3–22.

Pickup, I and Price, I (2008) *Teaching Physical Education in the Primary School: A Developmental Approach*. London: Continuum.

Race, R, Gill, D, Kaitell, E, Mahmud, A, Thorpe, A and Wolfe, K (2022) Proclamations and provocations: decolonising curriculum in education research and professional practice. *Equity in Education & Society*, 1 (1): 82–96.

Randall, V (2020) Becoming a primary physical educator. *Education 3–13: International Journal of Primary, Elementary and Early Years Education*, 48 (2): 133–46.

Randall, V and Griggs, G (2022) London's Olympic legacy: research reveals why £2.2 billion investment in primary school PE has failed teachers. *The Conversation*. Available at: https://Theconversation.Com/Londons-Olympic-Legacy-Research-Reveals-Why-2-2-Billion-Investment-In-Primary-School-Pe-Has-Failed-Teachers-178809 (accessed 16 June 2022).

11

PERSONAL, SOCIAL, HEALTH AND ECONOMIC EDUCATION (PSHE), AND RELATIONSHIPS AND SEX EDUCATION (RSE)

VICTORIA-MARIE PUGH

KEYWORDS: RELATIONSHIPS; LIFE SKILLS; FINANCIAL LITERACY: HEALTH EDUCATION; SELF-AWARENESS; GLOBAL CITIZENSHIP.

LINKS TO THE CORE CONTENT FRAMEWORK

High Expectations (Standard 1): 1.6

Subject and Curriculum (Standard 3): 3.1, 3.5

Classroom Practice (Standard 4): 4.1, 4.2

Adaptive Teaching (Standard 5): 5.2, 5.3

PART 1: EXPLORING PSHE AND RSHE

WHAT IS PSHE?

PSHE education is a subject that encompasses a wide range of topics. PSHE stands for Personal, Social, Health and Economic Education. However, many educators are unaware of the E for economic, confusing it instead for education (Shakespeare, 2020). The subject holds an important place in the education system as, unlike more traditional subjects, it promotes life skills, decision-making skills, as well as information relating directly to health and well-being. Recently, Relationships and Health Education were made a statutory requirement in Primary Education and Relationships, Sex and Health Education statutory within secondary education. These aspects of PSHE are referred to as RSHE or RSE (DfE, 2019). Changes to legislation will be discussed in more detail later in the chapter, but this shift in status within the curriculum has been instrumental in raising the profile of PSHE as a whole. For the purposes of this chapter, I will refer to the subject as PSHE, as it is clearly stated within the DfE guidance document that teaching RSHE within a wider PSHE curriculum is recommended.

PSHE, however, is not just a stand-alone subject. Ofsted's school inspection guidance calls for evidence to show how Personal Development is being addressed for pupils. Amanda Spielman, Ofsted Chief Inspector (2019), stated that:

> In the new inspection model, we are particularly interested in how schools contribute to the personal development of children. This area is now a judgement in its own right. This makes more space in inspection for discussing things like the PSHE lessons in which wider life issues can be explored.

PSHE must also be recognised as a tool to support safeguarding with key skills such as using scientific names for body parts playing a key part in clarity when disclosures have been made by young children around abuse. The Ofsted safeguarding guidance (2022) states that schools must ensure that the curriculum is robust and that:

> as part of the curriculum, children and learners are supported to understand what constitutes a healthy relationship both online and offline, and to recognise risk, for example risks associated with criminal and sexual exploitation, domestic abuse, female genital mutilation, forced marriage, substance misuse, gang activity, radicalisation and extremism, and are aware of the support available to them.

It is therefore imperative that PSHE is valued as a subject and is planned, delivered and assessed accordingly.

REFLECTION

In what ways does PSHE education impact on wider school and community aspects?

How can economic education help ensure that pupils have the opportunity to develop key life skills in ways that also meet their individual needs?

How can a strong PSHE curriculum support the wider needs of pupils and safeguarding?

WHY IS PSHE IN THE NATIONAL CURRICULUM?

PSHE is not currently part of the national curriculum. However, elements of it are statutory. In 2017, the Children and Social Work Act stated that relationships and sex education would be mandatory in all secondary schools, and relationships education statutory in all primary schools (UK Parliament, 2017). Health Education was then also given statutory status and is now mandatory in all schools, both primary and secondary. Other aspects of PSHE such as economic education, and bereavement and sustainability are still not statutory. However, the guidance strongly recommended that a full PSHE curriculum is taught in all schools and states that schools should not just 'teach to the guidance', but see it as the basic requirement that forms part of broader PSHE education. Economic and financial education provide valuable life skills, with Whitebread and Bingham (2013) stating that money habits may be formed as early as seven years old, with Strong et al. (2020) reporting that financial education in schools may lead to better outcomes for people and increased financial well-being. Similarly, the Young Enterprise organisation (2022) state that:

> Financial education enables young people to develop the knowledge, skills and attitudes towards money so that they can make informed financial decisions and thrive in today's society. Without the skills built through financial education, young people are at risk of financial difficulties, exclusion and debt.

Therefore, the areas excluded from the statutory guidance do not just support understanding of content but vital life skills, which can impact upon positive outcomes for pupils both now and later in life.

Given that not all PSHE topics are statutory within primary education, you may find the tables below useful when familiarising yourself with the key content.

STATUTORY RSHE ELEMENTS

Key topics covered in statutory Relationships Education:

- Families and people who care for me.
- Caring friendships.
- Respectful relationships.
- Online relationships.
- Being safe.

Table 11.1 Summary of requirements from DfE (2019, p10)*

Relationships Education	Relationships and Sex Education	Health Education
All schools providing primary education, including all-through schools and middle schools (includes schools as set out in the Summary section).	All schools providing secondary education, including all-through schools and middle schools (includes schools as set out in the Summary section).	All maintained schools, including schools with a sixth form, academies, free schools. Non-maintained special schools and alternative provision, including pupil referral units.
		The statutory requirement to provide Health Education does not apply to independent schools – PSHE is already compulsory as independent schools must meet the Independent School Standards as set out in the Education (Independent School Standards) Regulations 2014. Independent school however, may find the principles in the guidance on Health Education helpful planning an age-appropriate curriculu

*The statutory requirements do not apply to sixth form colleges, 16–19 academies or Further Education (FE) colleges, although we would encourage them to support students by offering these subjects. These settings may find the principles helpful, especially in supporting pupils in the transition to FE.

Key topics covered in statutory Health Education:

- Mental well-being.
- Internet safety and harms.
- Physical health and fitness.
- Healthy eating.
- Drugs, alcohol and tobacco.
- Health and prevention.
- Basic first aid.
- Changing adolescent body.

WIDER NON-STATUTORY PSHE TOPICS TO COVER AS RECOMMENDED BY THE PSHE ASSOCIATION

Key topics to cover in PSHE:

- Bereavement.
- Aspirations, work and careers education.

- Financial education.

- Global citizenship.

- Communities.

- Rules and the law.

- Sustainability and the environment.

HOW HAS 'KNOWLEDGE' IN PSHE DEVELOPED OVER TIME?

PSHE has been referred to by many names over the past 20 years in education. From PSHCE, which included citizenship education, to PSE to PRSHE, it has at times been an undervalued and undertaught part of the curriculum (Pugh, 2021). Often in schools, PSHE has been delivered through the use of circle time for 10 minutes at the end of a busy day. This perception of PSHE being an 'airy-fairy' subject which depended solely on talking about feelings is one that is thankfully changing, and the value of PSHE in supporting attainment, a sense of belonging as well as contributing to safeguarding and risk awareness is being acknowledged. Prior to the change in legislation and RSHE guidance release, the last RSE guidance was published in 2000 (DfEE, 2000). It was inevitable that key issues in society and childhood changed and developed over the 22 years, and this is apparent in the 2000 guidance as there was no reference to social media or online communication, for example.

Although the desire to communicate with friends has not changed over the years, the method of communication has. The Children's Commissioner's report on the effects of social media use on 8–12-year-olds, 'Life in Likes' (Children's Commissioner, 2018), states that 75 per cent of 10–12-year-olds have a social media account, despite the official age limit of 13 years. It also found that pupils were concerned with 'getting likes' and followers, and that this often led to them feeling anxious.

The Children's Society (2020) reported increases in issues with body image and young people with a rise in toxic masculinity from filters and adverts. It was reported that ITV aired adverts for cosmetic surgery in the breaks of their most-watched programme, *Love Island*, which have been attributed to rising mental health concerns in young people.

Increases in mental health concerns were also reported by Newlove-Delgado T, et al. (2022), who stated that the rates of probable mental disorders have increased since 2017: in 6–16-year-olds, from one in nine (11.6 per cent) to one in six (17.4 per cent), and in 17–19-year-olds from one in ten (10.1 per cent) to one in six (17.4 per cent). Rates in both age groups remained similar between 2020 and 2021. Possible reasons cited for these increases ranged from reduction of physical activity and increases in a sedentary lifestyle, inequalities in education and health services, pressure from social media and access to unrestricted online information.

The fast-paced developments in social media, phones and internet access were not a part of PSHE considerations in the past, with curricula focusing on emotional literacy, puberty education and friendships. The change in foci within society and technology means that PSHE is a subject that must continually develop and improve in line with greater sociological consideration and health research, as well as global priorities.

PSHE NOW

As previously discussed, topics in PSHE have developed over time. Issues around gender pronouns, peer-on-peer sexual harassment, vaping, climate crisis and financial literacy, given the current cost of living increases, are all key areas of concern within the PSHE curriculum currently. It is not possible to address all these areas within this chapter. However, the following sections will cover some of the current issues, and sustainability and climate crisis hold their own chapter within this book.

The recent publication of the Ofsted review of sexual abuse in schools and colleges (2021) and the Everyone's Invited campaign (2020), brought child-on-child abuse and conversations about consent to the forefront of education. As PSHE is a subject that teaches about personal safety, permission seeking and signposting for support, it was not surprising that the RSE elements of PSHE were considered as a support in preventing child-on-child sexual abuse.

The following objectives from the statutory relationships education guidance may support the prevention of child-on-child sexual abuse.

- The importance of respecting others, even when they are different from yourself – for example, physically, in character, personality or backgrounds – or make different choices or have different preferences or beliefs.

- The importance of self-respect and how this links to one's own happiness.

- That in school and in wider society, they can expect to be treated with respect by others, and that in turn they should show due respect to others, including those in positions of authority.

- Regarding different types of bullying (including cyberbullying), the impact of bullying, responsibilities of bystanders (primarily reporting bullying to an adult) and how to get help.

- What a stereotype is and how stereotypes can be unfair, negative or destructive.

- The importance of permission-seeking and giving in relationships with friends, peers and adults.

- That the same principles apply to online relationships as to face-to-face relationships, including the importance of respect for others online, including when we are anonymous.

- The rules and principles for keeping safe online, how to recognise risks, harmful content and contact, and how to report them.

- How to critically consider online friendships and sources of information, including awareness of the risks associated with people they have never met.

- How information and data are shared and used online.

- What sorts of boundaries are appropriate in friendships with peers and others (including in a digital context).

- How to recognise who to trust and who not to trust; how to judge when a friendship is making them feel unhappy or uncomfortable; managing conflict; how to manage these situations, and how to seek help or advice from others, if needed.

- Regarding the concept of privacy and the implications of it for both children and adults, including that it is not always right to keep secrets if they relate to being safe.

- That each person's body belongs to them, and the differences between appropriate and inappropriate or unsafe physical, and other, contact.

- How to respond safely and appropriately to adults they may encounter (in all contexts, including online) whom they do not know.

- How to recognise and report feelings of being unsafe or feeling bad about any adult.

- How to ask for advice or help for themselves or others, and to keep trying until they are heard.

- How to report concerns or abuse, and the vocabulary and confidence needed to do so.

- Where to get advice – e.g., family, school and/or other sources.

By teaching about respect, empathy, personal safety and consent, trainees and teachers can support pupils to navigate and make informed decisions about their own life choices, both now and in the future.

WHAT MIGHT KNOWLEDGE IN PSHE LOOK LIKE IN THE FUTURE?

The introduction of statutory RSHE was welcomed by PSHE educators, charities and school leaders in 2019. However, the addition of all elements of PSHE as statutory to ensure that PSHE education continues to develop as a valued and respected subject taught by teachers who are confident in the content and development of skills would certainly be on the wish list for the future. Considering the ways in which we can ensure that PSHE is inclusive and diverse must be a priority as we move forward with PSHE education and development of the curriculum. For example, when teaching about families, it is important that we celebrate the diverse nature of families rather than the heteronormative stance which is often adopted. Referring to 'mum and dad' as though it is the norm at home is a common phrase and can lead to stereotypes around what a family looks like. This change in perspective of curriculum planning and language is one that is also sought in ideas around decolonising the curriculum for PSHE. For example, Sperring, (2020, pp3) suggests that

> despite being a global ethnic majority, their [children and families of colour] experience of the curriculum is all too often white Eurocentric; more specifically, that of white, middle-class men, 'male, pale and stale' voices that need to be banished.

Fitzpatrick et al. (2021) continue this discussion by acknowledging that Relationships and Sex Education (RSE) needs to be addressed in a more culturally responsive way which considers social, environmental and political contexts. It is therefore vital to consider how you can introduce and embed opportunities to acknowledge and discuss discrimination, identify, representation and questioning perspectives of knowledge.

REFLECTION

Consider the following questions in relation to the decolonisation of the PSHE curriculum and inclusion:

How can you ensure that PSHE is taught sensitively, ensuring that a range of cultural, religious and social beliefs are respected?

How do your own experiences and beliefs influence your confidence and approach to PSHE education?

How can you ensure that you are a confident PSHE practitioner?

PART 2: FOUNDATION KNOWLEDGE IN PSHE

As previous stated within this chapter, PSHE encompasses a range of topics that include a number of sensitive and complex issues. This section will explore strategies that will support you to become a confident and informed PSHE teacher. In particular, this section will explore the use of distancing techniques, dealing with tricky questions and present a variety of questions to consider when teaching some example PSHE topics.

DISTANCING TECHNIQUES

It is important to remember that all pupils will come to the classroom with their own backgrounds, experiences, beliefs and attitudes, and that as teachers we do not always know the full story of their lives. Therefore, distancing techniques allow pupils to explore issues and concepts without having to directly share personal information about themselves or past experiences. The PSHE Association (2022, p3) suggests that the use of distancing techniques *allows pupils to engage more objectively with the lesson content.*

Below are examples of activities that can be used to engage pupils in topics and discussions that may require distancing techniques.

Table 11.2 *Pedagogical activity examples*

Activity example	Advantages	Considerations
Scenarios	Using a range of scenarios allows you to tailor the story of story board to fit the needs of your objective. It also allows pupils to depersonalise the situation as they are commenting or responding to characters rather than talking about their own experiences.	When writing or choosing scenarios to use with your class or a group of pupils, do make sure that the names used are not the same as any pupils in your class and that they are not exactly the same as situations that may have happened recently to individuals within the class. Some pupils may enjoy role playing their responses to the scenario. However, some may prefer to discuss them or give a written response - having a choice of response options can be a supportive tool for pupil engagement.

(Continued)

Table 11.2 (Continued)

Activity example	Advantages	Considerations
Picture books	Picture books offer a wonderful approach to a range of topics. They can be used as a whole story or broken down into storyboards with the ending left out so that pupils can discuss possible endings or resolutions to the characters' situations. Again, this can offer pupils distance from being personally involved with the situation but enable them to offer advice or strategies to the characters and think objectively about the situation presented. Picture books can serve as an inclusive tool with visuals, but can often be accessed as audio books, as well for those who would benefit from this option.	Choose picture books that allow pupils to identify a range of emotions throughout the story. Ensure that the picture books you use are representative of diversity of race, beliefs, disabilities, family structures, etc.
TV or podcast clips	Using clips from popular cartoons/TV programmes or podcasts are a great way to engage pupils and allow them to connect with characters.	Ensure that the clips are age appropriate and that any videos have subtitles enabled.
Advice pages	Using advice columns that pupils can respond to and allow them to consider situations or contexts from a wider perspective and give advice. These 'problem pages' can cover any objectives and can be written to meet the needs of the lesson.	Try to avoid gender stereotypes with 'problems' – for example, many examples focus on girls and friendship fall-outs or boys and physical fights. If these types of examples are used, it should be made clear to pupils that these situations can arise regardless of gender.

DEALING WITH TRICKY QUESTIONS

Woolley (2020, p3) suggests that:

> Each of us has issues that we find difficult to discuss. These may be because of past experiences, being unsure about our own viewpoints, being worried about causing offence or saying the wrong thing, or the fact that the issue is new to us. The same is true within our professional context and it is important to consider what can make an issue controversial within the setting of the primary school, particularly in the areas of Personal, Social, Health and Economic Education and Relationships Education.

Teacher confidence has also played a part in the past with research by Giles et al. (2012) stating that teacher confidence and enthusiasm influenced the effectiveness of PSHE teaching and learning. With little to no PSHE education taught as part of Initial Teacher Education programmes previously, it was suggested that teachers did not feel equipped or confident when teaching particular aspects of PSHE.

So how do we support pupils to feel safe and respected within the classroom while being able to answer their questions effectively?

Wölk (2003) suggested that student–teacher relationships were the most important elements of classroom management and that without them a strong community for learning could not be established. Therefore, designing class or discussion rules together and revisiting them often can allow for critical thinking around terminology, difficult concepts and topics that may be sensitive, as there is a strong emphasis on respect which has been built as a class community.

GROUND RULES

Co-constructing ground rules at the beginning of the year is a key strategy in developing a safe and respectful environment for PSHE lessons. It is vital that this is a co-constructed activity between the pupils and yourself, otherwise these are merely rules being 'done to them'. Creating a space where pupils feel that they can ask questions without the fear of judgement or getting terms wrong is essential, and this can be achieved by defining key terms clearly and ensuring understanding around terminology. A positive approach to rules can often be more effective than a list of 'do nots' and promotes the behaviours that are encouraged rather than those that are not. Some examples of ground rules might include:

- Everyone has the right to be included.

- Everyone has the right to be listened to.

- Anything confidential that is shared in class shouldn't be discussed with other people outside of the classroom.

- People have the right not to share personal experiences or take part if they don't want to.

- We will respect people's views even if we don't agree with them.

- We will use the correct vocabulary relating to the units we are studying and can ask for clarification without people being offended.

- We will agree that it's OK to get things wrong and we shouldn't make fun of people for this.

- There are no 'stupid' questions and people do not need to be afraid to ask questions.

(Pugh, 2020)

WHAT TO ANSWER AND WHEN

Every school must have a clear policy for PSHE (and in particular RSHE) (DfE, 2019, p3). Within this policy will be a breakdown of content taught in each year group and a clear outline of what is classed as relationships education and what is classed as sex education. The defining of these two areas is vital as relationships education is statutory and parents/carers cannot withdraw their children from these lessons; they do, however, have the right to withdraw their children from any sex education lessons. The policy is there to ensure that there is a shared understanding for all parties as to what is being taught and when, and this can be helpful to you as a trainee and as a teacher, as it offers further clarity on what questions might be appropriate to answer in class. See, for example, Figure 11.2.

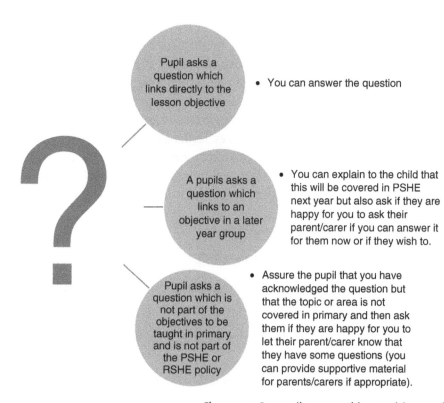

Figure 11.1 Responding to sensitive or tricky questions

Developing strong relationships with parents/carers is an important element of PSHE education, as the life skills learnt go far beyond the classroom and there are many topics such as puberty (which is statutory) and sex education (non-statutory) which parents/carers may wish to express their opinions on. A transparent approach to conversations with parents/carers and sharing of resources can often alleviate any worries they may have and support the home/school partnership.

PUBERTY EDUCATION

Puberty Education now sits within the statutory Health Education and is addressed by two main objectives.

Pupils should know:

- key facts about puberty and the changing adolescent body, particularly from age 9 through to age 11, including physical and emotional changes;

- about menstrual well-being, including the key facts about the menstrual cycle.

There are, however, several things to consider when delivering puberty education to ensure that the provision is informative, inclusive and supportive.

- Is it best to teach about puberty in single gender groupings or altogether? What are the benefits and limitations of each option?

- Have you included a range of sustainable menstrual products within your teaching of the menstrual cycle, such as menstrual cups, reusable sanitary pads, etc. How can this open up a discussion about sustainable personal care products in general?

- How can puberty education support the taboo around periods and open up conversations, particularly for boys and non-menstruating people?

- How would you deal with the discussion around wet dreams, and do you think that all genders need to be informed?

- Do you talk about girls menstruating or people who menstruate?

THE IMPORTANCE OF EMOTIONAL LITERACY

According to Sharp (2000, p8), emotional literacy has been defined by Southampton Educational Psychology Service as *the ability to recognise, understand, handle and appropriately express emotions*. Emotional literacy can support pupils to recognise their emotions and be able to regulate them accordingly, which is beneficial within their relationships, academic work and mental health. When we consider how emotional literacy can be developed across the key stages, it is important to note that for us to 'expect' pupils to be able to resolve conflict with friends, they must first understand how they feel, how this influences their behaviour and how they can manage this. Therefore, it is important to consider what these skills might look like in PSHE education.

Here are some questions to critically reflect upon when considering the teaching of emotional literacy:

- What does self-awareness mean?

- How can you support the development of self-awareness within a class of 30 children?

- What type of self-regulation strategies could be used to support the regulation of emotions within the classroom?

- What type of resources could you use with pupils to support and develop their self-regulation skills?

DIGITAL CRITICALITY

While the term 'life online' is frequently used, the NSPCC (2018) argue that life online for children is just real life. With the Covid-19 pandemic and lessons online, it could be argued that the need for pupils to acquire a sense of criticality while accessing information online is more important than ever. Taylor (2020) stated that

> school closures and strict containment measures mean more and more families are relying on technology and digital solutions to keep children learning, entertained and connected to the outside world, but not all children have the necessary knowledge, skills and resources to keep themselves safe online.

According to the survey on children's online behaviour in England and Wales, year ending March 2020, *around one in six children (17%) aged 10 to 15 years spoke with someone they had never met before (equivalent to 682,000 children) in the previous 12 months.* Although this survey extends to pupils up to 15, it must be acknowledged that KS2 pupils are also apparent in these figures and therefore developing their understanding of keeping safe online is paramount.

Here are some questions to critically reflect upon when considering the teaching of digital resilience and criticality:

- How can you involve parents and carers in developing digital criticality skills and support the school/home partnership?

- How would you deal with incidents that happen on apps, such as WhatsApp or Snapchat, when they have happened outside school time, but the issues are being brought into the school day?

- What strategies could you use to develop pupils' understanding of fake news and why people post information that is not true or accurate?

- How might you use apps and media to support your teaching of digital criticality?

- How might you support pupil's understanding of how data is used to influence our purchasing choices and advertising?

PART 3: UNDERSTANDING THE DEVELOPMENT OF CHILDREN'S KNOWLEDGE IN PSHE

It is recommended that development of knowledge and skills within PSHE education is based upon a spiral curriculum that allows for progression. Bruner (1960) developed the idea of a spiral curriculum as the planning and delivery of topics that spiral from basic concepts to those that are more advanced, with topics being continually revisited to ensure development of understanding and opportunities for application (Ireland and Mouthaan, 2020). This is key to supporting pupils' understanding of both concepts and skills, as it gives them time and space to reflect upon their learning and link it to other skills or knowledge they have acquired. As PSHE can present many topics that require personal responses, it may be that pupils' opinions or viewpoints change as they gain more knowledge in particular topics and reassurance given that this is OK, as it shows they are reflecting upon what they know and developing their own opinions.

Clarke (2020, p285) argues that

> an education system with the single agenda of knowledge acquisition is a reductionist vision. Not only would such a trade-off be harmful to the wellbeing of future citizens, it underestimates the transformative power of education to prepare children to live informed and worthwhile, emotionally textured, fulfilled lives.

It could be argued that PSHE is a key example of this type of 'transformational' power as it deals not only with knowledge and facts, but also with the acquisition of key skills such as communication, assertiveness, risk management and self-awareness. For example, a pupil may be able to recite or recall the dangers of taking illegal drugs or vaping, but do they have the skills and vocabulary to be able to articulate that they do not want to take part in the activity if a friend offers?

Below is an example of a sequence of learning for the topic of relationships. This shows the development of concepts from the relationships with self, to relationships with others across the EYFS and primary age phases. The learning outcomes are taken from the Early Learning Goals (ELG) and Development Matters (DM), and the Primary objectives from the statutory RSHE guidance. See Table 11.3 for examples.

Table 11.3 Progression of skills for PSHE across EYFS, KS1 and KS2 for the topic of relationships

Year group	Learning outcomes	Activities to develop the skills and understanding	Next steps
EYFS	ELG – Self-Regulation: show an understanding of their own feelings and those of others, and begin to regulate their behaviour accordingly. Development Matters: build constructive and respectful relationships.	Pupils could create a friendship potion using all the qualities that they think make someone a good friend. Have a different colour for each trait and use coloured sand or coloured water and oil to create a layered jam jar. This can also act as a sensory jar for pupils.	Discuss how they demonstrate these qualities and give examples of times when they have done this. Building an understanding of mutual respect through actions as well as words.
KS1	To know how important friendships are in making us feel happy and secure.	Pupils can identify a range of feelings which may be associated with friendship. They could draw pictures or write cards to celebrate their friends.	Pupils could use a range of books that show a variety of friendships and identify the feelings of each character at different points throughout the story.
LKS2	The characteristics of friendships, including mutual respect, truthfulness, trustworthiness, loyalty, kindness, generosity, trust, sharing interests and experiences, and support with problems and difficulties.	Display a range of statements about friendship that pupils can discuss and debate. These might include statements such as: • Friends never lie to each other. • It's important for friends to have things in common • It is OK for friends to fall out or argue at times. • Being best friends means not playing with other people.	Encourage pupils to design their own statements and use these as a basis for discussion they may wish to use a Philosophy 4 children-style approach to the discussion (see P4C in the resources recommendations).
UKS2	That most friendships have ups and downs, and that these can often be worked through so that the friendship is repaired or even strengthened, and that resorting to violence is never right.	To explore a range of active listening activities and consider the importance of listening to others. Role play or discuss in groups scenarios where friends have fallen out and suggest strategies to support communication and actions to resolve the conflict.	Begin to identify traits that could be negative within friendships such as manipulation, control, isolation, belittling, etc. Consider if there are any areas of their own friendships which they could develop or improve.

Another example looks at the concept of consent. This shows how consent does not always relate to sexual consent, and that it plays a wider role in self-worth, the ability to articulate feelings and wants, and an understanding of their own needs.

Table 11.4 Progression of skills across EYFS, KS1 and KS2 for the topic of consent

Year group	Learning outcomes	Activities to develop the skills and understanding	Next steps
EYFS	ELG – Self-regulation: show an understanding of their own feelings and those of others, and begin to regulate their behaviour accordingly.	There may be times when pupils want to hold hands with another pupil or play with their hair, etc and if the other child does not want this, it is important for them to be able to articulate their feelings. Giving a range of simple scenarios and having the pupils practise phrases such as 'no, thank you, I don't want you to do that' or 'no, thank you, I don't like that' is a great way to support their understanding of consent. Having pupils understand that this is not necessarily a rejection and that they can still be friends if both wish to be is also an important aspect.	Encouraging pupils to use these phrases (or their own phrases) when situations arise. Create role-play scenarios for pupils to act out with puppets which show a situation where someone is happy to hold hands/have their hair played with/sit together, etc. and situations when they are not happy about it.
KS1	That each person's body belongs to them, and the differences between appropriate and inappropriate or unsafe physical and other contact.	Using the NSPCC PANTS and Pantosaurus resources (see recommended list), discuss the importance of keeping private parts private and introduce scientific names such as vagina, vulva and penis when describing private parts. Ideally, the use of scientific names for body parts would be introduced in Nursery, but many schools have children coming from a range of settings, so it is important that it is covered in Year 1.	The pupils could write short stories or picture books to explain what PANTS means and these could be shared with younger pupils or put in a shared library area or on display.

(Continued)

Table 11.4 (Continued)

Year group	Learning outcomes	Activities to develop the skills and understanding	Next steps
LKS2	That in school and in wider society they can expect to be treated with respect by others, and that in turn they should show due respect to others, including those in positions of authority.	Explore communication online and what respectful relationships look like when using apps, messages, etc. Look at the rules around sharing images and discuss why it isn't OK to share or post images without a person's permission first.	Create a range of fake 'text messages' using an online app. Ask pupils to consider how they would respond to each message and what they would do.
UKS2	The importance of permission-seeking and giving in relationships with friends, peers and adults.	Give pupils a variety of scenarios and ask them to consider if permission from the other person is required or not. These situations might include giving someone a hug, wanting to join with a game, playing alone with a ball, changing clothes in front of a friend, etc. Discuss what might happen if the person did not give permission. How might the conversation go?	Move on to KS3 elements of consent, such as consent when kissing, engaging in sexual activity, consenting to share photos or digital images.

PART 4: DEVELOPING YOUR KNOWLEDGE OF PSHE FURTHER

READING

- Alldred, P, Fox, N and Kulpa, R (2016) Engaging parents with sex and relationship education: a UK primary school case study. *Health Education Journal*, 75 (7): 855–68. Available at: https://doi.org/10.1177/0017896916634114

- Asagba, K (2019) *Sex and Relationships Education for Young People and Adults with Intellectual Disabilities and Autism.* Hove: Pavilion.

- Brooks, R and Adoption UK (2020) *The Trauma and Attachment Aware Classroom: A Practical Guide to Supporting Children who have Encountered Trauma and Adverse Childhood Experiences.* London: Jessica Kingsley Publishers.

- Englander, EK and Lawson, C (2007) New approaches to preventing peer abuse among children. In NB Webb (ed.) *Play Therapy with Children in Crisis: Individual, Group, and Family Treatment* (3rd edn). New York: Guilford Press, pp. 251–69.

- Hallam, S (2009) An evaluation of the social and emotional aspects of learning (SEAL) programme: promoting positive behaviour, effective learning and well-being in primary school children. *Oxford Review of Education*, 35 (3): 313–30. Available at: https://doi.org/10.1080/03054980902934597.

- Howard, C, Burton, M and Levermore, D (2020) *Children's Mental Health and Emotional Well-being in Primary Schools: A Whole School Approach* (2nd edn). London: Learning Matters.

- Kara, B (2021) *Diversity in Schools*. London: SAGE.

- Pandya, A and Lodha, P (2021) Social connectedness, excessive screen time during COVID-19 and mental health: a review of current evidence frontiers in human dynamics. *Frontiers in Human Dynamics*. Available at: https://doi.org/10.3389/fhumd.2021.684137

- Pugh, V and Hughes, D (eds) (2021) *Teaching Personal, Social, Health and Economic and Relationships, (Sex) and Health Education in Primary Schools: Enhancing the Whole Curriculum*. London: Bloomsbury Academic.

- Wang, Y, Hawk, ST, Tang, Y, Schlegel, K and Zou, H (2019) Characteristics of emotion recognition ability among primary school children: relationships with peer status and friendship quality. *Child Indicators Research*, 12 (4): 1369–88. Available at: https://doi.org/10.1007/s12187-018-9590-z

- Wilder, R (2018) 'Knowledge' in English primary schools' decision-making about sex and relationships education, *Health Education Journal*, 77 (1): 30–42. Available at: https://doi.org/10.1177/0017896917737343

ONLINE COURSES

- Brook offers a range of free courses: https://learn.brook.org.uk/

- The DfE have created nine modules for teachers on aspects of RSHE: www.gov.uk/guidance/teaching-about-relationships-sex-and-health#train-teachers-on-relationships-sex-and-health-education

- The University of Worcester offers a University Diploma in PSHE. This course has a fee: www.worcester.ac.uk/courses/university-diploma-in-personal-social-and-health-education

WEBSITE RECOMMENDATIONS

https://pshe-association.org.uk/

www.sexeducationforum.org.uk/

www.nspcc.org.uk/keeping-children-safe/support-for-parents/pants-underwear-rule/

SPECIALIST ORGANISATIONS

The PSHE Association is the national body for PSHE education in the UK. There is a small charge for students to join the association. However, their website offers a range of policies, up-to-date training and a variety of high-quality resources.

OTHER HELPFUL NATIONAL RESOURCES

- Childnet International and UK Safer Internet Centre (2018) Myth vs reality: a practical PSHE toolkit for educators to explore online pressures and perceived 'norms'. Childnet International. Available at: www.childnet.com/wp-content/uploads/2019/05/Full-PSHE-Toolkit-Myth-vs-Reality.pdf

REFERENCES

Bruner, J (1960) The process of education. Cambridge, MA: Harvard University Press.

Children's Commissioner (2018) Life in Likes Report. Available at: www.childrenscommissioner. gov.uk/wp-content/uploads/2018/01/childrens-commissioner-for-england-life-in-likes.pdf (accessed 13 September 2022).

Clarke, T (2020) Children's wellbeing and their academic achievement: the dangerous discourse of 'trade-offs' in education. *Theory and Research in Education*, 18 (3): 263–94.

Department for Education (DfE) (2019) *Relationships and Sex Education (RSE) and Health Education: Statutory Guidance for Governing Bodies, Proprietors, Head Teachers, Principals, Senior Leadership Teams, Teachers*. London: DfE.

Department for Education and Employment (DfEE) (2000) *Sex and Relationship Education Guidance*. London: DfE.

Fitzpatrick, K, Mcglashan, H, Tirumalai, V, Fenaughty, J and Veukiso-Ulugia, A (2022) Relationships and sexuality education: key research informing New Zealand curriculum policy. *Health Education Journal*, 81 (2): 134–56.

Giles, SM, Pankratz, MM, Ringwalt, C, Jackson-Newsom, J, Hansen, WB, Bishop, D and Gottfredson, N (2012) The role of teacher communicator style in the delivery of a middle school substance use prevention program. *Journal of Drug Education*, 42 (4): 39–411. doi: 10.2190/DE.42.4.b

Ireland, J and Mouthaan, M (2020) Perspectives on curriculum design: comparing the spiral and the network models. *Research Matters*, 30: 7–12.

Newlove-Delgado T, Marcheselli F, Williams T, Mandalia D, Davis J, McManus S, Savic M, Treloar W and Ford T (2022) Mental Health of Children and Young People in England. Leeds: NHS Digital.

NSPCC (@NSPCC) (2018) To children, online life is real life. *Find out if the apps and social networks your kids are using are safe at: #netaware:* http://bit.ly/2epizj0Twitter, 12 July.

Ofsted (2021) Review of sexual abuse in schools and colleges. Available at: https:www.gov. uk/government/publications/review-of-sexual-abuse-in-schools-and-colleges/review-of-sexual-abuse-in-schools-and-colleges (accessed 10 September 2022).

Ofsted (2022) *Inspecting Safeguarding in Early Years, Education and Skills Settings*. Available at: www.gov.uk/government/publications/inspecting-safeguarding-in-early-years-education-and-skills (accessed: 13 September 2022).

PSHE Association (2022) Handling complex issues safely in the PSHE education classroom. Available at https://20248256.fs1.hubspotusercontent-na1.net/hubfs/20248256/Guidance/Documents/Handling%20complex%20issues%20safely%20in%20the%20PSHE%20classroom.pdf?Hsctatracking=c2552fae-621f-4b9e-bb0e-3f8d0a57a351%7c3661ba81-9241-436d-8299-e2c468e27f75 (accessed: 13 September 2022).

Pugh, V (2020) *My Life: PSHE Scheme of Work*. London: Collins.

Pugh V and Hughes D (2021) Teaching Personal, Social, Health and Economic and Relationships (Sex) and Health Education in Primary Schools. London: Bloomsbury Academic.

Shakespeare, B (2020) Developing the E in PSHE. In V Pugh and D Hughes (eds) *Teaching Personal, Social, Health and Economic and Relationships, (Sex) And Health Education in Primary Schools: Enhancing the Whole Curriculum*. London: Bloomsbury Academic.

Sperring, K (2020) Decolonising the curriculum: male, pale and stale voices that need to be banished. Available at: https://uclpimedia.com/online/lets-banish-thehierarchy-topped-by-male-pale-and-stale-voices-and-decolonise-the-curriculum

Spielman, A (2019) Amanda Spielman at Stonewall. Available at: www.gov.uk/government/speeches/amanda-spielman-at-stonewall (accessed 10 September 2022)

Strong, C, Ansons, T, Dabhi, K and Crossfield, J. (2020) Financial Wellbeing Behavioural Science Ipsos June 2020 final, *Money and Pensions Service*. Available at: https://moneyandpensionsservice.org.uk/wp-content/uploads/2020/09/Using-behavioural-science-to-improve-financial-wellbeing-Ipsos-Mori-June-2020.pdf (accessed 2 February 2023).

Taylor, H (2020) Children at increased risk of harm online during global COVID-19 pandemic – UNICEF. Available at: www.unicef.org/romania/press-releases/children-increased-risk-harm-online-during-global-covid-19-pandemic-unicef (accessed: 12 September 2022).

The Children's Society (2020) Children, body image and the media. Available at: www.Childrenssociety.Org.Uk/What-we-do/Blogs/Children-body-image-and-the-media (accessed 13 September 2022).

UK Parliament (2017) Children and social work bill. Available at: http://services.parliament.uk/bills/2016-17/childrenandsocialwork.html (accessed 10 September 2022).

Whitebread, D and Bingham, S (2013) Habit formation and learning in young children. London: Money Advice Service.

Wölk, S (2003) Hearts and minds. *Educational Leadership*, 67 (1): 14–18.

Woolley, R (2020) Teaching controversial issues. In V Pugh and D Hughes (eds) *Teaching Personal, Social, Health and Economic and Relationships, (Sex) and Health Education in Primary Schools: Enhancing the Whole Curriculum*. London: Bloomsbury Academic.

Young Enterprise (2022) Young Enterprise.org.uk Available at: https://www.young-enterprise.org.uk/home/impact-policy/research-evaluation/research/impact-of-financial-education/ (accessed 10 September 2022).

12

RELIGIOUS EDUCATION

JAMES D. HOLT

KEYWORDS: RELIGIOUS; RELIGION; WORLDVIEWS; SUBSTANTIVE KNOWLEDGE; DISCIPLINARY KNOWLEDGE; PERSONAL KNOWLEDGE; PROGRESSION; RELIGIOUS EDUCATION.

LINKS TO THE CORE CONTENT FRAMEWORK

Subject and Curriculum (Standard 3): 3.1, 3.2, 3.6, 3.7

Classroom Practice (Standard 4): 4.1, 4.2

Adaptive Teaching (Standard 5): 5.2

PART 1: EXPLORING RELIGIOUS EDUCATION

WHAT IS RELIGIOUS EDUCATION?

Religious Education (RE) is a multidisciplinary subject that encompasses our efforts to understand religion and worldviews and how they impact on the lives of individuals and communities today. It encompasses beliefs and systems that are religious and non-religious. As we explore the nature of religion and belief, it is important to note that its purpose is to help students understand others and their beliefs, rather than for them to become religious (or not), or to develop their own belief systems. The aims of RE have been articulated as:

- To stimulate interest and enjoyment in Religious Education.

- To prepare pupils to be informed, respectful members of society who celebrate diversity and strive to understand others.

- To encourage students to develop knowledge of the beliefs and practices of religions and worldviews, and informed opinions and an awareness of the implications of religion and worldviews for the individual, the community and the environment.

- To give all students equal access to Religious Education.

- To develop pupils' own responses to questions about the meaning and purpose of life (Holt, 2022, p16).

As we teach RE, we teach with a positive neutrality: 'Many Christians believe . . . ', 'Many Hindus believe . . . ', and so on. It is a subject that is important in helping children reflect on their own and others' experiences. The complexity of teaching RE comes in the diversity of expressions within and between religions and beliefs. Religions and worldviews are not neatly structured organisations; rather, they have a 'messiness' where people believe and behave differently. It is the teacher of RE's responsibility to help students understand this diversity and the lived reality of these beliefs for people today.

REFLECTION

What is the purpose of RE?

What do you hope children in your classroom leave being able to do/know/understand?

RELIGIOUS EDUCATION AND THE NATIONAL CURRICULUM

Religious Education, while being part of the statutory curriculum for all schools (including academies), is not part of the national curriculum; it is, for the most part locally agreed. Every local authority has a Standing Advisory Council on Religious Education (SACRE) which is responsible for overseeing and developing RE in schools in the local area. Every four years the SACRE establish an Agreed Syllabus working group to review and update the Agreed Syllabus. The Agreed Syllabus is the legal document for all local authority schools that outlines the content that should be taught from Early Years Foundation Stage all the way up to Year 13. Academies are free to design their own RE curriculum that should take account of the main religious traditions of the UK, with the recognition that Christianity is the main tradition. More recently, religious traditions have also been expanded to include non-religious worldviews. Many academies will choose to follow aspects of the local Agreed Syllabus. Faith schools will adopt an approach suggested by the sponsoring faith tradition. Although the Commission on RE (2018) recommended a national entitlement for RE be drawn up, this has not been acted upon by the government.

HOW HAS 'KNOWLEDGE' IN RELIGIOUS EDUCATION DEVELOPED OVER TIME?

Included in the 1944 Education Act, RE was initially focused around the tenets and practices of the Church of England, and in some schools was known as Religious Instruction. In the intervening years it has developed significantly and has undergone paradigm shifts. The first paradigm shift took place in the 1970s and 1980s when RE adopted a 'World Religions' paradigm. This involved agreed syllabi, as well as teaching within schools to shift to a more multi-faith RE that included what are seen to be the 'big six' in terms of numbers within the UK: Buddhism, Christianity, Hinduism, Islam, Judaism and Sikhism. This paradigm developed at different rates in the various parts of the country, but it had at its heart the idea that religions shared common characteristics or concerns that could be taught in a systematic way: first Christianity, and then Hinduism, and so on. Or they could be taught in a thematic way; the default themes were shared considerations such as holy books, rites of passage, and so on. However, the questions raised by shared human experience provided a more robust approach to themes teaching.

In the late 2010s, an approach, or paradigm, called the 'Religion and Worldviews' approach began to be favoured (see Norfolk SACRE, 2019; Chater, 2020; Hutton and Cox, 2021; Holt, 2022). A worldview is explained in this way:

> The shift in language to 'worldviews' captures, as best we can, the shifts in vision that we have outlined above, in particular the complex, diverse and plural nature of worldviews. The name also removes the ambiguity in the phrase 'Religious Education', which is often wrongly assumed to be about making people more religious. We are keeping the word 'religion' in the subject name both to provide continuity and to signify that young people need to understand the conceptual category of 'religion' as well as other concepts such as 'secularity', 'secularism' and 'spirituality'.

> (Commission on RE, 2018, p7)

In some ways, this is not as large a paradigm shift as some people might imagine or have indicated. It is a recognition that all people have different worldviews, even within the same faith tradition. It draws on the work of people such as Kimberle Crenshaw (1989) who discussed issues of intersectionality. This is the argument that all people have multiple influences and identities that coalesce to form a distinctive worldview or experience of life. Thus, the articulation that all religions shared similar constructs is rejected, as is the idea that individuals within religions and worldviews believe and act in the same way. To some extent, this is the way that 'good' RE classrooms always functioned, in recognising the diversity of the lived experience, but the worldviews paradigm formalises this.

This 'new' RE similarly challenges the received structure of religions. It is apparent that the way that individual religions are understood in today's world has been influenced by a Western colonial lens. For example, Hinduism and Buddhism especially are seen to have been defined in the modern world through a Christian lens. Thus, Buddhism becomes focused around a central figure in a similar way to Christianity, rather than understanding it on its own terms (see Holt, 2023). Even the appellation of 'ism' is a way that colonialists sought to impose a structure of a religion to be studied (see Holt, 2023a). Indeed, Wilfred Cantwell Smith has suggested:

> This process [of Western systematisation] normally took the form of adding the Greek suffix '-ism' to a word used to designate the persons who are members of the religious community or followers of a given tradition.

(1991, p62)

One of the further consequences of the worldviews paradigm is the inclusion of voices outside of the big six. The inclusion of non-religious worldviews such as Humanism and Secularism, as well as smaller religions such as Baha'i, Rastafari, Jain and Paganism is increasing, alongside smaller expressions of the bigger religions such as Shi'a and Ahmadiyya within Islam (see Holt, 2019).

REFLECTION

What religions have you experienced being taught in schools?

Is this reflective of the society in which you live? How can RE be truly representative?

RELIGIOUS EDUCATION NOW

Alongside the development of a worldviews paradigm is a discussion about how much of a world religions paradigm should be rejected. Certainly, the challenge to the way that religions have been structured and perceived is important, but to some extent taking the worldviews paradigm to its extreme, it would be simply an exploration of personal worldviews. Within RE, it is important that we explore institutional worldviews and the myriad of ways in which they are expressed. There has to be a recognition of essentialism; the idea that there are essential aspects that lie at the heart of each religion and worldview. Ben Wood has suggested:

Some argue that 'essentialism' narrows and limits understanding and fails to provide a realistic picture of the world and religion and belief. Others, myself included, accept this to a point, arguing that 'essentialism' may be limited, but it is a necessary part of the process of learning about religions in a progressive manner, in that what is learnt in this phase is essential for progress to more sophisticated learning.

(2020, p14)

What would this essentialism look like? In contrast to the one-size-fits-all world religions paradigm, it would be different for each religion and worldview. For example, it would be appropriate to explore the concept of God that lies at the heart of Christianity, but to try to explore the nature of the divine in Buddhism would be an unimportant aspect. What is essential within each religion and worldview will differ, and within the religion itself there will be room for debate and disagreement. There are ways that the curriculum might be organised. For example, people have often used Ninian Smart's (1998) dimensions of religions as an access point:

- The doctrinal
- The mythological (narrative)
- The ethical
- The ritual
- The experiential
- The social
- The material (aesthetic).

To some extent, this may still be drawing categories into which teachers try to force religions and worldviews, and they may not always be appropriate. A further effort has been made with the *Big Ideas in Religious Education* (Wintersgill, 2017), which has questions in which the curriculum is structured:

- Continuity, change and diversity.
- Words and beyond.
- A good life.

- Making sense of life's experiences.

- Influence, community, culture and power.

- The big picture.

These are questions and sections around which a curriculum can be structured. This is something with which the teacher of RE will need to grapple: how do we organise our curriculum in a way that is reflective of diversity but which has coherence?

One other area that is linked with the decolonisation and diversification of the RE classroom is the issue of representation. One concern of the world religions paradigm was to establish religions as monoliths that created stereotypes. As a teacher of RE, it is our responsibility to recognise the various aspects of diversity within the religion. This could be diversity of interpretation (different traditions), cultures, ethnicities, countries and practice. One such example is the representation of people within Christianity. Consider the representation of Jesus in the art of Christianity. The overwhelming majority is of a white man; this is because of the power dynamic at play throughout the history of Christianity, where those painting Jesus did so in their own image, so that those viewing the image could relate to him. This meant that marginalised groups often could not see themselves in the Christian message. For this reason, the use of different artworks as stimuli for learning is key. By the same token, is the image of a Christian we portray that of a white man or woman? It does not mean that we should not use such images, but that we diversify their expression in inclusion of people of all genders, ethnicities and background. This same principle is applied across all religions so that we do not reinforce stereotypes.

REFLECTION

Choose one religion other than Christianity.

How can you ensure that it is represented in a diverse way?

WHAT MIGHT KNOWLEDGE IN RELIGIOUS EDUCATION LOOK LIKE IN THE FUTURE?

RE is an interesting case study in being subject to interested parties who wish to shape the subject to their ideas of what it should be. It could be suggested that in some ways RE is a pie of which everyone wants a slice. There are not infinite slices to share, and so we need to consider how to balance the competing or complementary demands. In using the above discussion, it might be helpful to consider some questions as we begin to think about the future of RE in the curriculum, but most especially in the classroom.

- How do we include more than the main expressions of the big six in the classroom?

- How do we incorporate individual worldviews within traditions?

- How can we diversify the expressions of religions and worldviews that we teach?

- What priorities do we have for the teaching of RE? Do they surround the teaching of knowledge or the development of skills or attitudes?

- What are the key questions around which we can develop our curriculum?

- How can we help others understand the importance of the subject?

- How do our aims enable us to structure learning within the classroom?

PART 2: FOUNDATION KNOWLEDGE IN RELIGIOUS EDUCATION

This section is a chance to look at key foundation knowledge that you will need to teach RE. This is somewhat problematic to put into words. If we were to explore each religion individually, we could fill a number of books for each, but conversely to make a list of the basic facts of each of the religions we would be at risk of being reductive and returning to the world religions paradigm where everything fits into neat little boxes. Before we attempt an identification of knowledge within RE, mention should be made of the three types of knowledge that Ofsted has outlined as central:

- Substantive knowledge.

- Disciplinary knowledge.

- Personal knowledge.

This is not without its problems and detractors. In some way, it can be seen as a repackaging of existing approaches within RE, but also it can be seen to be reflective of a particular approach. It is seeming to be accepted as fact, perhaps because it has come from Ofsted. In some ways, it may be part of the pendulum swing to what is described as 'traditional' or knowledge-rich curriculum. In doing so, it might be a swing away from skills that form an imperative part of any RE curriculum. Indeed, in Part 3 below, we explore how skills and knowledge can be moulded together to develop effective learning. But what do each of these knowledges mean?

Substantive knowledge is the 'stuff' that is learned: the narrative of the nativity story; the reasons for the Great Schism in 1054; the positions of prayer within Islam; the features of a synagogue and the reasons for them. If we were to try to present an overview of this knowledge here, it would be problematic. Consider the presentation of the central concepts of Buddhism; in any textbook that can be found in classrooms around the country, these will be identified as the Four Noble Truths. This is only partially true: when we consider the difference between Theravada and Mahayana Buddhism, the way that the Noble Truths are viewed is different. In Mahayana, they are preparatory to the true understanding of the *bodhisattva* ideal. But this is the way that knowledge is presented. We therefore need to be aware of the qualifying nature of all the knowledge that we learn and teach. There are few things within each religion and worldview that is believed/ practised by all within that tradition.

Disciplinary knowledge is also described as ways of knowing. Within RE, this has developed into utilising multidisciplinary lenses to inform the learning that is taking place. Students could look at knowledge from lots of different perspectives, some include:

- theological;
- philosophical;
- social science;
- historical.

What this means is that there are different ways of exploring the phenomena called religion. From a theological perspective, scripture or stories might be used to explore concepts central to the religion. Hence, the parable of the Good Samaritan and its various layers may be read and explored as a way to understand who Jesus was referring to when he asked people to love their neighbour. In a social science lens, data might be explored or the experiences of individuals to attempt to draw conclusions as to what beliefs are and how they are expressed. In considering the question 'How important are the 5Ks', one might look at the writings of Guru Gobind Singh from a theological perspective, but from a social science lens we could use publications such as the British Sikh Report to suggest their centrality. Or we might look at stories of Sikhs in the modern day to try to see why the 5Ks are important to them. To some extent, the utilisation of lenses is a repackaging of skills, but the RE world is trying to articulate what the skills attached to each lens are.

Person knowledge in Ofsted's view is the beginning and end of the content in the RE classroom. Teachers begin by exploring what children already know/think: there is taught input and then children reflect on where they stand in relation to the content. This is a contested area and perhaps a move towards the 'Learning about' and 'Learning from' attainment targets that were prevalent in the 1990s and 2000s. Is it appropriate to have children reflect on where they stand in relation to religious content? There is a way of doing this that is not about developing religiously. In critical RE in the exploration of truth within the context of religion, there is a reflective process that enables pupils to engage in an exploration of their learning journey in terms of assumptions and skills.

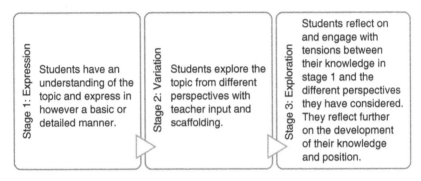

Figure 12.1 Three stages of CRE (Easton et al., 2019)

In developing a pedagogical approach to RE, it is important that certain principles are utilised to ensure that knowledge can be developed. With this as a background, it would be possible for a teacher to develop their substantive knowledge and then be able to apply it within their teaching. In exploring the pedagogical principles, we will use examples of religious knowledge, but this will necessarily only be a small taste, and teachers should extend their knowledge on this basis of these principles. I have articulated these 'bridges' elsewhere with regard to the secondary school (Holt, 2022), but with minor adaptations I now apply them to the primary classroom.

BRIDGE 1: WITH PUPIL'S PRIOR EXPERIENCES AND LEARNING

At its heart, I believe RE relies on a constructivist approach to learning. Just as in Piagian terms (McCleod, 2018) a child develops a schema based on the processes of disequilibrium, assimilation or accommodation, so this is how learning develops within RE. Central to this bridge is a conceptual pyramid of RE.

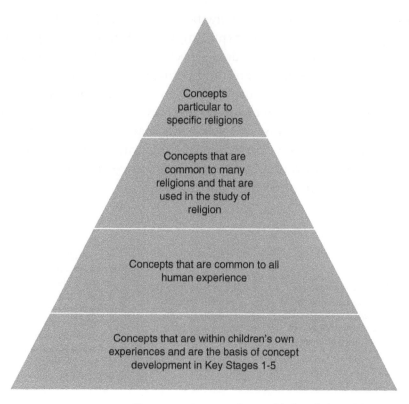

Figure 12.2 Conceptual pyramid of RE (adapted from Lowndes, 2012)

When we are teaching pupils, we are usually exploring aspects of religions that lie in the top layer of the pyramid. Concepts that are particular to specific religions, these might be atonement within Christianity, *dukkha* within Buddhism, *sewa* within Sikhism, etc. One of the problems is that for many children, these are new concepts that they are unfamiliar with. The teacher should therefore utilise concepts from lower down the pyramid to enable them to be able access the learning or, colloquially, 'to give them something to hang their hat on'.

Most effective are concepts that are within their own experience – those concepts that they experience just in the act of living. So, the teacher might begin an exploration of the Buddhist festival of Wesak by asking the questions 'What do you celebrate?' and 'How do you celebrate?'. This breaks down illusory barriers of 'them' and 'us', but at the same time opens up a schema on which to build learning. If teachers were building on prior learning, which might be the concepts that are common to many religions, the same concept of celebration might be used, but with the questions 'How do Hindus celebrate Diwali?' and 'How do Hindus celebrate?'. The difference here is that the teacher knows what has been taught.

Depending on the topic and the class, either is effective. Wesak is not the Buddhist Diwali, but it shares similarities and, most importantly, differences. Teachers do not use 'other' religions as a yardstick, but they can be used as a way in.

The knowledge that teachers need to have with regard to this bridge is the conceptual knowledge to see how 'everyday' concepts can link with religious concepts to ensure that learning is optimised.

BRIDGE 2: BETWEEN BELIEF AND PRACTICES

One of the things that can be noted in RE teaching is that there is often a disconnect between beliefs and practices. Sometimes the focus seems to be on what people do. For example, in teaching about Islam, most classrooms will focus on the Five Pillars of Sunni Islam. This is not problematic by itself; indeed, the example lessons below do just this. The problem arises when they are taught without the context of the beliefs that they reflect. Consider the example of *sujood*, where a Muslim will prostrate themselves on the ground in prayer. Without the context of the belief in living life in submission to Allah who is One, then it could appear odd. The belief is central to understanding practice. Teaching this is as simple as asking the question, 'Why?'

One further example is the task of labelling a place of worship. In labelling a synagogue, a child may be able to put an arrow to the *Ner Tamid* (Everlasting Light); but if we are to go beyond the observable, then the questions 'Why is it there?' or 'What does it represent?' should be asked. In understanding that it is a symbol of the Almighty, pupils begin to understand the religion and go beyond being able to list certain facts or practices.

BRIDGE 3: BETWEEN RELIGIONS AND WORLDVIEWS

In showing progression in RE between year groups, it is important that pupils are given the opportunity to draw links with prior and future learning about different religions. As you progress through your career, this will become easier as you begin to draw links. As with the first bridge, there are similarities and differences that should be outlined. Religions are not the same, they are different. Muslims and Christians do not believe in the same concept of God, even though there are similarities. The greatest sin in Islam is *shirk* – the ascribing of partners to Allah, compared with the greatest truth in Christianity that God the Father has a son, Jesus Christ. These two 'truths' are incompatible, even though Muslims believe Isa (Jesus) is a prophet.

BRIDGE 4: WITH LOCAL COMMUNITIES

There can be a tendency within RE to exoticise aspects of religious practice. The teacher may show a Hindu funeral taking place in Varanasi. This shows a body being wrapped in cloth, carried through the streets and then placed on a large funeral pyre. The ashes are then scattered in the Ganges. This is not wrong, but it gives the impression that Hinduism is a religion that happens elsewhere. Much more useful in the RE classroom is the 'Being Hindu' documentary from the BBC that shows a funeral in the UK at the local crematorium. It makes the religion less alien. It may be possible to compare the practices and see what is similar between the two, but when we focus purely on the 'overseas' nature of a religion, it is possible that religion is seen to be other. The utilisation of authentic voices from the local community or from the UK is effective. It enables students to see the reality of lived religion in the UK. There are a variety of different ways in which this can be accomplished.

- Visits to the local places of worship and discussions with members of the community.

- Inviting members of faith communities into the class to discuss questions from the children.

- Utilising videos of members of the faith communities or inviting them to join via a video call.

The interaction breaks down barriers and also helps humanise the 'abstract' religious person. If diversity is to be brought into the classroom and the recognition of individual worldviews, then the authentic voice is an important way that this will be accomplished.

BRIDGE 5: WITH OTHER SUBJECTS

RE often falls to the bottom of the pile in the primary school, and one way this can be avoided is through the utilisation of cross-curricular themes. Examples could include linking with D&T to make diva lamps for Diwali, or maybe even puppets to retell the story. Another example could be the utilisation of *Planet Omar: Accidental Trouble Magnet* and subsequent books (Mian, 2019) as a chapter reading book and a basis for literacy tasks. Omar is a child who has bizarre and fantastic experiences; he is also a Muslim and aspects of Muslim living are shown and can be explored. There is a caveat to this, however. Sometimes cross-curricular work means that one subject is the 'poor relation'. Consider the RE, History and Geography project on Egypt. History covers the pyramids and customs of ancient

Egypt, Geography explores the Nile Delta and RE explores the religion of ancient Egypt. This, for me, is inappropriate as it is exploring RE as something that happened in the past. Religion is based on aspects of history, but it is only one facet. A better inclusion of RE would be the exploration of religion in Egypt today, whether that is Islam as the majority religion of the area or smaller religions.

REFLECTION

Choose one religious topic.

How do these bridges help the teacher represent subject knowledge in the classroom?

PART 3: UNDERSTANDING THE DEVELOPMENT OF CHILDREN'S KNOWLEDGE IN RELIGIOUS EDUCATION

One of the most important aspects of RE in the classroom is the issue of progression. Many schools have examples of nicely designed curriculum maps that show what topics are to be covered within each year group. While they are useful to know what is being taught and when, they often do not function well at showing progression. Progression in RE is perhaps more complex than in other subjects where there is a neatly planned curriculum that is designed to build knowledge and skills, and is taught across the country. Within RE, depending on the local authority and school, there could be a myriad different maps. It is therefore imperative for the teacher of RE to understand how progress is made within RE. Ofsted (2021) has been clear that a well-designed curriculum is the progression model. Therefore, this curriculum should show links with content that has come before, content that will come afterwards and also highlights skills that are to be developed. Consider the topic of Diwali within Hinduism and the retelling of the story of the *Ramayana*. This may well be taught in Reception and then further up the school.

REFLECTION

How can progress be made in teaching the same/similar topic such as Diwali?

In Reception, we could focus on the retelling of the story of Diwali or the identification of practices that take place at Diwali. Indeed, the book *Mr. Men Little Miss Happy Diwali* (Hargreaves, 2020) is a useful introduction to the celebrations, but it does not link it to the story. Within Year 2 or 3, pupils might begin to link the story with the celebrations and identifying the meaning of aspects of the festival. Further up the school in upper Key Stage 2, it might be possible to compare versions of the story to consider the audience and the writer. New knowledge and new skills will be developed and progression will be made. This same type of skills and knowledge development can be seen between different festivals. In Year 1, we may have explored the story of the Nativity; in Year 3, we are looking at Passover within Judaism. We can assume that pupils can retell the story, so, after taught input introducing them to the story, the major focus would be on how the celebration of Passover reflects elements of the story. The progression is not just within a religion, but also utilising concepts as a thread between religions. This enables progression to be made among disparate religions and topics.

The RE Council of England and Wales (2013) have suggested that some of the skills that are developed in RE and should be within various units of work include:

- investigating religions and worldviews through varied experiences, approaches and disciplines;

- reflecting on and expressing their own ideas and the ideas of others with increasing creativity and clarity;

- becoming increasingly able to respond to religions and worldviews in an informed, rational and insightful way;

- critical and personal evaluation;

- find out about;

- investigate;

- respond creatively;

- enquiry;

- articulate beliefs, values and commitments clearly (13, 15 and 60).

The links between year groups is important; but it is also important that lessons build on each other to ensure that a range of skills and concepts are being developed.

As you explore the example of planning above, it is important to note that this is only a fragment of a longer medium-term plan. As indicated in the plan, there is a further exploration of the Night of Power, and the further pillars of Sunni Islam. Questions we could ask of this plan are:

Table 12.1 Learning plan – Year 4: The Five Pillars of Islam

Year 4: The Five Pillars of Islam		
Learning outcomes	Activities to develop the skills and understanding	Next steps
Focus of the lesson The Five Pillars of Islam. **Links to previous learning** Check for prior learning and knowledge of Islam. Students will be able to describe religious beliefs and actions. **Concepts** Islam; submission; peace; pillars; strengthen; faith. **Anticipated misconceptions** Reminder that not all Muslims accept the Five Pillars as understood in Sunni Islam – 'most, many and some'.	Pupils should brainstorm their previous knowledge of Islam. The word Islam and its meanings of submission and peace should be discussed: that through submission to Allah peace in this life and the next can be achieved. Teachers should introduce the Five Pillars through the use of 'Muslims in Britain: Introduction' and 'Basic Beliefs: Introduction' (or TrueTube video), and how they strengthen and uphold a person's faith. Pupils should complete a card sort exercise to provide themselves with a basic background knowledge of the Five Pillars on which to build future study. Students should watch the section of *Muslims in Britain* DVD, 'The World of Muslims in Britain' and answer the question 'Who is a Muslim in the UK?'	**Assessment strategies** Formative; think pair share; questioning; discussion; C card sort. **Assessment for future lessons** Next five sessions will build on this introduction.
Focus of the lesson Islamic belief in Allah. **Links to previous learning** Builds on previous understanding of the Five Pillars of Sunni Islam. Also, on Year 2 exploration of God in Christianity. Students will be able to explain why belief in Allah is important to Muslims. Students will be able to create images that portray how Muslims reflect on Allah in their lives. **Concepts** Allah; God; *Shahadah*; belief; symbol; *Tawhid*; characteristics. **Anticipated misconceptions** Portrayal of Allah in art.	**Outline of the lesson structure** The teacher should recap the two beliefs of the *Shahadah* and discuss that the focus will be on the first part, 'There is no god but Allah . . .'. Pupils should then investigate the reasons behind the non-portrayal of Allah and suggest reasons for themselves as to why it might benefit a Muslim to not visualise God. As an introduction to beliefs about God, students could watch the section of *Muslims in Britain*: 'Basic Beliefs/ Five Pillars/ Faith and Basic Beliefs/Articles of Faith'. The teacher should get the class to try to describe somebody using only one-word qualities. Does this convey what this person is like? Is it better than a physical description? Building on this, pupils should discuss the beautiful names and how they help a Muslim to understand Allah. Focus should be made on the concept of *Tawhid* as the most important belief about God. To textualise their understanding, pupils should answer a series of questions, then produce a piece of art showing some of the beautiful names and the centrality of *Tawhid*. Students should show their pictures and explain how they reflect the Muslim belief in God.	**Assessment feeding into this lesson** Pupils will be able to describe the Five Pillars of Islam. **Assessment strategies** Questioning; link with own experiences; art; formative; think pair share. **Assessment for future lessons** The belief in Allah underpins all other pillars: being able to explain Allah's importance is crucial for all follow-up stages of learning.

(Continued)

Table 12.1 (Continued)

Year 4: The Five Pillars of Islam		
Focus of the lesson Muhammad (PBUH).	**Outline of the lesson structure**	**Assessment feeding into this lesson**
Concepts: Prophet; revelation; *risalah*; angel.	List the qualities of a hero or role-model starter activity on a whiteboard.	Will understand what a prophet is (Year 3 Judaism).
Students will be able to explain why belief in Muhammad is important to Muslims.	Discuss what makes someone a hero or respected by a community. Compile a feedback of ideas.	Will understand the centrality of Allah.
Students will be able to describe the central events in the life of Muhammad.	Do people from different cultures have different role models?	**Assessment strategies**
Links to previous learning	Pupils should recap what the *Shahadah* is. Focus will be on 'and Muhammad is his prophet'.	Link with own experiences.
Links to work on religious leaders in Year 3; understanding of the place of Allah in Islam.	Teachers should provide a brief sketch outline of the life of Muhammad. As a form of a writing, frame pupils will be given a research notes aid. Pupils should use a variety of resources to fill in the research. The final section on what others think about him should include a personal view based on some of the quotes given. (A useful introduction to the Prophet and how he is viewed can be found in *Muslims in Britain:* 'Basic Beliefs/Muhammad') –differentiated materials are available.	recap; independent enquiry; formative; think pair share.
Anticipated misconceptions		
Portrayal of Muhammad (PBUH).		**Assessment for future lessons**
Use of PBUH.	Snowballing activity about events in the life of Muhammad (PBUH). (Snowballing is where one student writes one fact on a piece of paper and then passes it on.)	*Laylat al-qadr* will be explored in the next lesson.

- How does each lesson build on prior knowledge (both immediate and in previous years)?

- How dies each lesson prepare for future learning?

- What knowledge is being developed?

- What skills are being utilised?

PART 4: DEVELOPING YOUR KNOWLEDGE OF RELIGIOUS EDUCATION FURTHER

RE is a subject for which there is a myriad of different resources. This does create its own issues in that the teacher needs to sift the material that is out there for suitability. Fortunately, within RE there is a supportive community of teachers who are willing to share ideas, resources and help in designing lessons and increasing subject knowledge. The first stop for any teacher of RE is the National Association of Teachers of RE (NATRE). In joining NATRE (your school will usually fund this), a teacher receives a termly mailing of *RE Today, The British Journal of Religious Education* and a curriculum book for the age phase that they teach. There is also a members only area of the NATRE website that provides lots of materials.

Social media is also an important resource whether it is Facebook groups or the Twitter community. Particularly useful is the Facebook group *Primary RE – for everyone teaching RE in Primary Schools!*

Podcasts are really useful for increasing your subject knowledge. The RE Podcast is specifically designed to discuss issues that surround the teaching of RE. It talks about individual religions, as well as specific topics such as Hallowe'en and the importance of decolonising the curriculum.

One of the important aspects of RE that is central to developing our understanding of differing worldviews is the use of authentic voices. In exploring these myriad voices, we can learn more about religion and worldviews, and how they are lived in today's societies. Examples include:

- Allen, J (2007) *Rabble-Rouser for Peace: The Authorised Biography of Desmond Tutu*. London: Rider.

- Backer, K (2016) *From MTV to Mecca: How Islam Inspired my Life*. Cirencester: Memoirs Publishing.

- Frankl, V (2004) *Man's Search for Meaning (The Classic Tribute to Hope from the Holocaust)*. London: Penguin.

- Greene, M (2020) *Jew(ish): A Primer, A Memoir, A Manual, A Plea.* Seattle: Little A.

- Khan, M (2019) *It's Not About the Burqa: Muslim Women on Faith, Feminism, Sexuality and Race.* London: Picador.

- Rani, A (2021) *The Right Sort of Girl.* Chelsea: Blink Publishing.

- Sathnam, S (2009) *The Boy with the Topknot: A Memoir of Love, Secrets and Lies in Wolverhampton.* London: Penguin.

There are also fictional writings that help teachers understand the messages or experiences of various religions and worldviews:

- CS Lewis's *Chronicles of Narnia* are purposeful allegories of the Christian message. They help make difficult concepts intelligible. Consider the death and subsequent coming back to life of Aslan as a type for Jesus's sacrifice within Christianity.

- Philip Pullman's *Northern Lights* series of books. Pullman is an atheist and aspects of his worldview are evident in these books.

There are also many books and websites that support the development of subject knowledge around the different religions and worldviews:

- reonline.org.uk: this website has sections and ideas surrounding all the larger religions and worldviews, as well as some of the smaller ones. It also explores issues of research and pedagogy within RE.

- truetube.co.uk: this website produces films for use in the classroom across the key stages. These are valuable for children, but also for the development of teacher understanding.

- There are many introductory books about the different world religions. One of the newer series is titled . . . *in 5 minutes* with volumes on Buddhism, Hinduism and Atheism. These have a number of different authors who answer specific questions in short essay-style sections. A new series next year is *Understanding . . . A Guide for Teachers* from Bloomsbury. The first two are Sikhism and Buddhism. They are specifically written for developing teachers' subject knowledge.

Television and film are also a treasure trove for RE content. These range from children's programming that explore issues in religion. An 'oldie' is the Rugrats who retell the stories of Passover and Chanukah. A more recent documentary presented by Sue Perkins – *Ganges* – also provided some background into the teaching of Hinduism. A series of programmes in 2021 highlighted the birth, marriage and funeral rituals in many religions in the UK. It was entitled *Being . . .* and included Hindu, Sikh, Christian, Jewish, Buddhist and Muslim rituals. The teacher of RE becomes an expert at scanning the TV guide for series or short stories that can help develop their understanding of religion.

REFERENCES

Cantwell-Smith, W (1991) *The Meaning and End of Religion*. Minneapolis: Fortress Press.

Chater, M (2020) *Reforming RE: Power and Knowledge in a Worldviews Curriculum*. Woodbridge: John Catt Educational.

Commission on RE (2018) *Religion and Worldviews: The Way Forward. A National Plan for RE*. London: Commission on RE.

Crenshaw, K (1989) Demarginalizing the intersection of race and sex: a black feminist critique of antidiscrimination doctrine. Feminist theory and antiracist politics. University of Chicago Legal Forum. University of Chicago Law School. pp139–68.

Easton, C, Wright, A, Goodman, A, Hibberd, T and Wright, A (2019) *A Practical Guide to Critical Religious Education: Resources for the Secondary Classroom*. London: Routledge.

Hargreaves, A (2020) *Mr. Men Little Miss Happy Diwali*. London: Egmont.

Holt, JD (2019) *Beyond the Big Six Religions: Expanding the Boundaries in the Teaching of Religions and Worldviews*. Chester: University of Chester Press.

Holt, JD (2022) *Religious Education in the Secondary School. An Introduction to Teaching*. Abingdon: Routledge.

Holt, JD (2023) *Understanding Buddhism: A Guide for Teachers*. London: Bloomsbury.

Holt, JD (2023a) *Understanding Sikhism: A Guide for Teachers*. London: Bloomsbury.

Hutton, L and Cox, D (2021) *Making Every RE Lesson Count*. Carmarthen: Crown Publishing.

Lowndes, J (2012) *The Complete Multifaith Resource for Primary Religious Education: Ages 4–7*. Abingdon: Routledge.

McLeod, SA (2018) Jean Piaget's theory of cognitive development. *Simply Psychology*. Available at: www.simplypsychology.org/piaget.html (accessed 30 November 2022).

Mian, Z (2019) *Planet Omar: Accidental Trouble Magnet*. London: Hodder.

Norfolk SACRE (2019) *Norfolk Agreed Syllabus 2019: A Religious Education for the Future Understanding Religion and Worldviews for a Life in a Changing World*. Norfolk: Norfolk County Council.

Ofsted (2021) *Research Review Series: Religious Education*. Available at: www.gov.uk/government/publications/research-review-series-religious-education/research-review-series-religious-education

RE Council of England and Wales (2013) *A Review of Religious Education in England*. London: RE Council.

Smart, N (1998) *The World's Religions* (2nd edn). Cambridge: Cambridge University Press.

Wintersgill, B (2017) *Big Ideas in Religious Education*. Exeter: University of Exeter.

Wood, B (2020) Teaching worldviews at GCSE. In M Chater, *Reforming RE: Power and Knowledge in a Worldviews Curriculum*. Woodbridge: John Catt Educational. pp165–8.

13

SCIENCE

DEBORAH WILKINSON

KEYWORDS: SUBSTANTIVE KNOWLEDGE; DISCIPLINARY KNOWLEDGE; WORKING SCIENTIFICALLY; PROCESS SKILLS; ENQUIRY; SUBJECT-SPECIFIC VOCABULARY; MISCONCEPTIONS.

LINKS TO THE CORE CONTENT FRAMEWORK

High Expectations (Standard 1): 1.2, 1.6

How Pupils Learn (Standard 2): 2.2

Subject and Curriculum (Standard 3): 3.5, 3.7, 3.10

Classroom Practice (Standard 4): 4.2, 4.7

PART 1: EXPLORING SCIENCE

WHAT IS SCIENCE?

Science endeavours to understand the world and beyond, and is both a way of working and a 'body of knowledge'. Science 'builds' on the ideas and work of others, and is *not* a static body of knowledge consisting of immutable facts. Therefore, children need to learn that 'scientific knowledge' is constantly refining as new technologies open up possibilities, and that science theories, explanations and models 'best fit' the evidence available at the time (Harlen et al., 2015). The non-statutory guidance of the national curriculum references the work of scientists so that children can begin to comprehend that knowledge evolves through being curious, collaborating, asking questions and undertaking investigations to identify patterns so that conclusions can be formulated.

Science generates knowledge in the form of diagrams, tables, graphs, data, theories and concepts, and is viewed as being reliable and rigorous due to the 'objective scientific methods' employed. Scientific knowledge is 'proven knowledge' rather than being speculative or based upon personal opinions (Chalmers, 1994). However, science is a human process and influenced by humans. Powerful people often influence what is believed, produced and published. Indeed, the history of science is often neglected and, according to Russell (1981), bears little relationship to the history of science as told by historians and how ideas are supported.

WHY SCIENCE IS IN THE NATIONAL CURRICULUM

Science is essentially concerned with preparing children for the future, so pupils need skills, knowledge and values to make informed choices such as how to avoid wasting energy, the impact of poor diet and lack of exercise on well-being, or decisions about vaccinations (Harlen et al., 2015). Consequently, children need to understand scientific terminology, concepts, enquiry and the interaction between science and society. We live in a time when people have access to social media and it is easy for 'fake news' to be communicated and misconceptions embedded and/or reinforced. Therefore, children need to learn how to question the reliability and validity of sources of information in order to make informed decisions in their lives. Indeed, the national curriculum states that:

> Science has changed our lives and is vital to the world's future prosperity, and all pupils should be taught essential aspects of the knowledge, methods, processes and uses of science. Through building up a body of key foundational knowledge and concepts, pupils should be encouraged to recognise the power of rational explanation . . . They should be encouraged to understand how science can be used to explain what is occurring, predict how things will behave, and analyse causes.

(DfE, 2014, p168)

To realise the above, the 2014 national curriculum aims to ensure that pupils secure scientific knowledge through the disciplines of biology, chemistry and physics. In addition to this, pupils learn about the nature, processes and methods of science through different types of science enquiries and, arguably most importantly, *develop a sense of excitement and curiosity about natural phenomena* (DfE, 2014, p168). Science in the national curriculum should sustain learners' curiosity and wonder about the world and should support the enjoyment of scientific activity and understanding (Harlen et al., 2015).

HOW HAS KNOWLEDGE IN SCIENCE DEVELOPED OVER TIME?

Spielman (2018) argues that the national curriculum is *the accumulated wealth of human knowledge, and what we choose to pass on to the next generation through teaching in schools.* Science is complex and vast, so how is the 'knowledge' for science decided?

In October 2009, an international group of scientists, engineers and science educators identified a series of ten 'big ideas' that can explain the world. They asserted that these 'big ideas' are relevant to all students and can help educators to conceptualise and structure the science curriculum so that pupils *understand, enjoy and marvel at the natural world* (Harlen et al., 2015). The ten big ideas are as follows:

1. All matter in the universe is made up of small particles.

2. Objects can affect objects at a distance.

3. Changing the movement of an object requires a net force to be acting on it.

4. The total amount of energy in the universe is always the same but can be transferred from one energy store to another during an event.

5. The composition of the Earth and its atmosphere and the processes occurring within them shape the Earth's surface and climate.

6. Our solar system is a small part of one of billions of galaxies in the universe.

7. Organisms are organised on a cellular basis and have a finite life-span.

8. Organisms require a supply of energy and materials for which they often depend on, or compete with, other organisms.

9. Genetic information is passed down from one generation of organisms to another.

10. The diversity of organisms, living and extinct, is the result of evolution.

REFLECTION

How many of the ten 'big ideas' can you find in the science national curriculum?

Are there any surprises about the content of the national curriculum? For example, where is physics delivered?

HOW MIGHT WE BEGIN TO DECOLONISE THE CURRICULUM?

Education has the power to bring about equity. Patel (2019) argues that schools need to decolonise the curriculum and asserts that teachers need to deconstruct the knowledge that is taught in schools and to question what we accept as 'knowledge'. Consequently, teachers should challenge the 'White, British and European curriculum' so that pupils know the contribution of a diverse group of people to our society (see Table 13.1). Stereotypes form within early childhood, so showing a diverse range of what science is, and who does it should begin in the early years setting. With this in mind, teachers should consider using scientists of different genders, ethnicities, the LGBTQ+ community and those with disabilities so that *all* children can identify with science. This also links well to the core content framework and the importance of providing high-quality teaching, as this may impact on pupils' willingness to study science and consequently their life chances (Royal Engineering Society, 2016). STEM learning has created a child-friendly booklet called 'Future me' to highlight STEM professions and there are useful links on the 'research champions' website to modern scientists (https://thestemhub.org.uk/docs/future-me-wie-edition.pdf). There is also a useful website showing links to science and everyday life so that children learn that science is everywhere (https://primaryandstem.online).

The book *Standing on the Shoulders of Giants* by the PSTT (Sinclair et al., 2019) provides effective links between scientists identified in the national curriculum and their modern-day equivalents. For a full list of links to scientists, access 'Nurturing science'.

REFLECTION

Look at the following video by Pran Patel: www.ted.com/talks/pran_patel_decolonise_the_curriculum

How might we begin to achieve this aim in the primary national curriculum for science?

Table 13.1 Scientists who could be referenced when delivering the 'chemistry strand' of the national curriculum

Year 1: Everyday materials	Year 2: Uses of everyday materials	Year 3: Rocks	Year 4: States of matter	Year 5: Properties and changes of materials
• William Addis (toothbrush inventor). • John Dunlop (tyres). • Chester Greenwood (earmuffs). • Natalie Von Goetz (nanoparticles in clothing).	• Charles Macintosh (waterproof material). • John McAdam (tarmac). • Julie and Scott Bursaw (road surfaces).	• Anjana Khatwa (geologist). • William Smith (fossils and strata). • Inge Lehmann (Earth's mantle). • Katia Krafft (geologist and volcanologist). • Mary Anning (palaeontologist). • Alice Roberts (evolutionary biologist).	• Joseph Priestley (discovered oxygen). • Lord Kelvin (absolute zero). • Anders Celsius (temperature scale). • Daniel Fahrenheit (temperature scale/ invention of the thermometer).	• Humphry Davy (separating gases). • Jamie Garcia (invention of a new plastic). • Becky Schroeder (fluorescence material). • Spencer Silver (Post-it notes). • Ruth Benerito (wrinkle-free cotton). • Maya Warren (food scientist working on ice-cream manufacture – see Research champions website, above).

SCIENCE NOW

The world of science in schools often appears to be influenced by business, industrial and economic imperatives, and the 'STEM agenda'. Research highlights the link between the quality of science that children experience at primary school and later attitudes towards science – specifically, subject choices at GCSE (Royal Engineering Society, 2006). Research by Archer and DeWitt (2017) attempted to establish the variables that 'shape' student engagement with science and the concept of 'science capital' emerged from the ASPIRES (2013, 2020) project, a ten-year longitudinal study of science and career aspirations in young people aged between 10 and 19. Science capital consists of *all the science-related knowledge, attitudes, experiences and social contacts that an individual may have* (Archer et al., 2020, p6), and may explain why children engage or disengage with science and whether they go on to pursue it in post-secondary education (Archer et al., 2015). Science capital is a 'lens' to view variables that lead pupils to decide if science is 'for them'. There are eight dimensions to science capital:

1. Scientific literacy.

2. Science-related attitudes, values and dispositions.

3. Knowledge about transferability of skills.

4. Science media consumption.

5. Participation in out of school science learning contexts.

6. Family science skills, knowledge and qualifications.

7. Knowing people in science-related jobs.

8. Talking to others about science in daily life.

To meet the above aims, the curriculum should aim to build relationships between the child and science. This should begin with valuing what children already know, their interests and their communities and 'building' learning around contexts that they are familiar with. Teachers may also be mindful of upcoming science events happening in the locality and/or films or television so that these can be promoted to children and their families. Explorify have produced resources aimed to generate discussion and raise science capital on their website titled 'Have you ever?'

> **REFLECTION**
>
> A teacher's science capital will impact on how they deliver the curriculum. Look at p89 from *The Primary Science Capital Teaching Approach* (www.ucl.ac.uk/ioe/departments-and-centres/departments/education-practice-and-society/stem-participation-social-justice-research/primary-science-capital-project) and calculate your science capital 'score'. If you have a 'low science capital', what can you do to improve this?

HOW IMPORTANT IS SUBJECT-SPECIFIC LANGUAGE?

Subject-specific vocabulary is required when explaining concepts and communicating ideas. Therefore, pre-teaching vocabulary reduces cognitive load if scientific words and definitions have already been 'chunked' in their memory. Consequently, children are better positioned to use technical vocabulary when verbalising, writing their ideas, explaining concepts and when drawing conclusions. Ideally, scientific words should have a short, memorable and scientifically accurate definition (this may be accompanied by an action or an image – e.g., a tree trunk can be linked to the action of reaching up tall with straight arms). To commit the words to the long-term memory, actions and words must be repeated frequently, and modelled by the teacher and provided with opportunities to practise and recall words and definitions from memory. Vocabulary practice could form part of a 'starter' activity in every lesson, and attention should also be paid to identifying possible misconceptions or confusion with language when a familiar word has a specific meaning in science. For example, the word 'force' has a different meaning in science and everyday life.

Vocabulary could also be displayed on a working wall in the classroom or could form part of a title page/knowledge organiser/concept map that is glued into an exercise book at the start of each unit of work so that children (and teachers) can refer back to key terms and use it in lessons.

WHAT MIGHT KNOWLEDGE IN SCIENCE LOOK LIKE IN THE FUTURE?

According to Oates (2014), knowledge drives the national curriculum towards a position where revisions are only justified when there are *evidence-based shifts in foundational knowledge*. 'Shifts' in foundational knowledge – e.g., genetic manipulation in biological science in the 1990s – are rare. He continues to assert that:

While primary legislation is likely to continue to locate ultimate control in the office of the Secretary of State, the implication of the principles is that it is custodians and representatives of discipline knowledge who should drive evidence based, principled change in the detail of the specifications.

(p27)

Since the introduction of the science national curriculum in 2014, schools have continued to make minor changes to the curriculum to reflect community needs, local agendas, regional and national agendas. Changes will continue to be made as governments change and considerations of how to better prepare pupils for the future are considered. For example, in 2023, schools will be required to add climate change, and this should be developed in all subjects across the curriculum. In the science curriculum, children should learn about nature and their impact on the world around them, the aim being to encourage children and young people to get involved in the natural world and helping children to develop their skills and knowledge of biodiversity and sustainability so they can impact their locality (DfE, 2021).

Science education also needs to take account of changes in the workplace that require the ability to link science with engineering, technology and mathematics (STEM), the urgent need for attention to major global issues, student assessment and the growing contribution of neurosciences to the understanding of learning.

PART 2: FOUNDATION KNOWLEDGE IN SCIENCE

Ofsted (2021) asserts that there are two types of knowledge that pupils need to build when learning science: substantive and disciplinary knowledge. Substantive knowledge is knowledge related to concepts and in the national curriculum is organised into biology, chemistry and physics. Substantive knowledge also links to building knowledge relating to the products of science, models, laws and theories. Disciplinary knowledge is related to 'working scientifically' in the national curriculum and is linked to the practices of science and the procedures that scientists use to develop scientific explanations. Disciplinary knowledge helps pupils to learn about the diverse ways in which science establishes and grows through enquiry. Figure 13.1 below summarises the interplay between the different types of knowledge and highlights that both types are important when learning science.

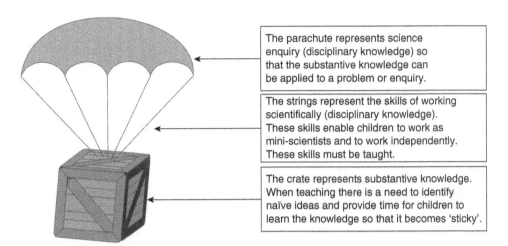

The parachute represents science enquiry (disciplinary knowledge) so that the substantive knowledge can be applied to a problem or enquiry.

The strings represent the skills of working scientifically (disciplinary knowledge). These skills enable children to work as mini-scientists and to work independently. These skills must be taught.

The crate represents substantive knowledge. When teaching there is a need to identify naïve ideas and provide time for children to learn the knowledge so that it becomes 'sticky'.

Figure 13.1 Knowledge types (image sourced from https://openclipart.org/)

For a video link explaining the knowledge types, see: www.facebook.com/watch/?v=4855350867887771

Ofsted (2021) argues that disciplinary knowledge is *beyond doing practical work and collecting data* and states that learners need to know:

1. Knowledge of methods that scientists use to answer questions and that they achieve this by using more than fair testing, modelling concepts, classifying, pattern seeking.

2. Knowledge of apparatus/technical equipment and taking measures, safety, planning, procedures.

3. Knowledge of data analysis and knowing a range of ways to communicate their understanding – graphs, tables, flow diagrams.

4. Knowledge of how science uses evidence to develop explanations and to draw conclusions and evaluations.

KNOWLEDGE OF METHODS

Pickford et al. (2013) argue that children need to apply their understanding of concepts to deepen and embed knowledge, and this can be achieved through an enquiry. Pupils link new ideas by connecting to existing knowledge and need to organise their knowledge into increasingly complex mental models. Enquiry can then be used to embed learning so that knowledge becomes 'sticky'. For example, if delivering a lesson on the circulatory system, a teacher may choose to plan for children to dissect a heart. This may be undertaken at the beginning of a unit of work to enthuse children, but in doing so the learning may be compromised as children do not necessarily have the subject knowledge to know what they are looking at. They may be enthused and may remember the practical (the 'doing') but not the required substantive knowledge (the 'knowing'). It is important that pupils do not just remember the experiment rather than the planned subject knowledge. For instance, when Ofsted (2019) questioned pupils during their research visits, they found that pupils could easily recall the task, but struggled to explain the subject knowledge or how the processes they were investigating worked. Therefore, knowledge needs to be made explicit. It is not just about 'doing' an activity. Time must be given for pupils to reflect on the evidence they gather to answer their scientific enquiry questions and use it to develop their 'substantive' knowledge. It should be highlighted to them that this process is how scientific knowledge is developed, revised and becomes established.

This aligns with the work of Skamp (2007) who discusses the interplay between *heads, hearts and minds-on science* to develop children's conceptual and procedural learning. During hands-on science, children are experiencing or 'doing' real science in order to observe a phenomenon for themselves. However, for hands-on science to be purposeful, it should support the teaching of science concepts (heads-on science), while sustaining children's interests in practical tasks that are enjoyable, comprehensible and useful (hands-on science). Children should be supported to ask questions and should be able to answer these via an enquiry during a unit of work. Enquiries involve more than fair testing. Over the duration of a year, children should engage with five types of enquiry identified in the national curriculum:

- Comparative and fair testing.

- Observation over time.

- Research using secondary sources.

- Identifying, classifying and sorting.

- Pattern seeking.

Table 13.2 highlights questions that children may pose to develop their substantive knowledge through investigative work, applying their disciplinary knowledge so that learning becomes embedded in their memory.

Table 13.2 Answering questions using different enquiry types

Which enquiry do I need to undertake in order to answer my question?	Identifying, classifying and grouping
	I will gather evidence by sorting and grouping items.
	Examples:
	• How can I sort the leaves?
	• Is this material magnetic or non-magnetic?
	• Is the material waterproof or not?
	• How can I sort the animals/plants/rocks?
Pattern seeking	**Comparative/fair testing**
I will gather evidence by changing one variable and measuring the other.	I will gather evidence by changing one variable and measuring the other. These usually involve biological investigations.
Examples:	Examples:
• Do people with bigger hands also have bigger feet?	• What are the conditions needed for healthy plant growth?
• Where on the school field do daisies grow?	• Do different surfaces affect how far a balloon car travels?
• What conditions do snails prefer?	• What is the 'best' material for sound proofing?
• Do bigger seeds result in bigger plants?	
Observing over time	**Research**
I will gather evidence by watching to see how something changes over time.	I will need to gather evidence by looking up information in secondary sources (or speaking to an expert such as a science ambassador).
Examples:	Examples:
• How do trees change over a year?	• How long is my intestine?
• What happens to my shadow length over the course of a day/year?	• Which is the closest planet to earth?
• How long does it take for a material to decompose?	• Where does our food come from?
	• Are all microbes harmful?

When children are engaging in enquiries, they should, according to the national curriculum, develop investigative skills (working scientifically) that become more developed as they move through primary school. Teachers usually elect to develop one or two of these skills during a lesson. Table 13.3 shows the investigative procedures that children should use across Key Stages 1 and 2. These are progressive and build upon prior learning. It may be noted that in Key Stage 1, children are not required to make predictions and interpret, as they may not yet have sufficient knowledge to do this effectively.

Table 13.3 Progression of investigative skills from Key Stage 1 to upper Key Stage 2 (DfE, 2014)

Key Stage 1 (Years 1 and 2)	Lower Key Stage 2 (Years 3 and 4)	Upper Key Stage 2 (Years 5 and 6)
• Asking simple questions and recognising that they can be answered in different ways. • Observing closely, using simple equipment. • Performing simple tests. • Identifying and classifying. • Using their observations and ideas to suggest answers to questions. • Gathering and recording data to help in answering questions.	• Asking relevant questions and using different types of scientific enquiries to answer them. • Setting up simple practical enquiries, comparative and fair tests. • Making systematic and careful observations and, where appropriate, taking accurate measurements using standard units, using a range of equipment, including thermometers and data loggers. • Gathering, recording, classifying and presenting data in a variety of ways to help in answering questions. • Recording findings using simple scientific language, drawings, labelled diagrams, keys, bar charts, and tables. • Reporting on findings from enquiries, including oral and written explanations, displays or presentations of results and conclusions. • Using results to draw simple conclusions, make predictions for new values, suggest improvements and raise further questions. • Identifying differences, similarities or changes related to simple scientific ideas and processes. • Using straightforward scientific evidence to answer questions or to support their findings.	• Planning different types of scientific enquiries to answer questions, including recognising and controlling variables where necessary. • Taking measurements, using a range of scientific equipment with increasing accuracy and precision; taking repeat readings when appropriate. • Recording data and results of increasing complexity using scientific diagrams and labels, classification keys, tables, scatter graphs, bar and line graphs. • Using test results to make predictions to set up further comparative and fair tests. • Reporting and presenting findings from enquiries, including conclusions, causal relationships and explanations of and degree of trust in results in oral and written forms such as displays and other presentations. • Identifying scientific evidence that has been used to support or refute ideas or arguments.

The above skills need to be taught in lessons. There are some skills that align well to enquiries and others that do not. For example, if children are being asked to research, they will not be required to apply observation skills, to take measurements or to predict.

KNOWLEDGE OF APPARATUS/EQUIPMENT AND MEASURES

Disciplinary knowledge is often framed as 'skills'. These skills need to be taught and are not learnt by simply just 'doing' science. For example, consider the skill of using a thermometer. To use a thermometer, children need to know:

- how to hold the thermometer;
- how to submerge the thermometer in the liquid;
- that they need to leave it in the liquid for at least a minute;
- how to read the temperature quickly after taking it out of the liquid;
- how to read the scale.

As children progress through primary school, they should also be able to identify health and safety issues.

KNOWLEDGE OF DATA ANALYSIS AND COMMUNICATION OF IDEAS

Pupils should seek answers to questions through collecting, analysing and presenting data. Recording and drawing conclusions from investigations is an important part of an enquiry and enables pupils to notice patterns in data so that they can make generalisations and draw conclusions. Recording is also a way to enable pupils to remember what they have done and to communicate this to others. Learners need to be introduced to a range of different recording approaches so that they are able to select their own ways of recording as they move into upper Key Stage 2. In Key Stage 1, children should be supported to talk and explain their observations, use drawings, annotate pictures, sequence pictures or to make models. As children progress through into Key Stage 2, they should be able to record data in a wider range of ways, including using bar charts, tables and line graphs, or, if looking for causal relationships between variables, scatter graphs may be produced. The type of investigation impacts upon the data that children can collect and how they can record their findings. For example, if children are sorting and grouping materials using a sorting enquiry, then they will use a simple table and/or a simple sorting exercise to prime learners to record using a Venn diagram.

As children progress through the school, opportunities should be provided for them to collect data to produce line graphs and scatter graphs. For example, the questions 'Do people with bigger feet also have bigger hands?' or 'Can people with bigger hands pick up more marbles?' will need to be answered by analysing data on a scatter graph. It is important to look at trends in the data and to talk to children about reasons for anomalies in the data. There will be an overall trend in the data, but there will always be some anomalies that are interesting to talk about.

EVIDENCE AND CONCLUSIONS

During enquiries, children should have the opportunity to organise their evidence and ideas in order to explain *how* and *why* something happens before checking that they have answered the question posed by the enquiry. Children need planned time to come back to their initial question and to use data to inform their conclusions. To assess 'mastery of learning', each topic could lead towards an 'outcome' in which pupils are asked to create an individual response to an open question (see Table 13.4). When planning 'open questions' for each topic, these could link to the 'big ideas' of science (concepts that pupils should know by the age of 17 years of age) and will ensure that children will learn ideas that are appropriate to their level of development. Indeed, Harlen (2010) argues that science is about connecting and extending children's understanding of smaller ideas to learn about 'big ideas'.

According to Harlen (2015), progression towards big ideas should result from studying topics that are of interest and relevance to the lives of all pupils.

PART 3: UNDERSTANDING THE DEVELOPMENT OF CHILDREN'S KNOWLEDGE IN SCIENCE

Primary teachers need to be conversant with the EYFS and the Key Stage 3 curriculum so that they know where the sequence of lessons that they are teaching contributes to children's knowledge base. Bruner (1999) stresses the importance of 'building' upon pupils' current level of understanding. He proposed the idea of 'spiral learning' where teachers work alongside children to develop new learning, such as extending their vocabulary, modelling new strategies, supporting collaboration and providing problem-solving tasks. He continues to argue that children need to construct knowledge, apply meaning to experiences and understand how ideas are relational. To achieve this aim, it is important that teachers are aware of concepts that have previously been taught so that they can consolidate ideas and build subject knowledge at an age-appropriate level.

Table 13.4 *Questions to guide learning of the 'big ideas' linked to primary science*

Biology					
Learning objectives posed as questions that children will be expected to answer at the end of the lesson/unit of work.					
Year 1	**Year 2**	**Year 3**	**Year 4**	**Year 5**	**Year 6**
What is alive?	What stays the same as we grow?	What is the function of the leaves/roots/stem/trunk/branches/petals?	How can we group plants and animals based on similarities and differences?	Are plants male or female?	How can you classify . . . ?
What is the same or different between these two plants?	How do we change?	How is water transported in plants?	Does toothpaste work?	What is the purpose of different parts of a plant?	How would your classification change if you included plants from a desert region?
How can you sort these leaves? Why have you sorted them in that way?	How can living things stay healthy?	What happens when we change the type of liquid/colour of light on plant growth?	How does our digestive system work?	Do all plants reproduce in the same way?	Which type of exercise affects pulse rate the most?
What happens to the tree over time?	Which offspring belongs to which animal?	Why do animals have a skeleton (or not)?	How does a habitat impact on food chains?	Do all life cycles look the same? Is there a relationship between a mammal's size and gestation periods?	How do our choices affect how our bodies work?
How do you know that a reptile is a reptile?	How does a cactus survive?	Why do we need muscles?	Why do different animals have different types of teeth?	Do all babies grow in the womb?	What is the impact of diet, exercise, drugs?
How can we organise the zoo animals?	How does a rainforest compare to a desert?	What should we eat?	What do our bodies do with the food we eat?	What change do we experience in puberty?	How do living things change over time and place?
What does a herbivore/carnivore or omnivore eat?	How do you look after a pet to keep it healthy?	Do living things need different things to survive?	Are living things in danger?	How do our bodies change as we get older?	How do plants and animals evolve?
Do living things change or stay the same?		Animals: how do nutritional requirements vary for different animals?	What are the dangers posed to life by environmental change?		
Where should I put my bug hotel?					
Can we recognise objects by touch? sound? smell?					

(Continued)

Table 13.4 (Continued)

Chemistry

Learning objectives posed as questions that children will be expected to answer at the end of the lesson/unit of work.

Year 1	Year 2	Year 3	Year 4	Year 5	Year 6
What are things made from? Which is the 'best' material for . . . ? (e.g., eggbox, gloves, bag) Which materials are most absorbent/flexible/waterproof?	How do we choose materials for a purpose - e.g., which sponge is best for mopping up a spill? Choosing materials for a purpose - why does it work best? Can we change materials - e.g., bending, stretching, twisting, squashing?	Are all rocks the same? How does the particle size affect the flow rate of water? Which ploughing pattern prevents erosion? Which materials are magnetic?	Is form fixed? Is water always a solid? Which material lets heat through easily? How does salt affect melting/boiling time of water? What is the difference between evaporation and condensation? How does the temperature affect how long it takes for sugar to dissolve?	What are things made from and why? Can we change materials? Is the change permanent? How will this science help you in the future?	

Physics

Learning objectives posed as questions that children will be expected to answer at the end of the lesson/unit of work.

Year 1	Year 2	Year 3	Year 4	Year 5	Year 6
		What is darkness?	Can we control electricity?	Sun, Earth and Moon: what is moving?	Can we vary the effects of electricity?
		How are shadows formed?	How do we use electricity?	Can you describe the movement of the planets and the Moon?	Achieved by:
		How does the distance from a screen affect the size of the shadow?	How does electricity travel?	How does the Earth's rotation affect the length of day and night?	investigating the effects of changing components in a circuit;
		How well does light reflect from different surfaces or colours?	How do we hear different sounds?	Do all objects fall through water in the same way?	representing circuits using symbols.
		What is a force?	Can you investigate how sound travels?	Which parachutes/cupcake cases take the longest to fall?	Which fruits make the best 'fruity' battery?
		What can magnets do?	How does the pitch, volume and distance vary?	Which shoe has the best grip?	How do we see?
		Achieved by:	Are two ears better than one?		Light travels in straight lines to be received by the eye.
		exploring how magnets and everyday materials interact;			How can we see around corners?
		exploring how two magnets interact.			

It is vitally important that they (learners) develop secure understanding of each key block of knowledge and concepts in order to progress to the next stage. Insecure, superficial understanding will not allow genuine progression: pupils may struggle at key points of transition (such as between primary and secondary school), build up serious misconceptions, and/or have significant difficulties in understanding higher-order content.

(DfE, 2014, p168)

REFLECTION

Look at the units that are taught in each year group and consider the ordering of these. For example, is it a good idea to teach sound before children have been taught about solids, liquids and gases? In Year 5, would it be better to teach forces prior to teaching Earth, Space and Beyond so that learners have a comprehension of gravity?

It is accepted that children have preconceptions before they begin school and that these may be different from the accepted understanding of science – hence the importance of knowing what has been delivered in the early years. The PLAN knowledge matrices, produced by the ASE, is a good reference point for teachers as it shows prior, current and future learning so that lessons can be pitched at the correct level for the age of the children. Sufficient time should be spent on each unit of work so that children are secure in the required knowledge and to ensure that they do not retain any naive ideas, as these present a *barrier to learning at all levels of education* (Allen, 2016, p5). Indeed, the curriculum is a planned journey that begins by identifying children's prior knowledge (along with misconceptions). Anticipating common misconceptions is an important aspect of curricular knowledge in the Core Content Framework.

Rosenshine (2012) acknowledges that if a learner's ideas are connected, then they are more readily used in new situations. Therefore, teachers can make links between areas of the science curriculum and build upon these ideas over Key Stages 1 and 2 so that children have the opportunity to revisit concepts. This prevents the curriculum being perceived by the learner as being like a series of disconnected facts (Harlen et al., 2015).

In terms of identifying examples to use in lessons, it has been suggested that teachers are aware of 'specificity'. For example, if teaching about plants, consider what is growing locally and use these examples; if there is a meadow nearby, children may learn about the names of flowers in a meadow, or if the school is near a beach, children may learn about the names of plants that grow on the shingle. Teachers may also carefully consider the animals that they reference when teaching children about animal groups and how this knowledge may be extended into Key Stage 2 when children learn about evolution. For example, teachers may choose a frog to teach children in Key Stage 1 about features of an amphibian and may use the frog again to consider how it has adapted to a number of different habitats. However, to engage learners, examples that pique their interests should be used.

Table 13.5 is a lesson plan showing a potential sequence of learning for light. This begins with the idea that we need light to see sources of light, reflective surfaces and finally the formation of shadows. In doing so, it is possible to build on prior learning and work towards application of knowledge to new and novel situations, and to demonstrate a secure understanding of taught concepts. The idea is that children also develop their enquiry skills (disciplinary knowledge) alongside the substantive knowledge.

Table 13.5 Sequencing learning for light

Prior learning	Learning outcomes	Activities to develop skills and understanding	Next steps
Describe the simple physical properties of everyday materials (KS1). Recognise that they need light in order to see things and that dark is the absence of light. Identification of light sources. Recognise that the sun can be dangerous and that there are ways to protect their eyes.	Notice that light is reflected from different surfaces.	Exploration of how different objects with different surfaces (shiny vs. matt) are more or less visible.	Recognise that shadows are formed when the light source is blocked by an opaque object. Find patterns in the way that the size of shadows changes.

PLAN have also produced examples of work that teachers can use to assess learning and to ensure that children are 'secure' with their understanding.

PART 4: DEVELOPING YOUR KNOWLEDGE

Secure subject knowledge helps teachers motivate pupils and teach effectively. Therefore, teachers need to be aware of their teaching practices and how to take their learning forward. This is known as 'metacognitive learning' (knowing about knowing). The metacognitive learner is self-aware, reflective and proactive about what they know and understand, and how they learn (Cross and Bowden, 2009).

The ASE is the subject association for science and they produce resources that will support subject knowledge development. The following websites are also worthwhile engaging with in order to develop the knowledge required to teach the national curriculum:

The Association of Science Education: www.ase.org.uk/

Explorify: https://explorify.uk

Institute of Physics: www.iop.org/explore-physics/at-home/more-to-explore#gref

The Ogden Trust: www.ogdentrust.com/

PLAN resources: www.planassessment.com/

Primary Science Education Consultancy: www.primary-science.co.uk/

Primary Science Teaching Trust: https://pstt.org.uk/

Principles and Big Ideas of Science: www.ase.org.uk/bigideas

Royal Society of Chemistry: https://edu.rsc.org/primary-science

Science and plants for schools: www.saps.org.uk/teachingresources/resources/?grouping=primary

STEM learning: www.stem.org.uk/

Welcome Trust: https://wellcome.org/what-we-do/our-work/improving-science-education

Facebook pages for science:

Dr Jo Science Solutions

Half Pint Science

Plymouth Science

Primary Science Coordinators

Unleash 1 – KS1: Science for Infants

Unleash 2 – KS2: Science for Juniors

REFERENCES

Allen, M (2016) *The Best Ways to Teach Primary Science: Research into Practice*. Maidenhead: Open University Press.

Archer, L and DeWitt, J (2017) *Understanding Young People's Science Aspirations*. London: Routledge.

Archer, L, Dewitt, J and Osborne, J (2015) Is science for us? Black students' and parents' views of science and science careers. *Science Education*, 99 (2): 199–237.

Archer, L, DeWitt, J, Osborne, JF, Dillon, JS, Wong, B and Willis, B (2013) *ASPIRES Report: Young people's science and career aspirations, age 10–14*. London: King's College.

Archer, L, Moote, J., MacLeod, E., Francis, B and DeWitt, J (2020) *ASPIRES 2: Young people's science and career aspirations, age 10–19*. London: UCL Institute of Education.

Bruner, J (1999) *The Culture of Education*. London: Harvard University Press.

Chalmers, AF (1994) *What is this Thing called Science?* (2nd edn). Maidenhead: Open University Press.

Cross, A and Bowden, A (2009) *Essential Primary Science*. New York: McGraw-Hill Education.

Department for Education (DfE) (2014) *The National Curriculum in England: Framework Document*. London: DfE.

Department for Education (DfE) (2021) Education Secretary puts climate change at the heart of education. Available at: www.gov.uk/government/news/education-secretary-puts-climate-change-at-the-heart-of-education--2

Harlen, W (2010) Principles and big ideas of science. Available at: www.ase.org.uk/bigideas

Harlen, W (2015) Working with the big ideas of science education. *Science Education Programme (SEP) of IAP*. Available at: www.interacademies.org/26703/Working-with-Big-Ideas-of-Science-EducationHarlen

Oates, T (2014) Progress in science education? The revised national curriculum for 2014. *School Science Review*, 95 (352): 21–9.

Ofsted (2019) Intention and substance: further findings on primary school science from Phase 3 of Ofsted's curriculum research. Available at: https://assets.publishing.service.gov.uk/government/uploads/system/uploads/attachment_data/file/777992/Intention_and_substance_findings_paper_on_primary_school_science_110219.pdfOfsted

Ofsted (2021) Research review series: science. Available at: www.gov.uk/government/publications/research-review-series-science/research-review-series-science

Patel, P (2019) Decolonise the curriculum TedXNorwichEd. Available at: www.bameednetwork.com/resources/video/decolonise-the-curriculum-pran-patel/

Pickford, T, Garner, W and Jackson, E (2013) *Primary Humanities: Learning through Enquiry*. London: SAGE.

Rosenshine, B (2012) Principles of instruction: research-based strategies that all teachers should know. *American Educator*, Spring, pp12–39.

Royal Academy of Engineering (2016) *The UKSTEM Education Landscape: A Report for the Lloyd's Register Foundation from the Royal Academy of Engineering Education and Skills Committee*.

London: Royal Academy of Engineering. Available at: www.raeng.org.uk/publications/reports/uk-stem-education-landscape

Russell, TL (1981) What history of science, how much and why? *Science Education*, 65 (1): 51–64.

Sinclair, A, Strachen, A and Threw, A (2019) *Standing on the Shoulders of Giants*. Bristol: Primary Science Teaching Trust.

Skamp, K (2007) Conceptual learning in the primary and middle years: the interplay of heads, hearts and hands-on science. *Teaching Science*. Journal of the Australian Science Teachers Association, Spring, 53 (3): 18–22.

Spielman, A (2018) HMCI commentary and the new education inspection framework. Available at: www.gov.uk/government/speeches/hmci-commentary-curriculum-and-the-new-education-inspection-framework

14

SUSTAINABILITY AND CLIMATE CHANGE EDUCATION

NASREEN MAJID

KEYWORDS: CLIMATE; CLIMATE CHANGE; CLIMATE ACTION; SUSTAINABILITY; CLIMATE JUSTICE; AGENCY; COMPETENCES; AUTHENTICITY.

LINKS TO THE CORE CONTENT FRAMEWORK

High Expectations (Standard 1): 1.6

How Pupils Learn (Standard 2): 2.1, 2.3

Subject and Curriculum (Standard 3): 3.1, 3.5

Classroom Practice (Standard 4): 4.1, 4.2

PART 1: EXPLORING SUSTAINABILITY AND CLIMATE CHANGE EDUCATION

It is said that teaching is a calling and many of us pursue the role because we want to make a difference to young people's lives. This chapter is unique in its framing of subject and pedagogical knowledge for trainee teachers in sustainability and climate change education. Climate change is the most pressing problem of our time and, as a trainee teacher, you are at the forefront of this debate. As a future educator, you can inform discussions and policy on changing the curriculum provision in England to embed sustainability and climate change education as a golden thread across all subjects.

The existing knowledge in the area needs reframing to support you, as busy trainee teachers, and indeed also support busy teachers in England, to assist the building of professional learning in the area. Hence, this chapter aspires to provide historical context, linked to education in the area of the sustainability and climate change debate: how it has evolved over time and how you can be supported to build competences and capabilities to teach sustainability and climate change education in an authentic way that intersects all aspects of the English national curriculum.

REFLECTION

What is your positionality as a trainee teacher in the teaching of sustainability and climate change education?

What is meant by climate justice? How can climate justice be explored at local level to inform global change?

What does personal action mean to you? How can you build opportunities for your pupils to empower them to take personal action towards a sustainable life?

(Questions adapted from *Climate Education and Sustainability Framework* (Majid et al., 2022))

WHAT IS SUSTAINABILITY AND CLIMATE CHANGE EDUCATION?

Climate scientists have been warning of the climate emergency for decades. The comprehensive Intergovernmental Panel for Climate Change (IPCC) reports have brought the science of the climate emergency to the forefront and what actions must be taken to reduce our carbon emissions (IPCC, 2021). Therefore, the knowledge in the area is vast and trainee teachers need guidance and clear support frameworks to enable them to develop agency in teaching about climate change.

UNESCO's competences for sustainability and the Sustainable Development Goals (SDGs) provide a structured framework to support pupils to develop knowledge, skills and understanding for living sustainable lives (UNECE, 2012; UNESCO, 2017). The notion of 'being' a global citizen is at the heart of developing these skills. This chapter, therefore, will go deeper into the subject and pedagogical knowledge and skills required to nurture trainee teachers' agency for the teaching of climate education and sustainability in an authentic and sustained way. Providing authentic opportunities to develop this work both from the trainee teacher and pupil perspective is essential in gaining lasting impact. Principles set out on 'forms of authenticity' by Barwell and Hauge (2021) will be drawn upon to facilitate understanding in fostering authenticity in the teaching of climate and sustainability.

WHY SUSTAINABILITY AND CLIMATE CHANGE EDUCATION IS IN THE NATIONAL CURRICULUM

Sustainability and climate change education does not feature explicitly within the primary national curriculum in England (DFE, 2013). Aspects are featured in the science and geography provision. In Key Stage 1, pupils learn about the weather, drawing upon the seasons and daily weather patterns. In science, they explore habitats, thus drawing upon the adaptation of plants and animals within their habitats. At Key Stage 2, in science, pupils learn about climate and habitats of plants and animals, and how environments can change. Additionally, in geography, pupils learn about climate zones. This level of work does not explicitly feature the principles of sustainability and climate change, and how to build habits for a sustainable future. Therefore, there is a push to thread through the principles driving sustainability and climate change education throughout the entire curriculum. This golden thread would aim to support pupils in developing their competences of *ways of thinking, ways of practising and ways of being* (Advance HE, 2021). In a recent survey (Majid, 2022), teachers shared their views on climate change and how they teach it in schools. When asked into which subjects teachers fit climate change, geography and science were the most common answers. A handful of teachers discussed a more holistic approach on developing this work through the framework of eco-schools and Forest School provision. However, these approaches are ones that schools invest into themselves and are not necessarily centrally funded to build knowledge, skills and understanding of sustainability and climate change education. Therefore, there is a gap, and this chapter aims to support trainee teachers to understand how sustainability and climate education principles can be threaded through all aspects of their curricular provision.

HOW HAS 'KNOWLEDGE' IN SUSTAINABILITY AND CLIMATE CHANGE EDUCATION DEVELOPED OVER TIME?

This chapter sets out to frame sustainability and climate change education within the parameters of the national curriculum for England. The chapter will share an insight into the historical context into this area and how trainee teachers can build their subject and pedagogical knowledge to teach this area authentically.

Sustainability and climate change education has not featured in official curricula in England, and therefore the subject and pedagogical knowledge and conceptual ideas cannot be critiqued with a chronological lens. Key international milestones will be drawn upon to understand and frame sustainability and climate change education.

The United Nations first discussed the environment over 50 years ago at its 1972 summit entitled 'Conference on the Environment' (UN, 1973). This led to key principles being adapted by nations to address the environmental emergency. Teacher training was mentioned in this report in recommendation 96C (UN, 1973). Similarly, the Earth Summit, held in Rio in 1992, set out a plan on sustainable development, including training for teachers, entitled 'Agenda 21' (UN, 1992). However, 50 years on, the embedding of training for teachers and trainee teachers on environmental issues has not been achieved. Similarly, in the Paris Agreement, article 12 specifically shared the need for *climate change education, training* (UNFCCC, 2016). Significant mobilisation of 'Education for Sustainable Development' (ESD) principles was achieved during the decade (2005–14) of ESD (UNESCO, 2022). However, the impact was short-lived and in the most recent IPCC AR6 [III] Report (Mitigation of Climate Change) states that *Changing from a commercialised, individualised, entrepreneurial training model to an education cognizant of planetary health and human well-being can accelerate climate change awareness and action* (IPCC, 2022a). In the recent government strategy on sustainability and climate change, the government sets out their key vision to become *the world-leading education sector in sustainability and climate change by 2030, with an emphasis on 'support for teachers'* (DFE, 2022). Therefore, introducing further curricular content in teacher training courses, specifically targeting the climate emergency and sustainability education, is a step in the right direction.

Structures used to develop sustainability and climate change education are not standardised and hence there is no clear way to monitor the effectiveness. UNESCO, through its work in the decade for sustainable development, has tried to establish frameworks such as the Millennium Developing Goals and the Sustainable Development Goals, and there are emerging curricula to support teachers and schools in developing climate change education.

SUSTAINABILITY AND CLIMATE CHANGE EDUCATION NOW

Sustainability and climate change education has gained much momentum over the past five years. The global pandemic, alongside the visible breakdown of our climate, has heightened the need to put decades' worth of policy into action. Many definitions exist for ESD. There is no consensus and developing a standardised definition is problematic. Cultural, historical, socioeconomic and local differences must be taken into consideration when thinking about ESD. For this chapter, the definition adopted by the United Nations in their 1987 report, *Our Common Future*, will be used as a standardised understanding. The United Nations define ESD as:

*Sustainable development is development that meets the needs of the present without com-
promising the ability of future generations to meet their own needs* (WCED, 1987).

Another vital aspect of sustainability and climate change education is how our
consumption in the global West may be having a detrimental effect on the global
South. This idea links directly to living more sustainably. Therefore, developing skills
that support pupils to look at their consumer habits through fact-finding around –
for example, how items of clothing such as jeans are made or the carbon footprint
of their lunch-box items can supports pupils' critical thinking and questioning of
where the products they are consuming come from. This level of work in schools
also builds on the notion of consuming less and supporting local enterprises.

WHAT MIGHT KNOWLEDGE IN SUSTAINABILITY AND CLIMATE CHANGE EDUCATION LOOK LIKE IN THE FUTURE?

The knowledge constructs around sustainability and climate change education will
continue to evolve and change. One vital component that would be welcomed
by teachers is the clear introduction of sustainability and climate change education as a strand within the national curriculum. Trainee teachers should develop
their subject knowledge in the area by using resources such as the IPCC reports
to gather peer-reviewed knowledge in the field. UNESCO's Office for Climate
Education (OCE) provides excellent resources to support training for teaching.
This is an underutilised resource and schools are encouraged to tap into this to
support their knowledge, skills and understanding of sustainability and climate
change principles – for example, a recent resource for teachers explaining the IPCC
Special Report on *Climate Change and Land* is broken down in an accessible way for
teachers. The facts from the report are broken down in an accessible format with
summary statements, as well as classroom activities that teachers can tap into. This
resource is one of many available on the OCE website (Connors et al., 2021).

PART 2: FOUNDATION KNOWLEDGE IN SUSTAINABILITY AND CLIMATE CHANGE EDUCATION

As sustainability and climate change education is not explicitly taught through
the programmes of study of England's national curriculum, this section will set out
approaches to learning to support trainee teachers in developing key aspects of climate and sustainability education in their settings. Therefore, this section will start
by sharing three core learning aims and outcomes for sustainability and climate
change education. It will then go on to share pedagogical approaches that can be
used to develop sustainability and climate change education. Up-to-date research

will be drawn upon, including a co-created Manifesto (BERA, 2021, Dunlop et al., 2022) to shape the thinking in this section.

Table 14.1 *Proposed aims and learning outcomes for sustainability and climate change education (adapted from Thew et al., 2021; Majid et al., 2022)*

Knowledge	Attitudes, values and behaviours	Competences and capabilities
1. Understanding of the causes and consequences of climate change – having a global and local perspective (IPCC, 2021, 2022a, 2022b). Know and understand the term 'Anthropocene'. 2. Linking climate change to sustainability education and creating a solution-based approach to developing this knowledge and skills. 3. Have an emphasis on social and environmental justice – teaching the impact our actions can potentially have on the most marginalised in society. 4. Building awareness of climate solutions through focused research on 'how' to affect change – e.g., insight into sustainable practices at a local, national and international level – 'act locally, think globally'.	1. Consider your positioning as a trainee teacher and future educator. How will your attitudes, values and behaviours towards sustainability and climate change education affect the way you engage learners? 2. Consider ethical issues driving the climate debate – e.g., how the consumption habits of the Global North have an impact on the most marginalised populations (Thew et al., 2021). 3. Develop an understanding of the Sustainable Development Goals (SDGs) and how this framework can support your attitude, values and behaviours and that of your pupils to teach 'approaches that cultivate knowledge and global citizenship, while preparing students for curious well-informed lives' (UNESCO, 2017). 4. Use the BERA Manifesto – co-creating with young people, teachers and researchers to promote shared attitudes, values and behaviours in the teaching of sustainability and climate change education (BERA, 2021; Dunlop et al., 2022).	1. Engage with competences that will enable trainee teachers to *critically engage with new information as it emerges and to recognise and advocate against denialism and fatalism* (Thew et al., 2021). 2. Engage with UNESCO's key competences that shape trainees' ways of thinking, ways of practising and ways of being for sustainability. Ways of thinking: • Systems thinking competency. • Anticipatory competency (future thinking). • Critical thinking competency. Ways of practising: • Strategic competency. • Collaborative competency. • Integrated problem-solving competency. Ways of being: • Self-awareness competency. • Normative competency. 3. Support pupils in developing routes into climate action. This will support the development of resilience and well-being and reduce eco-anxiety. Draw upon the work of Walshe et al. (2022) to support the development of eco-capabilities through nature connectedness.

The above aims and learning outcomes are shaped to support trainees in building their knowledge, attitudes, values, behaviours, competences and capabilities. These six areas will support trainees in understanding how to develop content to support their pupils in understanding the core principles of sustainability and climate change education. The pedagogical approaches will share concrete examples on how these aims and learning outcomes can support pupils' learning outcomes for sustainability and climate change education.

SYSTEMS THINKING

The notion of systems thinking and a systems approach is a core principle driving all aspects of sustainability. Therefore, understanding how to develop a system's thinking approach for all areas of sustainability and climate change education is vital for successful engagement and change.

Simply put, a system is a sum of its component parts where each part works within the system to achieve set objectives. A systems approach seeks to look at a problem as a whole system, seeing how different parts of the system interact and hence influence each other. Therefore, a systems approach is a powerful way to monitor and understand the causes and effects of our actions within a system. A systems approach requires individuals to identify parts of a system to understand their interconnected relationships. Systems thinking also requires anticipatory thinking, where individuals use the evidence gathered within a system to model how behaviours may change or respond to a modification. Therefore, a systems thinking approach is integral in shaping pupil understanding of the complex aspects of our climate emergency – e.g., schools can engage in a carbon literacy project first to understand how the school works as a system and then pupils can use this information to model ways of reducing the school's carbon emissions by looking at buying local produce for the school canteen or the reduction of food waste, etc. This would lead not only to an improvement and efficiency in the school's use of resources, but, more importantly, would collectively support the reduction of emissions locally and nationally. A *systems thinker positions themselves so they can see both the forest and the trees and keep one eye on each* (Richmond, 1994).

PEDAGOGICAL APPROACHES THAT CAN BE USED TO DEVELOP SUSTAINABILITY AND CLIMATE CHANGE EDUCATION

Table 14.2 Titles of sessions that trainee teachers could develop over time to support the development of sustainability and climate change education (Majid et al., 2022)

1. Teacher positionality	2. Climate justice	3. Climate action: personal and collective

It is suggested that trainees use the outlined model in Table 14.2, adapted from Majid et al. (2022), to deliver sustainability and climate change education. It is worth noting that understanding one's own positionality within this work is vital to build confidence and secure subject knowledge in teaching the complexities of sustainability and climate change education. The area of climate justice has a key part to play in this field as climate justice cuts across all aspects of life on a local, national and international level. Our histories are intertwined and hence, in a postcolonial world, the reshaping of reality must acknowledge the inequalities faced by many due to the legacy of colonial practices. Research shows that this is a particularly complex area of teaching due to the emotive and controversial nature of the discourse. Teachers are reticent to engage in such debate and thinking within the classroom so as not to come across as 'preachy' (Majid, 2022). Therefore, teachers need appropriate instructions and resources to teach this area well. Finally, climate action is put forward as a third and arguably most important component of pedagogy to support pupils to take action to live more sustainable lives. Each section from Table 14.2 will now be taken individually to provide context on how these complex ideas can be shaped and taught authentically to primary pupils.

TEACHER POSITIONALITY

Teacher identity is complex, and evolves and develops over time. The notion of positionality is valuable to understand what knowledge, understanding and lived experiences have been experienced to help shape a trainee teacher's understanding of sustainability and climate change education. This starting point can then be used to start discussions with pupils on sustainability and climate education. There are many ways to build this approach – examples are shared in Table 14.3.

Table 14.3 Sharing activities linked to developing positionality in developing foundation knowledge in sustainability and climate change education

Activity	How this will support pedagogical insight	Examples of types of activities
Showing video footage	Videos are a great way to start conversations to engage pupils, and to assess their insight and understanding into the complexities of sustainability and climate change education.	David Attenborough's *Witness Statement*. Newsreel from *Newsround* on recent climate breakdown news (UK temperatures on Tuesday, 19 July 2022). Sharing Dr Ella Gilbert's videos, explain complex climate science in a way that can be easily understood.

Activity	How this will support pedagogical insight	Examples of types of activities
Understanding what 'Anthropocene' means, sharing the term and its etymology with pupils.	Discuss the word 'Anthropocene' as an unofficial term used to describe the period of rapid change over the past 50 years that has resulted in significant changes to the earth's climate. Consider framing this carefully, as it is not an officially recognised term across the scientific world. Therefore, scientists are still debating it.	Share the etymology of Anthropocene: it originates from the Greek terms for human (*anthropo*) and new (*cene*) (Crutzen and Stoermer, 2000; Edwards, 2015; Ruddiman et al., 2015,Waters et al., 2014). As the debate continues regarding whether this era in the earth's history should be called the Anthropocene, it could be put out to a class to debate, using evidence they have gathered from a range of sources. As a teacher, you could play 'devil's advocate' in substantiating the claims or dismissing them.
Using imagery to start conversations about sustainability and climate change education.	Use the 'climate stripes' to understand the change in global temperatures since the late 1800s.	Use the climate stripes (Hawkins, 2021).

CLIMATE JUSTICE

Climate justice is an integral component of foundational knowledge in understanding sustainability and climate change education. The intersectionality of climate justice and how our actions impact on others plays a key role in building knowledge and understanding of the complex domains of sustainability and climate change education. The understanding of climate justice reinforces the notions of a systems thinking approach to understanding the complexities of sustainability and climate change education.

Trainee teachers are encouraged to look up the Sustainable Development Goals (SDGs) set out by the United Nations (UN, 2015). There are 17 goals that intersect and provide a framework to empower each citizen of the world to come together to enable a more sustainable approach to living. The 17 goals are underpinned with 169 targets and 232 unique indicators. Trainees are encouraged to study the SDGs carefully and use the goals as a framework to develop conversations about sustainability and climate change education. Table 14.4 provides examples of building climate justice into your curriculum.

Table 14.4 Sharing activities linked to climate justice in developing foundation knowledge in sustainability and climate change education

Activity	How this will support pedagogical insight	Examples of types of activities
Introducing the SDGs	This is a global framework to embed sustainability and climate change education. Therefore, understanding the 17 goals, the 169 targets and 232 indicators will build trainee teachers' foundational knowledge. Look at the SDGs as 17 key societal indicators that act like a system – how one interrelates to the other and links up as a system. Therefore, if we have a positive impact on one SDG, this can have a knock-on positive on another. However, if we have a negative impact on one SDG through our action, this can have a detrimental effect on others.	Trainee teachers are encouraged to make links with their local Development Education Centre. Details can be found at: Consortium of Development Education Centres (CoDEC). First, introduce the SDGs to students – this can be done via: • Whole-class discussion, each table is given a couple of SDGs to look into and then share their research back to the class. • Develop a learning trail across the school grounds with the SDGs. Pupils walk the trail to start developing an understanding. The trail can act as a continuous learning resource outside class time for pupils to embed their understanding of the SDGs. • As a whole-school approach, choose the most relevant SDGs and link them with each year group. This way each year group will focus on one SDG and look at it, in depth, over an academic year.
Oxfam resources	Have a look at the comprehensive set of resources developed by Oxfam on climate justice and use these to develop pupil understanding.	Look up the comprehensive range of resources from Oxfam (2022) to develop a layered and progressive insight into climate justice issues across the globe.
Using imagery	Use imagery to debate and make sense of the complex issues around climate justice.	Use images from *The Guardian* to look at food consumption from around the world to debate distribution of resources, ethics and fairness of this (Menzel, 2013).

Activity	How this will support pedagogical insight	Examples of types of activities
Indigenous practices	Much can be gained from the knowledge and insight that indigenous people hold. At COP26, indigenous communities had a platform to inform conversations to find sustainable solutions to achieve the Paris Agreement. Therefore, understanding the voice of indigenous communities will support the shaping of knowledge and understanding of work on climate justice.	Introduce the word 'indigenous' and get pupils to provide insight into what they think this means. Can they give examples of people they might know who identify as coming from indigenous communities? Why is the knowledge of indigenous communities important in tackling climate change and living more sustainably? Case study on a chosen indigenous tribe to provide greater depth in pupil understanding of the skills, knowledge and understanding that can be gained from the community. Have a focus on climate activists from indigenous communities such as Carlon Zackhras from the Marshall Islands.

CLIMATE ACTION: PERSONAL AND COLLECTIVE

There is growing evidence that young people are experiencing 'eco anxiety' (Dunlop et al., 2022; Whitehouse and Jones, 2021), where they share a concern for the planet and yet feel quite at odds in what actions they can take to support a more sustainable future. In a recent study, Majid (2022), the data suggest that pupils did share anxiety around the climate breakdown but positively did go on to list ways that they can take actions to build more sustainable lives. Actions such as planting more trees, walking more rather than driving to places and having more meat-free meals were some examples shared. Therefore, it is integral to build concrete ways to support pupils to take action to build more sustainable lives. This will not only support the building of sustainable habits, but also supports pupils in engaging in solutions and direct actions to combat the climate emergency. One way to facilitate this is engaging pupils with nature to develop sets of skills that build resilience, nature connectedness and support pupil well-being. The recent work on eco-capabilities, developed by Walshe et al. (2022), supports the notion of using nature and the arts to build 'eco-capabilities' that engage pupils in becoming more resilient while taking action to build a more sustainable future.

Table 14.5 Sharing activities linked to climate action that can be taken at a local level to develop foundational knowledge in sustainability and climate change education

Activity	How this will support pedagogical insight	Examples of types of activities
Using the school outdoor space	Using the outdoor space as nature trails, linking this to any aspects of the learning set out by the national curriculum to support the building of 'green skills'.	• Developing an eco-trail around the school to support science work on biodiversity. • Rewild parts of the school estate to support the reintroduction of wildlife. Watch the growth and the repopulation of the area over time. The data collected could be used in mathematics and science lessons.
Using the school outdoor space	Growing one's own food – using the seed to crop is the concept to facilitate learning in all aspects of the national curriculum.	• Monitor the growth of seeds for science. • Look at the crop yield by using different types of organic fertilisers – different approaches to growing – e.g., no dig method.
Carbon literacy projects	Utilising data from the school site to support the school to become net zero. This approach supports pupils in developing skills they can transfer to their everyday lives and future sustainable practices.	• Facilitate this through a structured programme such as the Green Schools Project (greenschoolsproject.org.uk)
Getting involved in charity work	Engaging with global issues through charity work. This will elevate the work from a local level to national and international action.	• Pupils could get involved in rewilding local spaces through involvement with local ecological groups. • Pupils could fundraise to plant trees internationally or help clean up oceans.

My final thought in this section is to engage your pupils and get them involved to support you in co-constructing curriculum outcomes. Emerging evidence in sustainability and climate change work demonstrates that engaging the younger generation is vital to develop approaches that will have a long-term impact. I would therefore ask that you read Dunlop et al.'s (2022) Manifesto sharing how the pupils can be supported to engage in environmental issues and support the development of curricular content. Although this Manifesto was constructed with secondary pupils, the principles are relevant for all age groups.

PART 3: UNDERSTANDING THE DEVELOPMENT OF CHILDREN'S KNOWLEDGE IN SUSTAINABILITY AND CLIMATE CHANGE EDUCATION

Sustainability and climate education are emerging areas for primary schools and, as such, there are no statutory guidelines in the progression of knowledge and skills across the primary age range. However, as demonstrated in Table 14.1, broad scaffolded structures can be deployed to support the development of knowledge, attitudes, values, behaviours, competences and capabilities. It is advised that trainee teachers draw upon the Programme of Study in each subject area they wish to embed sustainability and climate education, and see how the progression of skills can be achieved. The example in Table 14.6 illustrates how the area of nature connectedness can be explored across the primary age range.

Table 14.6 Illustrating how a sequence of lessons can be developed on nature connectedness

Year group	Learning outcomes	Activities to develop the skills and understanding	Next steps
Year R	Building nature connectedness through using the outdoor space for learning outcomes.	Nature trails – walks outdoors and connecting with the natural space. Using the materials collected to build display and create artwork.	This approach could be used to build collaborative artwork – e.g., a class nature collage.
Year 1	Building nature connectedness through using the outdoor space for learning outcomes.	Building science knowledge of common plants during outdoor learning opportunities. To be developed throughout the year to compare and link with seasonal change.	Using the senses to explore feelings – what can you see, hear, smell, feel in the outdoor space.
Year 2	Building nature connectedness through using the outdoor space for learning outcomes.	Develop work on habitats, understanding key aspects of habitats and how animals and plants co-exist. How we impact on habitats and what we can do to reduce this impact.	Use the local detail around habitats and explore broader habitats such as the oceans – how marine life is impacted from climate change and what we can do to build awareness.

PART 4: DEVELOPING YOUR KNOWLEDGE OF SUSTAINABILITY AND CLIMATE CHANGE EDUCATION FURTHER

SOME READING TO SUPPORT YOUR DEVELOPMENT

Gilio-Whitaker, D (2019) *As Long as Grass Grows: The Indigenous Fight for Environmental Justice, from Colonization to Standing Rock*. Boston, MA: Beacon Press.

If you wish to develop a deep insight into indigenous knowledge and work being developed to support the work on social and climate justice, this is a good read.

Lack, B (2020) *The Children of the Anthropocene: Stories from the Young People at the Heart of the Climate Crisis*. London: Penguin.

This book provides a contemporary lens from climate activists across the world on their vision for a better future.

OPEN ONLINE COURSES

Communicating Climate Change for Effective Climate Action. University of Glasgow: www.futurelearn.com/courses/communicating-climate-change-raising-engagement-for-climate-action

This site gives you details of all online courses available on climate change: www.my-mooc.com/en/categorie/climate-change?search%5Blocale%5D%5B0%5D=en

The UNE Learn platform on climate change has a range of courses you could take to further your knowledge and understanding: https://unccelearn.org/

WEBSITES RECOMMENDATIONS

Earth Warriors is a site that supports teachers with developing climate and sustainability education using the outdoor space. There is a cost involved in using their resource, but it is worth a mention here: www.earthwarriorsglobal.com/

The Green Schools Project is an excellent organisation supporting schools in developing carbon literacy. You can certainly get their support to build carbon literacy skills with your pupils: www.greenschoolsproject.org.uk/

UNESCO's Office for Climate Education: this is an excellent site with a range of free, accessible resources for teachers: www.oce.global/en/resources/ipcc-summaries-teachers

United Nations site for climate change: https://unfccc.int/

University of Reading's Partnering for the Planet site has a range of resources for both primary and secondary teachers to support the development of sustainability and climate change education: www.reading.ac.uk/planet/

SPECIALIST ORGANISATIONS

Eden Project Change Makers CPD: there is a cost involved with this. Details can be found at: www.edenproject.com/learn/schools/teacher-training-and-school-development/eden-project-changemakers-cpd

OTHER HELPFUL NATIONAL RESOURCES

UCL Centre for Climate Change and Sustainability Education. I would encourage you to join the mailing list for this centre: www.ucl.ac.uk/ioe/departments-and-centres/centres/ucl-centre-climate-change-and-sustainability-education

REFERENCES

Advance HE (2021) *Education for Sustainable Development Guidance*. York: QAA and Advance HE.

Barwell, R and Hauge, KH (2021) *A Critical Mathematics Education for Climate Change: A Post-Normal Approach. Applying Critical Mathematics Education*. Leiden: Brill.

British Educational Research Association (BERA) (2021) A manifesto for education for environmental sustainability. Available at: www.Bera.Ac.Uk/News/Manifesto-For-Education-For-Environmental-Sustainability-Efes-Published-By-Bera-Research-Commission (accessed 21 March 2022).

Connors, S, Yaahid, FR, Klein, D., Nicetto, S, Pathak, N, Schlüpmann, M, Tricoire, J, Van Diemen, MR and Wilgenbus, D (2021) *Climate Change and Land*. Summary for Teachers. Based on the IPCC (SRCCL). In Education, UAOFC (ed.). Paris: Office for Climate Education.

Crutzen, P and Stoermer, E (2000) The 'Anthropocene'. *Global Change Newsletter*. Sweden.

DfE (2013) *The National Curriculum in England: Key Stages 1 and 2 Framework Document*. London: DfE. Crown copyright.

DfE (2022) Sustainability and climate change strategy. In *Education, DO* (ed.). London: DfE. Crown copyright.

Dunlop, L, Rushton, EAC, Atkinson, L, Ayre, J, Bullivant, A, Essex, J, Price, L, Smith, A, Summer, M, Stubbs, JE, Diepen, MT-V and Wood, L (2022) Teacher and youth priorities for education for environmental sustainability: a co-created manifesto. *British Educational Research Journal*.

Edwards, LE (2015) What is the Anthropocene? *Eos, Earth and Space Science News*, 97: 6–7.

Hawkins, E (2021) #Showyourstripes. University of Reading. Available at: https://Showyourstripes.Info/S/Globe (accessed 1 August 2022).

IPCC (2021) *Climate Change 2021: The Physical Science Basis Summary for Policymakers* Geneva: IPCC.

IPCC (2022a) Climate Change 2022. Mitigation of Climate Change. In *Change, WGICTTS AROTIPOC* (ed.). UNEP; WMO. Geneva: IPCC.

IPCC (2022b) IPCC outreach material. Available at: www.Ipcc.Ch/Outreach-Material/

Majid, N (2022) *Teachers' and pupils' perceptions of climate change. ISATT Conference: Inclusive Ethics in Education as a New Horizon for Teachers and Teaching*. Bordeaux. International Study Association for Teachers and Teaching.

Majid, N, Reed Johnson, J, Marston, S and Happle, A (2022) University of Reading Climate Education and Sustainability ITT Framework. University of Reading.

Menzel, P (2013) Hungry planet: what the world eats – in pictures. *The Guardian*, 6 May.

Oxfam (2022) Learn about climate justice. Available at: www.Oxfam.Org.Uk/Education/Classroom-Resources/Human-Impact-Climate-Change/Resources-For-Primary-Schools/ (accessed 1 August 2022).

Richmond, B (1994) Systems thinking/system dynamics: let's just get on with it. *System Dynamics Review*, 10: 135–57.

Ruddiman, WF, Ellis, EC, Kaplan, JO and Fuller, DQ (2015) Defining the epoch we live in. *Science*, 348: 38–9.

Thew, H, Graves, C, Reay, D, Smith, S, Petersen, K, Bomberg, E, Boxley, S, Causley, J, Congreve, A, Cross, I, Dunk, R, Dunlop, L, Facer, K, Gamage, KAA, Greenhalgh, C, Greig, A, Kiamba, L, Kinakh, V, Kioupi, V, Lee, M, Klapper, R, Kurul, E, Marshall-Cook, J, Mcgivern, A, Mörk, J, Nijman, V, O'brien, J, Preist, C, Price, E, Samangooei, M, Schrodt, F, Sharmina, M, Toney, J, Walsh, C, Walsh, T, Wood, R, Wood, P and Worsfold, NT (2021) Mainstreaming climate education in higher education institutions. Glasgow: COP26 Universities Network Working Paper.

UN (1973) *Report of the United Nations Conference on the Human Environment*. Stockholm, 5–16 June. New York: United Nations.

UN (1992) *United Nations Conference on Environment and Development*. Rio de Janeiro, 3–14 June. *Agenda* 21.

UN (2015) United Nations Sustainable Development Goals. Available at: https://Sdgs.Un.Org/Goals (accessed 17 February 2022).

UNECE (2012) *Learning for the Future: Competences in Education for Sustainable Development*.UNECE: Geneva.

UNESCO (2017) *Education for Sustainable Development Goals: Learning Objectives*. UNESCO: Paris.

UNESCO (2022) UN decade for ESD. Available at: https://En.Unesco.Org/Themes/Education-Sustainable-Development/What-Is-Esd/Un-Decade-Of-Esd

UNFCCC (2016) Paris Agreement text. UNFCCC: New York.

Walshe, N, Moula, Z and Lee, E (2022) Eco-capabilities as a pathway to wellbeing and sustainability. *Sustainability*, 14: 3582.

Waters, CN, Zalasiewicz, JA, Williams, M, Ellis, MA and Snelling, AM (2014) A stratigraphical basis for the Anthropocene? *Geological Society*, 395: 1–21.

World Commission on Environment and Development (WCED) (1987) *Our Common Future*. Oxford: Oxford University Press.

Whitehouse, S and Jones, V (2021) 'It makes me angry. Really angry': exploring emotional responses to climate change education. *Journal of Social Science Education*, 20.

INDEX

Page numbers followed by "f" indicate figures; those followed by "t" indicate tables.